Internationalism or Russification?

Internationalism or Russification?
A Study in the Soviet Nationalities Problem
Ivan Dzyuba

Resistance Books, London
and the International Institute for Research
and Education, Amsterdam

Resistance Books
resistancebooks.org
info@resistancebooks.org

The International Institute for Education and Research
iire.org
iire@iire.org

Internationalism or Russification? A Study in the Soviet Nationalities Problem is issue 77 of the Notebooks for Study and Research published by the International Institute for Research and Education.

The original Ukrainian text was published under the title Інтернаціоналізм чи русифікація? by Sucasnist Publishers, Munich, July 1968.

The first and second English editions were published in Great Britain by Weidenfeld & Nicolson in 1968 and 1970.

The text in this edition is from the third edition published in 1974 by the Monad Press, New York, and distributed by Pathfinder Press. It is being republished in this edition with their kind permission.

Design by
Michael Wallace
Gareth Lindsay

Typefaces used
Karrik by Jean-Baptiste Morizot and Lucas Le Bihan
Cardo by David Perry

ISBN: 978-0-902869-18-9 (pbk)
ISBN: 978-0-902869-16-5 (e-pub)

Acknowledgements

Resistance Books is grateful to Halya Kowalsky, Chris Ford, Jim Ryan and Dave Kellaway for their help and advice in the production of this book. Fred Leplat organized the production, and Michael Wallace and Gareth Lindsay designed the book. Without their contribution, it would not have been possible to publish *Internationalism or Russification? A Study in the Soviet Nationalities Problem*.

Resistance Books is grateful to Pathfinder Press for granting us permission to republish *Internationalism or Russification?* based on the text of their 1974 edition. We also thank Bohdan Krawchenko, who gave us permission to use his texts originally published under the name of M.I. Holubenko.

Internationalism or Russification? was written in 1965 while there was a wave of political repression in Ukraine. Ivan Dzyuba analyses from a Marxist position the national and cultural policy of the Soviet Union in Ukraine. The book was distributed as a samizdat, and first published abroad in 1968. In 1972, Dzyuba was expelled from the Writers' Union and subsequently arrested and sentenced to five years' imprisonment. Ivan Dzyuba died on 22 February 2022 at the age of 91 on the eve of the invasion of his country by Russia.

The word інтернаціоналізм translates internationalism in the original title. In the context of this book it should be understood to have the meaning (which is also that given it by Soviet lexicographers) of: the defence of freedom and equality of all peoples and struggle against chauvinism (S.I. Ozhegov).

I have always endeavoured to consider nationality problems just as, in fact, all other problems – from the viewpoint of the principles of scientific Communism and of the teaching of Marx, Engels and Lenin, perceiving the prospects for their successful solution to lie along the road towards the fulfilment of Lenin's legacy and Communist construction.

Ivan Dzyuba, 26 December 1969

Contents

Preface, by John-Paul Himka
17

The author and his book, by Bohdan Krawchenko
23

Letter to P. Yu. Shelest and V. V. Shcherbyts'ky
30

Internationalism or Russification?
39

Introduction
41

1. The possibility of mistakes and the admissibility of criticism on the nationalities question
56

2. The importance and place of the nationalities question
62

3. The forces that prepared the revision of the Leninist nationalities policy
70

4. The future of nations; nations under communism
79

5. National sentiment, national consciousness, national duties
92

6. The socialist republics and the forms of their cooperation
98

7. The phantom of 'Ukrainian bourgeois nationalism' and the reality of Russian GreatPower chauvinism as the principal obstacle to national construction in the USSR
103

8. Actual equality and formal equality
174

9. Ukrainization and its repression
191

10. Russification and its mechanics
200

11. The Russification of other peoples and denationalization run counter to the interests of the Russian people itself
245

12. The gap between theory and practice: covering up the tracks by deliberately false phraseology
251

13. The national question is simultaneously a social and a universal historic question
280

14. The government of the Ukrainian SSR as the spokesman of national integrality; its responsibility for the nation
285

Conclusions
291

Postscript to the second edition
308

Editors' notes
327

Tables
329

People
335

Index
347

Abbreviations
359

Appendix Speech by Ivan Dzuba at Babyn Yar
360

About the Publishers
368

Preface
John-Paul Himka

Like many classics, Ivan Dzyuba's *Internationalism or Russification?* is more honoured than read. Of course, we live in an age where the very idea of reading an entire book seems daunting. And more to the point, Dzyuba's brilliant critique of russification in the former Soviet Union might, deceptively, seem to be no longer even relevant. But *Internationalism or Russification?* remains a fundamental access point for understanding contemporary Ukraine, which – at the time of this writing – is engaged in what is literally a life-and-death struggle with Russia. Dzyuba's analysis also makes for captivating reading.

Consider its opening. A brash thirty-four-year-old writes to the first secretary of Ukraine's Communist Party. The letter's style (and indeed most of the book's style) wavers between informative explanation, outrage and cheekiness. One hears here the tone in which young people were addressing authority in Paris and Chicago and in Warsaw and Prague in the rebellious 1960s. Dzyuba bewails the absence of basic civil rights in his country, such as freedom of expression and freedom of assembly. He documents cases in which poetry is treated as a dangerous substance, visual art is destroyed on ideological grounds, and scholars are fired for their opinions. He wants to figure out what lies behind these developments, their primary causes. And then the rest of the book looks for these causes in the Soviet Union's deviation from Marxist-Leninist principles on issues of nationality.

The topic 'socialism and the national question' has a long and distinguished history in Ukrainian political thought.

Many voices lately have been calling for an indigenization of socialist thought, and revisiting the texts produced by Ukrainian Marxists and socialists should be high on their agenda. Ukraine's most impressive political thinker, Mykhailo Drahomanov, returned again and again to the issue of how nationality and socialism intersect. One of his major works, *Istoricheskaia Pol'sha I velikorusskaia demokratiia* (Historical Poland and Great Russian Democracy), published in Geneva in 1881, analysed the stance of Polish and Russian revolutionaries toward Ukrainians and called upon them to recognize the distinctiveness of the Ukrainian nation, to shed pretensions to polonize and russify Ukraine's population, and instead to work among Ukrainians in the Ukrainian language. In his view, socialists who wanted to work in Ukraine had to acculturate at least linguistically to the Ukrainian nationality. And for Ukrainians, as an exploited people, the only sensible political path was that of socialism. Unfortunately, almost nothing that Drahomanov wrote is available in English, and even his works in Ukrainian and Russian are nowhere near as accessible as they should be.[1]

To jump to the revolutionary period, there is the extraordinary work of two Ukrainian Bolsheviks, Vasyl Shakhrai and Serhii Mazlakh, who made the case for the independence of a Soviet Ukraine.[2] Valuable critiques of Lenin's position on the national question were penned by the social democrats Lev Yurkevych and Volodymyr Levynsky. A classic work on Marxism and the national question – not just for Ukraine, but for global Marxism – is Roman Rosdolsky's work, *Engels and the 'Nonhistoric' Peoples: The National Question in the Revolution of 1848*.[3] And the most recent addition to what is really a very much longer list is Marko Bojcun's *The Workers' Movement and the National Question in Ukraine 1897–1918*.[4] Dzyuba's *Internationalism or Russification?* fits perfectly into this tradition.

The main thrust of Dzyuba's book is to contrast the views of Lenin, the author most frequently cited in his text, and the views of other old Bolsheviks with the historical narratives obligatory in the Soviet Union from the 1930s into the 1980s. Lenin's views on nationality and Ukraine have been completely ignored by many self-styled Leninists, then and now. It should be noted, too, that Lenin defended Ukrainian national aspirations at a time when Ukrainian national consciousness was much weaker than it is today.

Dzyuba exposes the betrayal of the ideals of many revolutionists who had called for an end to the russification of Ukraine. He draws productively on such pre-revolutionary figures as Herzen and Turgenev. But he also cites numerous old Bolsheviks who criticized Russian chauvinist tendencies within the party, including Mykola Skrypnyk, Hryhorii Hrynko, Volodymyr Zatonsky, Georgii Safarov, Yakov Yakovlev and Khristian Rakovsky. All their writings were banned in the USSR under Stalin, who left us a deformed, bowdlerized version of Bolshevik thinking on the national question. And Stalin was not content to simply edit the socialist heritage by banning particular texts, he also edited by killing the authors of these texts. Not one of the old Bolsheviks listed above survived beyond 1941.

Nationality is rooted in culture, Dzyuba observes. Art of every sort is produced within a particular cultural context. True, there is some assimilation of nations at an all-human level. For example, smartphones are ubiquitous globally, and American music has influenced musical culture worldwide. But this is something quite different from one national culture completely absorbing and thereby destroying another national culture, such as russification aims to do. The vigorous defence of nationalities should be an obvious duty of progressives. They are obliged to oppose genocide, including cultural genocide. African-Americans are correct to demand their own history and to have that history included in mainstream American classrooms. And Indigenous Peoples throughout the world wage a righteous struggle to reclaim their vulnerable cultures. The world is slowly coming to recognize the value of diversity – biodiversity, ethnic diversity, neurodiversity and cultural diversity.

Diagnosing the Soviet mentality, Dzyuba identifies a severe case of Russian imperialism: 'The "rehabilitation" of the colonial heritage of the Russian Empire as the "ancestor" of the USSR is entering more and more widely into contemporary Russian literature, criticism and journalism.' This Soviet attitude of adopting as its own the tsarist heritage involves also pretending that tsarist expansionism was a progressive step forward for all the peoples it affected. Marxists back in the days of tsarism certainly didn't think that. Friedrich Engels, as Dzyuba reminds us, had this to say on the topic: 'No spoliation, no violence, no oppression on the part of Tsardom, but has been perpetrated under pretext of "progress", "enlightenment", "liberalism", "the deliverance of the oppressed".' Of course, tsarist imperialism and colonization actually oppressed the indigenous populations it conquered, be they Poles or Chukchi. It was not just tsarist political thought that the Stalinists adopted, but Russian imperialist practices. At the beginning of World War II, thanks to its alliance with Nazi Germany, the Soviet Union expanded into Western Ukraine and Western Belarus, and after the war it established satellite regimes westward into the middle of Europe. Since the fall of the Soviet Union, not one of these conquered peoples has expressed its gratitude to the USSR for its control of their governments and cultures – in fact, all of them have been eager to join the NATO alliance against Russia. Dzyuba's passionate and penetrating book guides us to a mental reordering of how we should understand Russia and Russian imperialism.

Dzyuba emphasizes how expressions of attachment to Ukrainian culture are identified as 'Ukrainian bourgeois nationalism' and denounced, while Russian Great-Power chauvinism, which Lenin considered the greatest danger to the Soviet state, was never called out. It is a telling fact that many dissidents in the post-Stalinist period were arrested and sent to the Gulag on suspicion of Ukrainian nationalism, but no one was ever arrested for Russian chauvinism.

Perhaps the most illuminating section of the whole book is the section on the mechanics of russification. One of Dzyuba's most compelling insights is how 'voluntary' russification occurred. The state turned Ukrainian culture into damaged goods that no one wanted. For example, in the post-Stalinist period, it was possible to publish an eight-volume collection of the works of the great Russian historian Vasilii Kliuchevsky; his biography was also published and a street was named after him. His younger contemporary, an equally fine historian, the Ukrainian Mykhailo Hrushevsky, could not be published or even mentioned unless in the context of a condemnation of 'Ukrainian bourgeois nationalism'. This created the impression that serious history was written only by Russian intellectuals, and in the Russian language. Scientific journals were overwhelmingly published in Russian, even in the Ukrainian SSR. To enter a university in Ukraine, you had to have an excellent command of Russian and did not need to know any Ukrainian at all. It is no wonder that when Khrushchev in 1959 allowed parents in Ukraine to choose between Russian- and Ukrainian-language education for their children, the result was the further russification of the Soviet educational system. One might add that not only was Ukrainian culture presented as damaged goods, but it was risky for Soviet citizens to take too much of an interest in it.

Because of his championing of national rights, Dzyuba rather overlooked the dark side of nationalism. For example, he writes: 'The Ukrainian people has never been aggressive and intolerant towards others; never in its history has it enslaved other peoples. To the overwhelming majority of Ukrainian intellectuals, because of their democratic spirit, narrow nationalism has always been alien and chauvinism quite unnatural.' This passage does not take into account the aggressiveness, intolerance and murderous nationalism exhibited by the

Organization of Ukrainian Nationalists during World War II. Nor does it take into consideration the conduct of Ukrainian cossacks and haidamaky in earlier centuries. I note, too, that one of the figures that Dzyuba defends in his work, Matvii Shestopal, wrote an antisemitic tract that was published after the collapse of the Soviet system. But, as I have pointed out elsewhere,[5] such pathologies are to a great extent the traumatic symptoms of violent national oppression. And as Dzyuba points out, the only cure for nationalism's dark side is the free development of nations.

1   The best introduction to Drahomanov's political thought is Ivan L. Rudnytsky, 'Drahomanov as a Political Theorist', in Ivan L. Rudnytsky, *Essays in Modern Ukrainian History*, ed. Peter L. Rudnytsky (Edmonton: Canadian Institute of Ukrainian Studies, University of Alberta, 1987), 203–53.
2   English translation: Vasyl' Shakhrai and Serhii Mazlakh, *On the Current Situation in the Ukraine*, ed. Peter J. Potichnyj (Ann Arbor: University of Michigan Press, 1970). The Ukrainian original has been republished: Serhii Mazlakh and Vasyl' Shakhrai, *Do khvyli (Shcho diiet'sia na Vkraini i z Ukrainoiu?)*, ed. Andrii Zdorov (Odesa: Astroprynt, 2019).
3   Glasgow: Critique Books, 1986.
4   Historical Materialism Book Series (Leiden: Brill, 2021).
5   John-Paul Himka, 'Radikaler ukrainischer Nationalismus: Geschicte und Gegenwart,' in *Die Ukraine in Europa. Traum und Trauma einer Nation*, ed. Franziska Davies (Darmstadt WBG/ Theiss, forthcoming).

The author and his book
Bohdan Krawchenko

Ivan Dzyuba was born into a peasant family on 26 July 1931 in a village in the Donbas coal mining region of the Ukrainian SSR. In 1949 he left his secondary school and entered the faculty of philology at the Pedagogical Institute in Donetsk (then Stalino). After graduating, he did research work in the T. Shevchenko Institute of Literature of the Ukrainian SSR Academy of Sciences. Subsequently he worked as an editor for the State Literary Publishing House of Ukraine, was in charge of the department of literary criticism of the journal *Vitchyzna* (the leading organ of the Writers' Union of Ukraine), and was a literary adviser for the publishing house Molod (Youth).

Dzyuba's work in literary criticism has been appearing in print since 1950; in this genre he has displayed remarkable insight, opening up for his readers entirely new approaches to literature. He carries his readers with him by a striking lucidity of exposition, and is no respecter of accepted opinion. His work has done much to encourage new trends in Soviet Ukrainian literature, and he is held in high esteem among the younger generation of writers and readers. His articles have been published not only in various periodicals in Ukraine but also in a number of Russian journals; he has also contributed to journals in Georgia, Czechoslovakia and Poland. The first publication of his work in English was in the Moscow journal *Soviet Literature* (No. 10, 1960).

Dzyuba's boldness and originality have not remained unchallenged by the conservative *literati* who have reproved him from time to time, as in June 1962 for instance, when the Presidium of the Writers' Union of Ukraine accused him of 'giving a distorted view of the real state of contemporary Ukrainian literature' and of uttering 'politically erroneous statements',[1] and threatened him with expulsion from the Union.[2]

In late August and early September 1965, a week or two before the arrests of A. Sinyavsky and Yu. Daniel, a number of political arrests among young intellectuals took place in Ukraine. On 4 September, Dzyuba, together with V. Chornovil and V. Stus, appealed to an audience in the 'Ukraina' cinema in Kyiv to protest against these arrests. No official statements were issued regarding them, nor was any answer given to enquiries about them addressed to the Central Committee of the Communist Party of Ukraine by eminent people – deputies of the Supreme Soviets of the USSR and the Ukrainian SSR, Lenin Prize laureates and holders of the Order of Lenin. Instead of clear official statements in the press, rumours about the arrests of 'nationalists' gained ground. Motivated by his conviction that those arrested were not 'nationalists' but people genuinely concerned for the condition of Ukrainian culture, and himself witnessing numerous instances 'of an indefatigable, pitiless, and absurd persecution of the national cultural life' of Ukraine, Dzyuba wrote the present book in the last months of 1965 in order to show that 'the anxiety felt by an ever-widening circle of Ukrainian youth' was the result of the abandonment of the Leninist nationalities policy by Stalin and Khrushchev. Dzyuba asserts that a policy of persecution is no answer; in his opinion, the restoration of the Leninist policy is indispensable for the good of Communism and its future progress.

His book, consisting of a thorough examination of the historical background of the nationalities problem, of the Leninist policy on it, of its subsequent abandonment, and the means whereby it should be restored, was presented to the leaders of the Communist Party and the Government of the Ukrainian SSR and also, within a month, in a Russian version, to the Central Committee of the CPSU. Shortly after receiving it the Central Committee of the CPU distributed it in a limited number of copies for internal circulation among the regional (*oblast*) Party secretaries (there are twenty-five regions in Ukraine) requesting their comments (these have so far not been revealed). The book subsequently began to circulate in Ukraine and beyond its borders.

Following the protest, he staged in the Ukraina cinema, in September 1965 Dzyuba was dismissed from his post with the Molod publishing house, and was given the post of language editor with the *Ukrainian Biochemical Journal* as from the January 1966 issue. Six months later, the Secretary of the Kyiv Communist Party Committee, writing in the Party organ *Komunist Ukrainy*, attacked Dzyuba (together with two other writers) for 'ideologically harmful statements' and other equally vaguely formulated offences,[3] and in September the satirical journal *Perets'* published a rather scurrilous lampoon of him,[4] soon answered by three journalists, among them Dzyuba's fellow-protester Chornovil, who courageously came to his defence in a letter to the *Perets'* editorial board (which has remained unpublished). Then in November, Dr S. Kryzhanivs'ky, a poet of the older generation, a literary critic and scholar and Party and Writers' Union member, vindicated Dzyuba from the rostrum of the Fifth Congress of Writers of Ukraine, naming him, together with another critic, as the only ones who dared to speak the truth (this *was* published).[5] In January 1968, Dzyuba returned to his first post as an editor with the State Literary Publishing House (now renamed Dnipro), and was also readmitted into print in the USSR for the first time in two and a half years. He was also busy with other books (his first, entitled *An Ordinary Man or a Philistine?*[6] appeared in 1959); they included a history of thought in Ukraine, a book on T. Shevchenko (*He Who Chased out the Pharisees*) and one on V. Stefanyk.

In the meantime, the arrests of 1965 (which impelled Dzyuba to write the present work) were followed by a series of trials.

The first two, in January–February 1966, were conducted in a way similar to the well-known one of Sinyavsky and Daniel, which also occurred that February, and the charges brought, of anti-Soviet propaganda and agitation, were also similar. The remaining nine trials, although the charges brought were again similar, were held in February–April and in September *in camera* (in breach, it must be noted, of the Soviet law on this point). Sentences of from eight months to six years were passed, and five of the accused are still, at the time of preparation of this edition (June 1970), in strict regime camps or prison.

Among the considerable number of inquiries about the fate of those arrested and of protests against their harsh sentences, that from Chornovil stands out by the fullness of its documentation and its convincing argumentation. In his letter, like Dzyuba's book, addressed to the First Secretary of the Central Committee of the CPU, P. Yu. Shelest, as well as to the highest legal and security authorities of the Ukrainian SSR, he demonstrates, by referring to specific articles of the Soviet Constitution and Soviet legal codes, that the majority of the trials were illegal because they were not public, and, moreover, that the investigation and trial procedures contained a number of grave breaches of certain fundamental and specific legal safeguards, thus invalidating both the trials and the sentences passed. Chornovil's serious specific charges against the judiciary and the security services remained unanswered for nearly fourteen months; in the meantime, by April 1967 he had compiled another document – a 'White Book' on the accused,[7] which, in early August, the security authorities did answer: Chornovil was arrested, and sentenced fifteen weeks later to three years' labour camp, halved under a general amnesty; he is now free.[8]

Louis Aragon declared that the Moscow sentences create 'A precedent, more harmful to the interest of socialism than the works of Sinyavsky and Daniel could be. It is to be feared, in fact, that one could think that this kind of procedure is inherent to the nature of communism,'[9] and John Gollan's conclusion was that 'The court have found the accused Guilty, but the full evidence for the prosecution and defence which led the court to this conclusion has not been made public. Justice should not only be done but should be seen to be done. Unfortunately, this cannot be said in the case of this trial.'[10] It must be remembered that there was at least some (though admittedly one-sided) discussion of the Sinyavsky and Daniel case in the Soviet press, that the trial *was* (though incompletely) reported in Soviet papers, and that *some* members of the public were admitted to the trial; but *not a single word* appeared in the Soviet press about the arrests and trials in Ukraine, and all the proceedings from late February 1966 were held *in camera*. Compared with them, even the 1968 Moscow trial was much more public, although the *Morning Star* wrote this about it in its leader of 13 January 1968:

> Outsiders are in a difficulty when forming an opinion of the trial and sentences on Yuri Galanskov and others in Moscow.
> Neither friends nor enemies of the Soviet Union in Britain know what went on in the courtroom, what evidence was produced, or what the witnesses said.

Louis Aragon's fears may well now be reinforced, and one cannot but say with John Gollan that justice most definitely has not been seen to be done; more than that, allegations of a grave miscarriage of justice can no longer be brushed aside, under the circumstances as they are now known.

In fact, a recent report of a Canadian Communist Party delegation to Ukraine also speaks of 'cases of violation of Socialist democracy and denial of civil rights' there, and continues: 'When inquiries were made about the sentencing of Ukrainian writers and others, we were told ... that they were convicted as enemies of the state. But the specific charges against them were not revealed. Although we do not claim to know what considerations of state security led to the trials of these writers being conducted in secret, we must make the point that such *in camera* trials never serve to dispel doubts and questioning.'[11]

Dzyuba's work shows the historical and contemporary background, the social, cultural and political processes in the light of which these events must be viewed. But he himself does not view these processes from the outside; he is deeply involved in them, feels responsible for what is happening, and ardently advocates a return to Leninist justice. A man of letters, Dzyuba is always mindful of these words of Jean-Paul Sartre which have now gained fresh poignancy:

> The writer is in a situation in his time: every word has repercussions. Every silence too.
> I hold Flaubert and Goncourt responsible for the repression that followed the Commune because they did not write a line to prevent it. It was not their business, one may say. But was the trial of Galas Voltaire's business? The condemnation of Dreyfus, was it Zola's business? Each of these authors, in a particular circumstance of his life, measured his responsibility as a writer.[12]

1   This he was supposed to have done in a lecture delivered in L'viv which has remained unpublished, and therefore it is difficult to ascertain the reality of these allegations.
2   'U prezydiyi SPU', *Literaturna Ukraina*, 29 June 1962.
3   V. Boychenko, 'Partiyni organizatsiyi ta ideologichne zahartuvannya tvorchoyi inteligentsiyi', *Komunist Ukrainy*, No. 6, June 1966, p. 17.
4   *Perets'*, No. 17, September 1966, p. 5.
5   *Literatuma Ukraina*, 20 November 1966, p. 5. It is said that at the mention of Dzyuba's name the audience's thunderous applause nearly raised the roof.
6   I. Dzyuba, *'Zvychayna lyudyna' chy mishchanyn? Litnatumo-krytychni statti*, Kyiv, 1959, 277 pp.
7   Both documents in *The Chornvil Papers*, McGraw-Hill, 1968.
8   Full documentation of his case, as well as more recent writings by some of these, and certain earlier, prisoners, appeals on their behalf by Dzyuba and others, and other relevant documents, with a survey of events in Ukraine from 1965 to 1968, published Macmillan in M. Browne (ed.), *Ferment in Ukraine*. Conditions in the camps are well documented in *Rights and Wrongs*, Penguin, 1969, and A. Marchenko, *My Testimony*, Pall Mall, 1969.
9   L. Aragon, 'Apropos d'un procés', *L'Humanité*, 16 February 1966, p. 3. [Translation by the editors]
10 'British Communist Protest at Soviet Sentences', *The Times*, 15 February 1966.
11 *Viewpoint* (Central Committee Bulletin, CP of Canada), Toronto, January 1968, p. 11.
12 J.-P. Sartre, 'Presentation', *Les Temps Modernes*, No. 1, October 1945, p. 5. [Translation by the editors].

Letter to P. Yu. Shelest and V.V. Shcherbyts'ky

To

Comrade P. Yu. Shelest,
The First Secretary of the Central Committee of the Communist Party of Ukraine and a Member of the Presidium of the Central Committee of the Communist Party of the Soviet Union;

Comrade V. V. Shcherbyts'ky,
The Chairman of the Council of Ministers of the Ukrainian Soviet Socialist Republic and an Alternate Member of the Presidium of the Central Committee of the Communist Party of the Soviet Union.

Honourable Comrades,

This letter which I am addressing to you concerns a matter that has alarmed a large section of the Ukrainian public. I am referring to the political arrests carried out in a number of Ukrainian cities – Kyiv, L'viv, Ivano-Frankivsk, Ternopil', Lutsk – towards the end of August and the beginning of September 1965, mainly among young people, as well as the house-searches and interrogations being widely carried out at present in Kyiv and other cities.

It has become known that an inquiry regarding this matter has been addressed to the Central Committee of the Communist Party of Ukraine (CPU) by the deputy of the Supreme Soviet of the USSR and a Lenin Prize laureate, Mykhaylo Stel'makh, and by the deputies of the Supreme

Soviet of the Ukrainian SSR and Shevchenko Prize laureates Andriy Malyshko and Heorhiy Mayboroda. They have received no answer. Finally, a group of intellectuals from Kyiv have recently applied to the Central Committee of the CPU asking for an explanation of the nature of the arrests and the fate of the detainees. Among them were the chief aircraft designer Oleh Antonov, the film director Sergey Paradzhanov, the composers Vitaliy Kyreyko and Platon Mayboroda, and the writers Leonid Serpilin, Lina Kostenko and Ivan Drach. It would seem that they are still waiting for an answer. Meanwhile, more reports come in of continuing house-searches, of new people being summoned for interrogation by the KGB, and occasionally also of further arrests.

All this intensifies the understandable alarm and occasionally gives rise to wild rumours. In any case, a totally abnormal and disgraceful situation has arisen which offends elementary civic feelings and gives rise to very natural misgivings as to whether it is compatible with the norms of socialist legality, and whether such legality is possible under these circumstances. After all, several dozen people have been under arrest for nearly four months. These people are not black-marketeers, embezzlers or hooligans. Each is a competent, eminent and respected man in his own field (for instance, the well-known men of letters Ivan Svitlychny, Bohdan Horyn' and Mykhaylo Kosiv, the talented painter Panas Zalyvakha, Mykhaylo Horyn', one of the leading specialists in industrial psychology in the country whose innovatory projects were discussed quite recently in *Izvestia*, Mykola Hryn', one of the leading specialists at the Geophysics Institute of the Academy of Sciences of the Ukrainian SSR, the geodesist Ivan Ru, the student Yaroslav Hevrych, Oleksandr Martynenko and others).

These are the people who are being 'isolated'. No explanation of the matter has been forthcoming, nor is there any information as to the reasons for their arrest or the charges preferred against them. To date, the majority of the detainees have not even been permitted to see members of their family. This is in itself inhumane and undemocratic. Furthermore, it creates an atmosphere of uncertainty and alarm. In this atmosphere the most disparate and absurd rumours and conjectures are spreading. The very possibility of such conjectures and reports and the very manner of the handling of the 'case' which is their cause compromise that socialist legality which we have supposedly restored. Even more ominous is the fact that before and after the arrests, statements prompted by malice could be heard from certain official quarters about a nationalist underground supposedly existing in Ukraine and about other absurd 'horrors', invented by somebody, after all, for some reason ... In such an atmosphere, and under circumstances in which there is the desire to furnish the proof of a fabrication beforehand, can justice be done to the men under arrest? It is not by chance, after all, that some time ago certain persons, in both official and semi-official positions, taking advantage of the authority invested in them, spoke with very serious and even doleful countenances about the ostensible discovery of a 'centre', about the detection of arms, a clandestine press and the like. Since then, a month has passed and already no one dares repeat these tragicomic fabrications.

Now launched, the irresponsible rumour is spreading among the Philistines, taking on even more absurd proportions, giving rise to totally unjustified reactions, and preparing the ground for the acceptance of a most frightful injustice. Imagination, aroused by indirect insinuation, is taking the place of unavailable factual information. 'I heard it from people who don't lie.' This is the very same atmosphere that made the crimes of the cultist period possible. Do we have any guarantee that after a month or two a ridiculous new canard will not be circulated, a canard which in spite of all its primitivism might prove costly for the arrested? Indeed, one can quite obviously feel the desire to 'put them away' and to 'show them'. (It is not by chance that the investigation has gone on for four months in total secrecy; if there had been facts, they would have been elucidated within a week.) There is obviously spite in the air against a certain category of people (the 'nationalists'), and 'in politics', as Lenin said, 'spite ... plays the basest of roles'.[1]

This is the very same psychological complex which incited the terrorists of the Stalinist era to their crimes. I recall the words spoken to one of them by Stepan Chauzov, the hero of S. Zalygin's novel *On the Irtysh River*: 'Why do you look for an enemy in a peasant like me? And since you have not found one, you hold a grudge against me.'[2] This 'since you have not found one, you hold a grudge against me' is a most terrible and typical trait of despotism and of its psychology. The fewer the proofs, the greater the spitefulness, for you must blind yourself with a bestial hatred against the victim in order to prevent injustice from tormenting your conscience and to make this injustice appear to be valour.

The only guarantee of justice has always been and still remains open public knowledge, the opportunity for the public and for every individual citizen to know and to control the actions of all officials and authorities, particularly penal authorities. 'The masses,' Lenin said, 'must have the right ... to know and check each smallest step of their activity.'[3] But in a situation of secrecy and non-existent control (by the general public) mistakes, abuses and crimes are bound to arise.

This is why a growing number of people are alarmed, and it is publicity as the only legal guarantee of justice which they desire in this matter. Let the competent agency inform the public just who have been arrested and why, and what the arrested men are charged with. If this agency believes that proof of guilt exists or has been assembled against any one of the arrested, let this proof become the object of an open judicial inquiry, let both the accusers and the accused take the floor, and the people will judge for themselves who is right and who is wrong. After all, this is not simply the kind-hearted wish of some over-sensitive people, this is what ought to be according to Soviet law and the elementary principles of justice and common sense.

However, there is yet another, and no less important, aspect to the matter under discussion. Although no official or public explanations of the arrests have been offered, there is a constant, quite purposeful amassing of rumours that 'nationalists' have been arrested. In newspapers, lectures and at meetings the word 'nationalism' has again run riot as in the years 1947–9. The obviously absurd tales about an underground movement, arms, a printing press, etc., have been supplanted by a new tale about 'nationalist propaganda'. What next? (Apparently the investigating agency is not yet sure itself which articles of the criminal code it will use, what 'legal' shape its malice and prejudice against the detainees will take.)

From past and recent history, it may be seen that in Ukraine it was permissible to label as 'nationalist' anyone possessing an elementary sense of national dignity, or anyone concerned with the fate of Ukrainian culture and language, and often simply anyone who in some way failed to please some Russian chauvinist, some 'Great Russian bully'.[4]

It is no secret that during recent years a growing number of people in Ukraine, especially among the younger generation (not only students, scientists and creative writers and artists, but also now, quite often, workers), have been coming to the conclusion that there is something amiss with the nationalities policy in Ukraine, and the actual national and political position of Ukraine does not correspond to its formal constitutional position as a state, that is to say as the Ukrainian Soviet Socialist

Republic within a Union of other socialist republics, and that the condition of Ukrainian culture and language gives cause for great alarm, etc. – all this resulting from perpetual, flagrant violations of Marxism-Leninism on the nationalities question, and the abandonment of scientific principles in communist national construction. This constantly growing circle of people have expressed their alarm openly, publicly and on principle, taking up a perfectly Soviet and socialist position, showing concern about the plenitude and health of the spiritual and cultural life of our socialist and future communist society and denouncing merely unnecessary and costly losses and deviations on the path forward. Those believing these people to have been mistaken in some way ought to have answered them in the same open and principled way in which they behaved. Instead, the response was terror, first moral, now also physical. Over the last two or three years it has been possible to count several dozen instances of repression for these reasons. Dozens of people have been punished by dismissal from their jobs, by expulsion from establishments of higher education, by disciplinary action from the Party or the Communist Youth League for participation or involvement in some affair or other arbitrarily and malevolently qualified as 'nationalism'. Here are some recent examples: expulsion from the university (and from the Communist Youth League) of a fifth-year student and young poet, M. Kholodny, for his speech during a discussion of A. Ishchuk's novel *The Villagers of Verbivka*,[5] an expulsion contrary to the decision of the Youth League meeting itself, which did not deem it necessary or possible to expel him; expulsion from the Party of a research worker at the Institute of Literature of the Academy of Sciences of the Ukrainian SSR, the author of a number of books on literature which were rated highly, Mykhaylyna Kotsyubyns'ka, niece of the classic Ukrainian writer, Mykhaylo Kotsyubyns'ky; expulsion from the Party and dismissal from her job on the newspaper *Druh chytacha* of Rita Dovhan' who, it is alleged, organized a poetry reading in the Scientific Research Institute of Communications on 8 December 1965. In general, it must be said, hardly a single reading of young poets in the last two or three years has escaped such or similar 'repercussions', and the majority of readings, though already prepared and announced, have simply been forbidden ('cancelled') on various pretexts. This borders on the farcical! (Is it not a joke, for instance, that according to an official directive no poetry readings are to take place without the sanction of the City Party Committee, and for members of the Writers' Union, without the additional permission of the Union! It is worth pondering a while this acme of bureaucratic order, this ultimate word on the theory that 'Art belongs to the People'!)

If all the facts of this kind were to be amassed, the resultant picture of an indefatigable, pitiless and absurd persecution of national cultural life would frighten the very 'stage managers' of this campaign themselves, and would force a great many people to do some thinking. But who knows about this in our present conditions of unobstructed public knowledge?

It is not possible to discuss all these facts here: listing them alone would take up too much space. I shall name only the 'highlights', incidents of, so to speak, a collective nature: the dissolution of the Club of Young Writers and Artists in Kyiv; the story of the Lesya Ukrainka memorial evening in the Central Park of Culture and Rest, 31 July 1963; the destruction of the Shevchenko stained-glass window panel in Kyiv University in March 1964 with the subsequent hounding of the young artists who had created it; the prohibition of a meeting at the Shevchenko monument in Kyiv on 22 May 1964 and 1965;[6] the subsequent punishment of those who did go to the monument; the prohibition of a Shevchenko memorial evening in the

Automatic Machine Tool Factory in March 1965, with the result that the evening took place in the neighbouring park, again with subsequent sanctions against the participants (as a result of staying out in the cold wearing indoor clothes, and no less as a result of mental shock, the young organizer of the evening, a technologist, Oleksandr Mykolaychuk, died two days later); the punishment of several dozen young journalists, graduates of Kyiv State University, who had signed a declaration protesting against the groundless dismissal for 'nationalism' of the popular university lecturer, assistant professor M.M. Shestopal, towards early spring of 1965; finally, the dispersal (in the literal sense of the word) by the KGB of a group discussion on the state of Ukrainian culture, organized by university students with the participation of several hundred young people on 27 April 1965, and similar cases. As early as that the first arrests, although only short-term, were made, while at the same time men in plain clothes kept whispering stories about 'American dollars' which mysteriously instigated these 'assemblies' of youth (indeed, it is difficult for a bureaucrat who has gone wild from irresponsibility to hit upon something more intelligent! He understands and knows how to do one thing: sell himself for money, and this is why he is incapable of finding any other motivation in others.) The present arrests and the present tales about arms, a printing press, and again those inevitable 'dollars', are the logical culmination of that policy of forcibly repressing the interest of youth in national culture. Whether the organizers of the repressions want it or not, they assume the form of a 'Terror'. But terror, whether moral and psychological or physical, offers no positive solution to any problem, but only creates new ones. 'Terror,' Engels wrote, 'implies mostly useless cruelties perpetrated by frightened people in order to reassure themselves.'[7]

    Whoever earnestly desires to solve a particular problem which has arisen in life ought to give some thought to its causes. One can arrest not only several dozen, but several hundred or several thousand citizens: all the same, every day, more and more people in different ways, here, there and everywhere, will in one way or another express their dissatisfaction, bitterness and disagreement with many aspects of the present nationalities policy. They will feel anxiety about the fate of Ukrainian culture and the Ukrainian nation, and will ponder ways and means of redress.

These are honest people with good intentions. They number thousands. They are Soviet people. Who has the right, and by whom granted, to sever them from the living body of the nation, to suppress their civic activity, to place them under suspicion? Would he who took such a road not commit another horrible crime against communism and society?

Is he who really thinks about the interests of communism, he who is really motivated by the interests of society, not duty-bound to repress his personal emotions and irritation and, instead of suppressing and severing, should he not rather take a more fundamental approach, attempt to seek out the primary causes and to correct the phenomena of life themselves, the political mistakes and enormities themselves which produce undesirable results and give rise to undesirable public reactions?

Today a Ukrainian, if he at all thinks himself a Ukrainian, cannot fail to feel a profound bitterness and alarm about the fate of his nation, and if that is so, nobody in the world has the power to prevent him from speaking out about it.

I am firmly convinced that the anxiety felt by an ever-widening circle of Ukrainian youth is the inevitable result of grave violations of the Leninist nationalities policy, or more precisely: a total revision of the Leninist nationalities policy of the Party carried out by Stalin in the 1930s and continued by Khrushchev in the last decade.

I am firmly convinced that for the cause of building communism, for a future communist society, and for the fate of world communism, it is difficult to find today anything more useful, noble and imperative than the restoration of the Leninist nationalities policy, since the fate of entire nations lies in the balance.

This is what I want to speak of in greater detail.

For this purpose, I am enclosing herewith material I have prepared on this topic (*Internationalism or Russification?*).

Ivan Dzyuba, December 1965

---

1 Lenin, *CW*, XXXVI, p. 606.
2 S. Zalygin, 'Na Irtyshe (iz khroniki sela Krutyye Luki)', *Novyy mir*, XL, 2, February 1964, p. 44.
3 Lenin, *CW*, XXXVI, p. 608.
4 Lenin, *CW*, XXXVII, p. 212.
5 A. Ishchuk, *Verbivchany. Roman-khronika*, Kyiv, Bk. x, 1961; Bk. 2, 1965.
6 22 May 1964: the date of a large spontaneous gathering in the park outside the University of Kyiv in which stands the monument to T. Shevchenko, held in memory to him; this resulted in official action being taken against a number of the participants. 27 April 1965: the date of a mass meeting in the same park, devoted to the problems of Ukrainian culture and nationality, dispersed by the authorities and followed by arrests and interrogations.
7 Marx and Engels, *SC*, pp. 302–3.

Here we have an important question of principle: how is internationalism to be understood?

V. I. Lenin, CW, XXXVI, p. 607.

We must create our own proletarian context for questions of Ukrainian culture ... Only the proletariat can be an active factor of Ukrainian culture. The building of Ukrainian culture can proceed only along proletarian paths, and we can say at the same time: only in its Ukrainian forms can culture develop in Ukraine, only in its Ukrainian forms can the Soviet state exist in our country.

M. Skrypnyk's speech in *X z'yizd KP(B)U*, Kharkiv, 1928, p. 458.

And the dark dungeons are full now. Who are the prisoners there? The police have spread slander among the people that they are incendiaries. They are interrogated, judged, tormented and tortured, but cannot be proven to be incendiaries, for in reality they are not incendiaries but men devoted to the people, desiring a different, genuine kind of freedom for the people.

'Tysyacheletiye Rossii', *Kolokol: Obshcheye veche*, No. 4, London, 15 October 1862, p. 26.

Internationalism or Russification?
A Study in the Soviet Nationalities Problem

Ivan Dzyuba

Introduction

One young Ukrainian poet has written a poem with these painful words:

> I bear no malice towards any people,
> Towards no people on this earth do I bear malice.
> Why then is it ever more difficult?
> To live on earth in spiritual plurality?

This is the grief of many Ukrainians, a *cri de coeur* of many Ukrainians.

The Ukrainian people has never been aggressive and intolerant towards others; never in its history has it enslaved other peoples. To the overwhelming majority of Ukrainian intellectuals, because of their democratic spirit, narrow nationalism has always been alien and chauvinism quite unnatural. These are now all the more alien to the overwhelming majority of Ukrainians, after so many bitter lessons of history, now that socialism has become the sole philosophy of Ukrainians and is shared by dozens of peoples of the great socialist commonwealth.

It is all the more painful for a Ukrainian (if he feels the least bit as a Ukrainian) to see today that something incomprehensible and unjustifiably disgraceful is happening to his socialist nation. Not all Ukrainians are equally aware and conscious of what is taking place (for these processes themselves are of such a nature that they do not appear on the surface nor in their own guise), but almost all feel that 'something' evil is going on.

Marxism-Leninism defines a nation as a historically evolved community characterized by unity of territory, economic life, historic fate, language and mental mould as revealed in its culture.

In all of these aspects the Ukrainian nation today is not experiencing a 'flowering', as is officially proclaimed, but a crisis, and this must be admitted if one takes even a moderately honest look at actual reality.

Territorial unity and sovereignty are being gradually and progressively lost through mass resettlement (by the *orgnabor*[1] and other means) of the Ukrainian population in Siberia, Kazakhstan, the North, etc., where it numbers millions but is quickly denationalized; through an organized mass resettlement of Russians in Ukraine, not always with economic justification and not always motivated by economic reasons (as, for instance, in Stalin's time, particularly in the cities of Western Ukraine); through administrative divisions that remain a formality and through the doubtful sovereignty of the government of the Ukrainian SSR over the territory of Ukraine. This latter reason, coupled with excessive centralization and a total subordination to all-Union authorities in Moscow, makes it equally difficult to speak about the *integrity and sovereignty of the economic life* of the Ukrainian nation.

A common historic fate is also being lost, as the Ukrainian nation is being progressively dispersed over the Soviet Union, and as the sense of historic national tradition and knowledge of the historic past are gradually being lost due to a total lack of national education in *school* and in society in general.

Ukrainian national *culture* is being kept in a rather provincial position and is practically treated as 'second-rate'; its great past achievements are poorly disseminated in society, and this chiefly lives by Russian culture assimilated just anyhow. The Ukrainian language has also been pushed into the background and is not really used in the cities of Ukraine.

Finally, during the last decades the Ukrainian nation has virtually been deprived of the natural increase in population which characterizes all present-day nations. As far back as

1913 one would hear about 'the 37 million Ukrainians'.[2] The 1926 census speaks of 29 million Ukrainians in Ukraine; if over 7 million in the Russian SFSR are added (a figure quoted at the XII Congress of the RCP(B) in 1923), this also gives some 37 million. The same 37-million-odd appear also in the 1959 census. Even with a minimal natural increase (not to mention official tables of increase for Ukraine,[3] the number of Ukrainians, allowing for war losses, should have increased by 10–20 million. After all, the total population within the present boundaries of the USSR has risen from 159 million in 1913 to 209 million in 1959, and the number of Russians has doubled in spite of war losses: 55.4 million in 1897, 60–70 million in 1913, and 114.1 million in 1959

Even if there had been no other alarming facts, this alone – the absence of a normal natural growth of a people – would have been sufficient attestation that the nation is going through a crisis. But there are countless other facts. These facts, and various aspects of the national crisis experienced by the Ukrainian people, will be the theme of the present work. We will show, in particular, how this crisis has resulted from the violation of the Leninist nationalities policy, from its replacement by Stalin's Great-Power policy and Khrushchev's pragmatism, all irreconcilable with scientific communism.

However, I should first like to say a few words to those who do not understand why we should be alarmed by the perspective of denationalization of one people or another, or why we should attach any importance at all to the question of nationality.

There are various kinds of negative attitudes to this question. There is one sort of negation of nationality which springs from elementary ignorance and a total deafness to spiritual interests. Another negation at least has its source in an instinctive feeling of danger connected with the idea of nationality ('politics'!); however, self-deception conceals its source in fear and seeks a 'noble' motivation. Finally, there is a negation based on a misunderstanding, on a superficial understanding of nationality as something that in one way or another is opposed to humanity and to the ideal of universality, and thus causes humanity to retrogress. All of these views have something in common. In the first place, those who hold them consider their position very noble (although in actual fact it is not, as we shall see below) and with ludicrous scorn regard any concern about the nationalities problem as 'nationalism', not noticing that all human culture is permeated with such 'nationalism'. Secondly, as history shows, any indifference to the national problem, attitudes of neglect, obscuring of it and apathy towards it, have always and everywhere been connected in some way or other with social reaction, anti-civic attitudes, or a decay of civic principles. In short, their common source is social despotism, not freedom. Such views have to a large degree been passed on to us by the petty bourgeoisie of the Russian Empire which was characterized by the greatest social and national oppression in the world and thus also by the greatest national nihilism. It is also typical that this national nihilism in the fancy-dress of alleged 'all-human' or 'all-Russian universality' was preached precisely by reactionaries, serf-owners and learned 'pillars of the Fatherland' and refined 'philosophers of the rod', while democrats and revolutionaries like Chernyshevsky, Dobrolyubov, Herzen, Bakunin, Pryzhov and others stressed the universal cultural value of nationalities and pointed out the important place of national movements on the wide revolutionary-democratic front of the struggle against the despotic empire of the Russian tsars. They supported with all their strength the liberation movements of the non-Russian peoples that were directed against the Russian Empire, thus becoming genuine internationalists and true sons of the Russian people, the honour and conscience of their nation. Let us remember how Lenin spoke of Herzen as having saved the honour of Russian democracy by coming to the defence of Poland against Russian tsarism.[4]

The great Herzen with his typical social perceptiveness and his unerring diagnosis of any falsehood and injustice firmly grasped and indefatigably stressed the inner connection between political despotism and an anti-national attitude. He was the first to reveal the political essence of that deliberate dislocation, depersonalization and artificial 'crossing' of nations which Russian tsarism carried out under the slogan of 'unity, a common fatherland, common blood, fraternity' and similar official formulas. In particular, there was written in Herzen's *Kolokol* about this:

> Our government, which dislikes pure nationalities, has always tried to mingle and reshuffle them as much as possible. Disjointed tribes are usually meeker, and it seems that the governmental stomach digests mixed blood more easily, there is less sharpness in it.[5]

Herzen's *Kolokol* constantly stresses the reactionary character of official 'all-Russianness', of bureaucratic 'nationlessness' and speaks with bitter sarcasm about the overpowering and obtuse bureaucratic principle which wipes out nationality and personality in the name of official 'convenience' and bureaucratic progress.

> Is it possible that you, writers, publicists and professors, have not understood yet that official rank by far outweighs any nationality, that it evens out and equalizes all national peculiarities and shortcomings, abstracting the frail human personality and raising it to a higher mathematical power? Is it possible that you do not know yet the great sacrament of governmental anointing, by virtue of which a Jew or a Moslem, having risen to the rank of colonel, may not only teach his Russian subordinates

their Christian duties, but also direct their religious consciences? Where then do you live, on what planet? The ideal official remembers no kinship. Or do you suppose that only a Russian is capable of achieving such a gentle disposition?[6]

It is interesting that these sarcastic passages are echoed in analogous taunts of Marx (for instance, about the *canaille* who barter away their nationality for rank and privilege)[7] and of Lenin ('The bourgeoisie, who put forward most insistently the principle "my country is wherever it is good for me", and who, as far as money is concerned, have always been international ...').[8]

Addressing myself again to people who are remote from consciously 'selling out their nationality', but consider a concern for the national problem to be incompatible with human nobility of mind, and want to feel 'simply as men', above any national bounds, I would like to tell them that they are profoundly (though, perhaps, sincerely) mistaken in considering such a position as the ultimate attainment of universal culture. Quite the contrary. For all the great figures of world culture – philosophers, sociologists, historians, writers, artists, psychologists and pedagogues – their membership of humanity and their work for humanity are inseparable from their membership of their own nation and their work for it. They have all derived their universal humanistic enthusiasm from their highly developed national feeling and national consciousness, without which they did not conceive of genuine internationalism.

We could cite hundreds of relevant statements from great men and great authorities (since in this case we are addressing those for whom authorities count). However, this would take up too much space.

Therefore, we shall limit ourselves to quoting a kind of *résumé* drawn from a review of all these opinions by a distinguished student of the nationalities question, the Russian scholar Professor A.D. Gradovsky, who, far from being a 'nationalist', was a conscientious scholar and was well acquainted with the attainments of European thought.

After drawing attention to the sad ignorance and inanity of the contemporary public on the nationalities question, Gradovsky goes on to summarize the current negations of nationality and the most popular arguments of the 'anti-nationals':

> There is but one culture; its results must be identical everywhere. Each people, though proceeding along its own path, is bound to arrive at the same results. If the results are to be common, why should we trouble ourselves about different paths? Would it not be better and simpler to adopt the institutions, methods and means of those peoples which have outstripped us in their civilization? Why should we exert our minds, if others have thought about the same matters earlier and better than we? The principle of nationality, flattering our self-esteem, will alienate us from the general cultural movement of civilized mankind. We will arrive at the conviction that everything which is our own, merely because it is *our own*, is infinitely higher than everything foreign, merely because it is foreign. The very source of national sentiment is suspect. Does it not consist in a hidden hostility towards other nations? Civilization must lead all peoples to intercourse and possible unity. Civilization will give us general peace and will consolidate general welfare. And what does our principle of nationality do? It gives rise to enmity and envy between various tribes, it is the source of endless wars and diverts peoples from productive work on their domestic tasks. Let us suppress

> within ourselves these feelings which may befit savage tribes. Let us banish this principle in the name of loftier demands of culture! Such are the current opinions; such are the objections we could hear quite recently at every turn; you can be sure we will hear them in the not-too-distant future. But I intend to challenge something more than these current opinions. We must get to the root of the matter, we must dwell on those factors that inspire these opinions which are only a particular echo, a symptom, so to speak, of a more profound world view.[9]

After examining this 'anti-national' philosophy, Gradovsky reaches the just conclusion that it is a product either of superficial thought or of an attempt to give a refined theoretical basis to a regime of national oppression.

On the basis of the facts of the universal historic process on the one hand, and of the views and doctrines of great philosophers, historians and sociologists on the other, synthesizing this mass of material, Gradovsky summarizes the concept worked out by nineteenthcentury scholarship (and, let us add, accepted and developed later by our contemporary scholarship) about the interrelation of the nation and humanity, of individual, national and universal life:

> No thinking man can help noticing the following significant fact:
> As the European states take on freer forms, as the principle of equality is consolidated in them, as education develops, as the initiative of society and its participation in political matters increases – in each society a consciousness of its own individual peculiarities takes root ...
> Catholic and feudal Europe of the Middle Ages knew no nationalities question. Neither

did the Europe created by the Westphalian peace, the Europe of artificial states ...

The nationalities question was raised and formulated in the nineteenth century. It follows from the recognition of a people's free moral personality which has the right to an independent history and therefore to its own statehood. This philosophic and political principle is reinforced by the conclusions of sciences created in our time: anthropology and linguistics; it is corroborated by the conclusions of history which has undergone so great a development in the nineteenth century. Before anthropology and linguistics had taken shape, prior to the contemporary achievements of history, 'humanity' was pictured as some formless mass of 'atoms' hardly differing from each other. Now we see humanity as a system of heterogeneous human groups loudly proclaiming their right to an individual existence ...

The diversity of national traits is the primary condition for the regular progress of *universal civilization*. Any one people, no matter how great its capabilities and how rich its material resources, can realize only one of the facets of human life in general. To deprive humanity of its different organs means to deprive it of the possibility of manifesting in human history the rich substance of the human spirit. The exclusiveness of a single civilization, the uniformity of cultural forms run counter to all conditions of human progress. Science does not reject the concept of a universal civilization, in the sense that the most important results of the intellectual, moral and economic life of each people become the property of all the others. But history offers incontrovertible evidence that each of those results was achievable on the basis of national history; that Phidias's statues and Plato's philosophy were Greek creations, that Roman law is a product of Roman history, and the constitution of England is its national heritage ...

In the name of the plenitude of human civilization, all nations are called to activity and life equally removed both from isolated alienation and from blind imitation. Each people must give humanity what is latent in the forces of its spiritual and moral nature. *National creative work* is the ultimate goal marked for each people by nature itself, a goal without which the human race cannot achieve perfection ... The subordination of all races to one 'all-redeeming' civilization has the same pernicious effect on international life as 'all-redeeming' administrative centralization has on the internal life of a country ...

A man deprived of the feeling of nationality is incapable of a wise spiritual life ...

Only a people speaking its own language is capable of progress in intellectual life ... Only a man who has overcome his feeling of self-interest and cold-hearted cosmopolitanism, who has devoted himself to the people's cause, who believes in the strength and calling of his people, is capable of creative work and of truly great deeds; for he acts in view of the living eternity of the people with all its past and its future.

Under such conditions a people accustomed to serious and persistent self-improvement will not strive for external predominance; common endeavour will breed the genuine esteem of one people for

> the individuality of another, and national liberty will become the rule of universal life.
>
> Nationality and work, nationality and creativity, nationality and education, nationality and liberty are words which must become synonymous ...
>
> The enunciation of the national principle is the attainment of an age-old culture, of a common endeavour of all European peoples. It has been enunciated in the name of civilization and for civilization ...
>
> Self-awareness! A great word indeed ... [10]

We repeat: similar judgements of highly authoritative and competent men can be cited indefinitely, as this is not someone's personal conclusion but, as Gradovsky justly pointed out, 'the attainment of an age-old culture, of a common endeavour of all European peoples'.

Marxism-Leninism, as is known, arose not as a result of the ignoring of this 'age-old culture', but as a result of the mastering and adapting of it. In particular, it did not reject the tremendous historic social-cultural significance and value of the nation, of national self-knowledge and self-awareness, of national thought and material creativity, of national liberation struggle, etc.

This is how the contemporary American Marxist philosopher, H. Selsam, sums up the attitude of scientific communism towards the nationalities question:

> But, the question is asked, why maintain national groups and national cultures at all? Why not a world culture, one language, one historical tradition? These questions are raised by the doctrinaire who sees in nationalism only a limitation upon a world society, who sees it only in the form of the worst bourgeois national chauvinism ...

> It is with nations as with individuals.
> A healthy society depends not on individual
> uniformity and regimentation but on the
> fullest and freest development of each in
> the interests of all. A healthy world requires,
> not the extinguishing of certain national
> differences but their cultivation and widest
> interplay, creating a universal culture through
> each people's unique contributions.[11]

Marxism-Leninism has related the nationalities question to the revolutionary class struggle of the proletariat, to the struggle for a new and just classless society – communism. Marx in a letter to S. Meyer and A. Vogt, 9 April 1870:

> Hence it is the task of the International everywhere to put the conflict between England and Ireland in the foreground, and everywhere to side openly with Ireland. And it is the special task of the Central Council in London to awaken a consciousness in the English workers that *for them* the *national emancipation of Ireland* is no question of abstract justice or humanitarian sentiment but *the first condition of their own social emancipation.*

Engels in a letter to Marx, 15 August 1870:

> The case seems to me to be as follows: Germany has been driven by Badinguet[12] into a war for her national existence. If Badinguet defeats her, Bonapartism will be strengthened for years and Germany broken for years, perhaps for generations. In that event there will no longer be any question of an independent German working-class movement either, the struggle to restore

> Germany's national existence will absorb everything, and at best the German workers will be dragged in the wake of the French ... The whole mass of the German people of every class have realized that this is first and foremost a question of national existence and have therefore at once flung themselves into the fray.

And further on:

> I think our people can ... join the national movement ...

Engels in a letter to K. Kautsky, 12 September 1882:

> In my opinion the colonies proper, i.e. the countries occupied by a European population – Canada, the Cape, Australia – will all become independent; on the other hand, the countries inhabited by a native population, which are simply subjugated – India, Algeria, the Dutch, Portuguese and Spanish possessions – must be taken over for the time being by the proletariat and led as rapidly as possible towards independence...The victorious proletariat can force no blessings of any kind upon any foreign nation without undermining its own victory by so doing.

Engels in a letter to F. Mehring, 14 July 1893:

> ... The plundering of German territory on a large-scale sets in. This comparison is most humiliating for Germans but for that very reason the more instructive; and since our workers have put Germany back again in the forefront of the

historical movement it has become somewhat easier for us to swallow the ignominy of the past.[13]

Marxism-Leninism has developed a tremendous wealth of ideas concerning the nationalities question, and if we really cherish the interests of communism and of the people, and not the mere eventualities of the current political situation, we have no right to forget them or to distort them for our current needs.

By subordinating the national problem to the general proletarian cause, to the cause of revolution and communism, Marxism-Leninism did not reduce but rather added to its weight and importance, establishing quite clearly that, as long as it remains without a just solution, a just society, communism is impossible, and committing us to foster the enrichment and proliferation of national cultural attainments which will pass into the universal treasury, instead of lopping off their branches and cutting through their roots.

Marx, Engels and Lenin gave proof of great perception and humanity, of a broad humanistic approach and a lucid understanding of the sacred needs of each nation and of the perspectives for the most favourable historic development of all humanity. When it sometimes turned out that a certain judgement was made in haste, with insufficient knowledge of the matter, that a certain opinion might be used in such a way as to bring harm to the cause of some nation or other, they did not hesitate to make all the necessary corrections, and even changed their minds. Let us recall the evolution of Marx's and Engels's views on the Irish question, or how they introduced greater clarity into their attitude towards Slav problems and Russia. Let us recall how Engels, who was extremely favourably disposed towards the Polish revolutionaries, nevertheless refused to support Polish claims to the territories 'up to the Dvina and Dnieper rivers' as soon as he learnt that 'all the peasants there are Ukrainians while only the nobles and some of the townsmen are Poles'.[14] Let us recall how Lenin, observing the growth of Russian chauvinism in the Soviet Union, sounded the alarm and declared 'war to the death' against it.[15] Let us recall how he advised the drawing of more 'nationals' into the elaboration of the nationalities policy and into its local implementation, and recommended that their advice should be sought, an ear lent them and their initiative encouraged.

The national cause is the cause of the entire people and of each individual citizen. It is a basic concern of the whole people and of the civic conscience of each of us; it does not displace all other problems, interests and ideals, but is inseparably linked with them, and nobody has the right to keep silent when he sees something disgraceful, just as nobody has the right to turn a deaf ear to troubled voices.

If, of course, communism is a matter of vital concern to us, our mutual responsibility for each other and for mankind, the blossoming of the human in men and the triumph of the universal human nobility and truth – and not endless square-bashing under sergeant-majors for some, for the many, and a showy stage for a high and mighty power game for others, the few. And yet we all seem to want the first – the communism of the truth, and not the second – the pseudo-communism of the barracks, against which we were so much warned by Marx and Engels. Communism devoid of humanity, said Rosa Luxemburg, turns into its opposite.

---

1 Orgnabor: organizovannyy nabor rabochikh, organized manpower recruitment.
2 Lenin, CW, XIX, p. 379.
3 2 Cf. V.I. Naulko, *Etnichnyy sklad naselennya Ukrains'koyi RSR*, Kyiv, 1965.
4 Lenin, CW, XVIII, p. 30.
5 'Osvobozhdeniye krest'yan v Rossii i pol'skoye vosstaniye', *Kolokol*, No.195, 1 March 1865, p. 1602.
6 Ibid., p. 1602.
7 Marx and Engels, SC, p. 283.
8 Lenin, CW, XXIX, p. 201.
9 A. D, Gradovsky, *Sobraniye sochineniy*, VI, St Petersburg, 1873, p. 228.
10 A. D. Gradovsky, *Sobraniye sochineniy*, VI, St Petersburg, 1873, pp. 3–4, 14–15, 157–8, 263.
11 H. Selsam, *Socialism and Ethics*, London, 1947, pp. 186–7.
12 Badinguet: Napoleon III.
13 Marx and Engels, SC, pp. 287, 294–5, 423, 544.
14 Ibid., p. 91.
15 Lenin, CW, XXXIII, p. 372.

1
The possibility of mistakes and the admissibility of criticism on the nationalities question

In our country decisions on the nationalities policy appertain to those prerogatives of higher leadership which are not subject to any criticism or doubt. It is held that the nationalities question was solved once and for all in 1917, that the internal nationalities policy took final shape on that date and has remained unchanged ever since. Any doubts about the wisdom of any of its features at any stage are regarded as a relapse into bourgeois nationalism, while any attempt at a meaningful discussion 'plays into the hands of our enemies', as our obliging demagogues are quick to point out. In addition to the facts already mentioned I shall cite further instances of reprisals taken against people who dared to express reservations about certain features of the present-day nationalities policy (the pertinent facts from Stalin's time are common knowledge). This, however, is far from a Leninist approach.

First of all, Lenin stressed more than once that the victory of the revolution alone had not resolved the nationalities question, that we were only taking our first steps in that direction, and that the road from the formal equality of peoples proclaimed by the revolution to actual equality led only through a whole historic period of social and national construction in which unforeseen problems might arise.

Secondly, Lenin often spoke sharply of the fact that the Party had committed grave errors in the nationalities policy (especially in its implementation), particularly in that it had missed a number of important cues in the national situation, that many Party leaders were unconsciously imbued with Great Russian nationalism and Great-Power ideas, that they did not understand the national needs of other peoples and gave rise to the suspicion that they intended to bring them 'their Great Russian chauvinism in the guise of communism'.[1]

Thirdly, Lenin never concealed that several, often opposing, views on the nationalities question existed in the Party, and he considered discussion useful and indispensable; and for the purpose of successfully subduing the Great-Power ideology and Great Russian chauvinism, which were the main obstacles to the elaboration of a policy that would be best adjusted to the national needs of other peoples, he deemed it necessary first of all to lend an ear to the voices and complaints of local workers and 'nationals' ('A detailed code will be required, and only the nationals ... can draw it up at all successfully').[2]

All these views of Lenin are well known from his reports and speeches at the VIII and X Congresses of the RCP(B) and from his notes 'The Question of Nationalities or "Autonomization"', published in 1956.[3]

Much less well known are similar statements by many delegates to the VIII, X, XII and other Congresses of the RCP(B) and the CP(B)U. I shall quote some of them.

At the X Congress it was said in a joint report on the nationalities question (by Comrade Safarov) in the spirit of Lenin's pronouncements:

> On the nationalities question the Party has not up to now held to a firm line that would genuinely normalize the process of revolutionary development in those borderlands which under the rule of tsarism and the bourgeoisie vegetated as colonial or semi-colonial countries.

> We must admit in all fairness that up to
> now our Party has shown precious little interest
> in the nationalities question. This has resulted
> in a whole series of unforgivable mistakes and
> in delay in the process of revolutionary devel-
> opment in many borderlands. Quite uncon-
> sciously sometimes our communist comrades, our
> foremost proletarian elements, entered into contra-
> diction, into conflict, with the toiling masses of
> the oppressed nationalities, not knowing how to
> approach them and how to get to know them.
>
> The entire history of the former Russian
> Empire, which Engels called an immense amount
> of stolen property, was a history of coloni-
> zation. And since the proletarian revolution found
> its support mainly in the cities, in the border-
> lands the opposition between city and village
> took on the character of a national antagonism.[4]

And here is a fragment from the speech of V. Zatons'ky:

> You cannot evade the issue by a bare proclamation
> of the right of nations to self-determination
> or even of the right of nations to state secession ...
> Now the national movement is assuming very
> great importance.
>
> The national movement has apparently been
> engendered by the revolution. It must be said
> bluntly that this we have overlooked and most
> certainly let pass. This has been the greatest
> mistake of the Communist Party working
> in Ukraine. We have let it pass, we are all to
> blame for it. We have missed the upsurge of the
> national movement which was perfectly natural
> at the moment when the broad ignorant peasant
> masses awoke to conscious life. We have missed

the moment when a perfectly natural feeling of self-respect arose in these masses, and the peasant, who before had regarded himself and his peasant language, etc., with disdain, began to lift up his head and to demand much more than he had demanded in tsarist times.⁵ The revolution has aroused a cultural movement, awakened a wide national movement, but we have not managed to direct this national movement into our own course, we have let it pass by, and it has gone wholly along the road where the local petty-bourgeois intelligentsia and the kulaks led it. This must be bluntly said. This has been our greatest mistake.⁶

Serious mistakes in the nationalities policy were also made by communist parties in other European countries. This is why the V Congress of the Comintern noted in its resolutions:

> Nihilism and opportunistic errors in the nationalities question for which a number of communist parties are still noted are the weakest points of those parties which will never be able to fulfil their historic task unless they rid themselves of this weakness ...
> Nihilism and carelessness in the nationalities question (and, even more, a concession to the 'Great-Power' point of view of the ruling national group) have done considerable harm ...⁷

These examples, which could easily be multiplied, attest that in Lenin's time the Party did not conceal errors, difficulties and changes in the nationalities policy, did not shun broad and principled discussion on the nationalities question, but on the contrary considered such discussion indispensable for the assessment of all the factors, sometimes unforeseen, in a nationality situation or in the building of a nation.

It would be perfectly natural to take the same view of this today as well. It would be un-Leninist to ignore these obvious facts:

1. that the nationalities policy in our country kept changing: Leninist nation-building in the 1920s; Stalin's revision of the nationalities policy in the early 1930s, in particular the termination of so-called ukrainization; Stalin's liquidation of national Party cadres in the 1930s; Stalin's notorious repression of entire nationalities during and after the war; the restoration after the xx Party Congress of the rights of the nationalities 'liquidated' under Stalin; the extension of the rights of Union Republics, accompanied, however, by a number of subjectivist chauvinist measures taken by Khrushchev, especially in the field of education;
2. that in the nationalities policy miscalculations, errors and even crimes were committed, such as the above-mentioned destruction of entire nationalities, as well as Stalin's obvious ukrainophobia and antisemitism, revealed in particular at the xx Party Congress;
3. that even now there are a number of difficulties and ambiguities in the nationalities policy, that some things remain unclarified and some principles undefined, and most important of all, that all too often practice does not conform to theory.

Here Lenin's approach and Lenin's example teach us, and not only teach us but commit us to the open and honest discussion of all unsolved questions, all accumulated mistakes, all painful problems. Only along the path of such free and honest discussion, discussion showing sincere concern and constantly mindful of the needs of a harmonious development of the communist commonwealth of nations, only by taking such a road can a truly scientific communist solution be found. However, 'backroom' procedures behind closed doors, contempt for the thoughts of others, neglect of the interests and views of some social group or other, of some stratum of people or other, precedence given tacitly to some motives (let us say economic) over others (let us say national-cultural), the practice of secret instructions, insincere manoeuvring, discrepancy between word and deed, between promises and intentions – none of these have ever produced good results anywhere. Precisely such means and such procedures 'play into the hands of our enemies'.

1 Lenin, *CW*, XXIX, p. 175.
2 Lenin, *CW*, XXXVI, p. 610.
3 Ibid., pp. 605–11.
4 X s'yezd RKP(B), p. 189.
5 It is worth noting how Zatons'ky quite justly links the awakening of national consciousness with human and civic dignity, with human and civic rights.
6 X s'yezd RKP(B), pp. 202–3.
7 *Kommunisticheskiy Internatsional v dokumentakh, 199–32*, Moscow, 1933, pp. 405, 488.

2
The importance and place of the nationalities question

In a discussion at the x Party Congress one of the delegates declared:

> At this time, comrades, when our thoughts are turned in quite a different direction, when we think more about fuel, foodstuffs and our policy towards the peasantry, somehow one doesn't feel much like speaking on such a topic as the nationalities question.[1]

This was a very typical declaration. Similar declarations were frequently made at the VIII and x Party Congresses, and not only by oppositionists such as Zinov'yev, Pyatakov, Kamenev, Bukharin and others, who stood essentially for nationality liquidation until Lenin made his declaration concerning 'Autonomization', which was a kind of ultimatum to Great-Power adherents and chauvinists. Only after a number of extremely sharp interventions by Lenin, in which he showed how very harmful the Party's national nihilism was to the cause of the building of socialism, and in which he exposed its chauvinist-colonialist roots, only then did the nationality liquidators and Great-Power adherents lay down their arms, some of them with sincerity, others only pretending to do so, while waiting for the right time to arrive (which it eventually did). A dominant theme at the XII Party Congress of 1923 was Lenin's great concern for the building of national states and national cultures in the republics, and his active struggle against chauvinist-colonialist inertia. Even those who at the VIII and X Congresses smiled at the mere mention of the nationalities question, now started talking about the development of socialist nations and about the danger of chauvinistic levelling.

Lenin's profound and extensive understanding of questions of nationality, his incredible intuition in these matters is by no means the least of those links joining him in a purely human way with Marx and Engels, not only as a theoretician but also as a type of politician and a type of citizen. There is a widespread impression that the nationalities question is of third-rate importance in authentic Marxism. This is precisely the basis of the attitude of all past and present nationality liquidators. But in reality this is not so at all. Marx and Engels often ridiculed those who pinned the labels of 'anachronism, superstition and reaction' on nations and nationality problems. Naturally, we shall find very little about the nationalities question in Marx's *Capital* or in his theory in general. After all, this was a theory of the *class struggle* of the proletariat, not a theory of nations. But when this theory of class struggle was transposed into historical practice and became strategy and tactics, an unending panorama of the lives of nations emerged in all its immense historical scope in the tense dynamics of political reality. Thus, we find literally a tremendous wealth of ideas about national relations and the national tasks of proletarian parties in Marx's and Engels's 'more concrete' political works and especially in their correspondence. As Lenin says, 'his[2] theory is as far from ignoring national movements as heaven is from earth'.[3]

It is worth recalling here that both Marx and Engels more than once gave sharp warnings against a superficial and one-sided acceptance of their views, against a reduction of those views to 'phrases about historical materialism' and 'the primacy of economic conditions', etc. In his letter to C. Schmidt, Engels wrote: '... Marx used to say, commenting on the French "Marxists" of the late seventies: "All I know is that I am not a Marxist".'⁴ And in a letter to J. Bloch, Engels admitted:

> Marx and I are ourselves partly to blame for the fact that the younger people sometimes lay more stress on the economic side than is due to it. We had to emphasize the main principle vis-à-vis our adversaries, who denied it, and we had not always the time, the place or the opportunity to give their due to the other elements involved in the interaction. But when it came to presenting a section of history, that is, to making a practical application, it was a different matter and there no error was permissible. Unfortunately, however, it happens only too often that people think they have fully understood a new theory and can apply it without more ado from the moment they have assimilated its main principles, and even those not always correctly. And I cannot exempt many of the more recent 'Marxists' from this reproach, for the most amazing rubbish has been produced in this quarter, too ...⁵

Lenin considered Marxism not only as a series of basic principles, but also as an enormous treasure-house of the human spirit and nobility and the endowment, as he said, of all humanity's greatest attainments in the course of its whole history. Hence his incomparable sensitivity and susceptibility also in matters of nationality, hence his uncommon *feeling for national equity*, which is the true mark of a genuine communist leader and which strikes everyone who has read his notes 'The Question of Nationalities ...',⁶ all the more since this *feeling* is well-nigh lost and scorned today ...

Lenin felt profoundly his great responsibility in the handling of the nationalities problem in the Union of Socialist Republics. He was persistent and tireless in stating the Ukrainian case, thus causing numerous complaints from 'centralists', who according to the 'good old tradition' considered this question to be an AustroGerman invention, among other things. 'Some comrades', Lenin testified, 'accused the writer of these lines of giving too much "prominence" to the national question in Ukraine,' and he went on to explain that such reproaches sprang from a complete lack of comprehension of the weight andww complexity of this question, from a failure to comprehend the true interests of communist coexistence of nations, and from the 'jaw breaking' complex of Great-Power chauvinists. '... To ignore the importance of the national question in Ukraine,' he continued, '– a sin of which Great Russians are often guilty (and of which the Jews are guilty perhaps only a little less often than the Great Russians) – is a great and dangerous mistake.'[7]

When Stalin proposed the idea of 'Autonomization', that is to say, the withdrawal of state sovereignty from the independent socialist republics and their reduction to only locally autonomous status, Lenin sharply contradicted this antinational centralizing tendency and considered the mere fact of the emergence and toleration of such an attitude as his own personal guilt before the communist cause.

> I suppose I have been very remiss with respect to the workers of Russia for not having intervened energetically and decisively enough in the notorious question of 'Autonomization', which, it appears, is officially called the question of the union of Soviet socialist republics.[8]

Lenin spoke more than once about the enormous importance of the nationalities question, both in its internal aspect ('the fundamental interest of proletarian solidarity') and in its external ramifications:

> It would be unpardonable opportunism if, on the eve of the *début* of the East, just as it is awakening,

we undermined our prestige with its peoples, even if only by the slightest crudity or injustice towards our own non-Russian nationalities.[9]

The Party leaders of that time well knew what efforts Lenin had to expend to re-orientate the Party's nationalities policy toward practical national construction and protection from Great-Power rapacity, toward actual and not formal internationalism. Besides deep gratitude to Lenin, they expressed concern about the further fate of this policy and about its continuation without Lenin.

It is not by chance that at the XII Congress of the RCP(B) the eminent communist Yakovlev said:

> It has been enumerated here that the nationalities question was discussed at the VIII Congress, at the X Congress, and now at the XII Congress. It has been forgotten that the nationalities question was discussed at the December conference in 1919, where Comrade Lenin delivered a speech on the nationalities question. This speech did not even get into his collected works. This is a lost document, it was not published at the time, and I fear it may become another dead letter. (Interjections: 'Hear, hear!') Would you, at this Congress, have discussed the nationalities question as you do, if there had been no *letters* of Comrade Lenin? No. I think there is one basic safeguard against our ending up with another dead letter, which will ensure our taking a number of concrete steps, and that is to circulate as widely as possible in the Party the ideas and thoughts developed by Comrade Lenin in his letters. For these are documents that will force every member of our Party to ponder how foul Russian Great-Power chauvinism penetrates through his machinery.[10]

The same idea was also stressed by delegate Makharadze:

> We all know whose teaching[11] it is and what it is, what our whole programme means and who shouldered it. Every comrade knows this well, knows who said the first word on Great Russian chauvinism and who was the first to raise his standard against this very thing. It was Comrade Il'ich.[12] You all know this well. Now I ask you: do the words pronounced here today resemble the words spoken by Vladimir Il'ich? I hope that the present Congress from which Vladimir Il'ich is now absent, though his spirit walks among us, I think that this Congress will pass such a resolution and adopt such measures as will really ensure the implementation of that very programme whose father and creator he was.[13]

Even Rakovsky, who at the time was Chairman of the Council of People's Commissars of the Ukrainian SSR and can hardly be suspected of separatism or particularly pro-Ukrainian sympathies (rather the contrary, since for a long time he had been close to those in the opposition who promoted the policy of national nihilism), even he was at that time forced to speak in these terms:

> For a great many reasons, we must regret the absence from our midst of Vladimir Il'ich, and the nationalities question is one of them. We have needed his authority, and his understanding, not only of the domestic, but also of the international situation, we have needed him to strike out at our Party with his authoritative word and to show it that it is committing fatal errors in the nationalities question. I must say frankly, when I look at the calmness with which the Russian

section of our Party in particular regards the disputes ... I feel anxiety for the fate of our Party.[14]

What triumphed later as regards the nationalities policy: Lenin's 'torments', the 'calmness' of the Philistine circles, or its end-product – Stalinist-style 'harshness'? Anyone who has the faintest recollection of recent history knows. But even now, when the miracle-working 'red-hot iron' has dropped from Stalin's weary hands, Lenin's 'torments' have remained buried in oblivion. To them, we still have a long way to go. A spirit of conscious or unconscious disdain for the nationalities' cause and of incomprehension of the nationalities question prevails everywhere. In recent decades almost no attention has been paid to it, neither in the press, in literature, in history, nor in social or educational work. Only perhaps in the fields of literary and art scholarship might you still hear the last gasps of piteous scholastic talk about 'national form' ...

But under this external crust of calm, indifference and neglect the ominous internal process of russification and assimilation has been flaring up all the more widely and fiercely.

In 1923 the XII Congress of the RCP(B) resolved (and this was reaffirmed later by a number of other congresses) that the Party cannot remain neutral in questions of national development. Its prime duty is to support the national development of each people in each national Republic. As regards Ukraine, the policy of 'neutrality' of the Party in the so-called 'struggle of two cultures', Russian and Ukrainian, was especially condemned, and the Party was made responsible for the development of Ukrainian national culture. A special point was even inserted into the 'Programme of the Comintern' about 'the Soviet state using all the forces at its command to safeguard and support the national cultures of nations that have liberated themselves from capitalism'.[15]

And now in 1961 Khrushchev has declared: we 'will not conserve ... national distinctions'[16] (as if it were just a question of this! What an original conception of 'national distinctions'!). In practice this meant: the mincing-machine of russification may continue turning at full speed, we will not interfere with it, quite the contrary!

1   X s'yezd RKP(B), p. 201.
2   Marx's.
3   Lenin, CW, XX, p. 436.
4   Marx and Engels, SC, p. 496.
5   Marx and Engels, SC, p. 500.
6   Ibid., XXX, p. 270.
7   Lenin, CW, XXXVI, pp. 605–11.
8   Lenin, CW, XXXVI, p. 605.
9   Ibid., pp. 609–11.
10 XII s'yezd RKP(B), pp. 595–6.
11 The 1923 edition of XII s'yezd RKP(B), which was used by Dzyuba, has in the first line of the Makharadze quotation mucheniye 'torment' (p. 474). This may have been a misprint; the 1968 edition has instead ucheniye 'teaching' (p. 519).
12 Lenin.
13 XII s'yezd RKP(B), p. 519.
14 Ibid., p. 576.
15 Kommunisticheskiy Internatsional v dokumentakh, 1919–32, Moscow, 1933, p. 22.
16 N.S. Khrushchev, On the Communist Programme, Moscow, 1961, p. 88.

3
The forces that prepared the revision of the Leninist nationalities policy

The concern for the nationalities policy without Lenin, expressed by the delegates to the VIII, X and especially XII Party Congresses, twas neither accidental nor abstract. The people who sounded this alarm well knew that there were forces in the Party which were indifferent or hostile to this policy; they well knew what efforts it had cost Lenin to overcome this indifference and to check this hostility; they well knew that with Lenin's death these forces could again assert themselves.

I shall cite several speeches from the XII Party Congress in which the greatest obstacles and dangers menacing the Leninist nationalities policy were vividly described. If we read these speeches carefully it is not difficult to see that the anti-Leninist tendencies and sentiments censured in them are not only alive today but sometimes even triumph under the guise of 'Leninism'.

In his address to the XII Congress of the RCP(B), the Ukrainian delegate and well-known Party worker, Comrade H. Hryn'ko, expressed his profound concern about the gap between theory and practice in the nationalities question, about the fine resolutions adopted unanimously and then forgotten. Hryn'ko saw the reasons for this pernicious 'tacit sabotage' of the nationalities policy as lying first of all in the 'inertia of centralism' and secondly in the peculiar Great-Power psychology of many 'Party apparatchiks':

I will begin by informing you how the nationalities question followed its course at the last All-Ukrainian Party Conference. After a speech by Comrade Frunze, followed by lively debates, one of the oldest members of our Party, Comrade Skrypnyk, with his fine knowledge and intuitive understanding of the Party, said that although all the circumstances of the Conference guaranteed the unanimous adoption of the Central Committee's theses, he still had a pessimistic feeling that they might again remain a dead letter. Comrade Frunze in his final address also stressed that he felt some pessimism, provoked by his conviction that there were a great many comrades in the conference hall who could have, but had not, raised objections, and who did not in fact subscribe to the present line of nationalities policy. And I think that this impression of one of the most significant Party Conferences brings us face to face with those difficulties and obstacles that we meet first and foremost within our Party when implementing our nationalities policy ...

I want to stress these obstacles in two fields: inter-state relations within the Union and national culture. It is no secret that not only in our Soviet state machinery ... but also within our Party there exists a profound centralizing inertia. And this profound centralizing inertia presses, often considerably, upon responsible leaders and is one of the greatest obstacles to the normalization of inter-state relations within the Union ...

According to Hryn'ko, the second important obstacle to nation-building was 'an extremely widespread attitude of mind among us, which at the present moment as a rule causes us to remain silent on the nationalities question. Sometimes, however, we speak, but the most dangerous thing is precisely that we remain silent.' Ironically, though in fact accurately, Hryn'ko thus sets forth 'the basic trait of this ideology or psychology':

> The nationality factor was important to us in 1919–20, when it was the weapon of the peasantry that went against us. We overcame and liquidated it. Now the nationality factor represents no danger to us. The second motive, which we could call a kind of pseudoeconomic disdain towards the nationality factor, sounds like this: the question of the union between workers and peasants is solved by economics – tobacco, agricultural implements, etc., the nationality factor is of no importance here... Furthermore, you can often see people trying to substitute personal impressions for an analysis of social facts. Highly responsible comrades from Ukraine speak thus: 'I have travelled all over Ukraine, I have spoken to the peasants, and I have gained the impression that they don't want the Ukrainian language.' Instead of analysing large-scale social movements, the period of the Central Rada, of Petlyura, of the national insurrections, etc., they are content with the uncritical method of personal impression and build their nationalities policy on this basis ...

Let us be honest: do not these words, uttered in 1923, strike straight home at some of today's statesmen? Is not this 'psychology' still alive today? Has it not burst into luxuriant bloom?

> It is this psychology which is the greatest and most fundamental obstacle to the implementation of the new line in the nationalities policy. I think the basic task of this Congress consists

in smashing this massive, inert psychology which is widespread among the ranks of our Party, in putting an end to this obtuse indifference on the nationalities question, and in instilling immediately some vigour into the implementation of our nationalities policy.[1]

Let us judge for ourselves whether this 'massive, inert psychology' was successfully 'smashed', or whether it has become even more 'massive' ...

And here is a *cri de coeur* from M. Skrypnyk's speech:

> We are used to following the age-old path and do not understand that the theses adopted by us in the nationalities question commit us to certain things.
>
> What does this mean? Where does this contradiction between theory and practice originate? Not only at our Congresses, but also at the II Congress of the Comintern we adopted a resolution on the nationalities question. It was precisely the Russian delegation that proposed this resolution which said that in the sphere of the nationalities question the proletariat must be ready for enormous self-sacrifice in order to form an alliance with the colonial peoples and with the peasants of oppressed nations. This is the question that we must now consider.
>
> Well, has this readiness for self-sacrifice been demonstrated? Not at all. There are only theoretical acknowledgements on the part of the majority, but when it comes to action we have neither the strength nor the will. Great-Power prejudices imbibed with their mother's milk have in the case of many, many comrades become second nature ...

Why then do we make virtually no headway in the nationalities question, and why do we actually remain powerless, although we have solved it correctly in principle? The thing is that we are making a balancing act of the nationalities question. There are those who constantly attempt to find a middle road. They feel that every reference to Great-Power chauvinism must always be compensated by a counter-reference to the chauvinism of stateless peoples, and thus we always get double book-keeping. They always try to dismiss every mention of Great Russian chauvinism by advancing the counter-claim: 'Try to overcome your own nationalism first.' Thus, in point of fact we have waged no struggle against Great-Power chauvinism.[2] We must put an end to this ...

In our Party there were differing points of view on the nationalities question: the point of view of Rosa Luxemburg and the point of view of Comrade Lenin. Alas, Comrades, there is still a third point of view, upheld by the greatest number of supporters, the point of view of the Party morass, the point of view of people who are afraid to speak up here with a clearly defined line. Are there comrades in our Party who are in principle Great-Power Russophiles? Why then don't they speak up here but only in practice distort the Party line? The important thing is not to adopt a resolution but to carry it out.

At our All-Ukrainian Party Conference, the resolution on the nationalities question was adopted unanimously, but for four abstentions. But I was told that after the adoption of the resolution one of those who voted for it, the chairman of a provincial executive committee, after leaving the conference hall was addressed in Ukrainian by some non-Party cooperative worker and answered without batting an eyelid: 'Why don't you speak in an intelligible language?' He 'voted for' the resolution on the nationalities question, he 'fully agrees' with it. This absolute contradiction between theory and practice, this line from the Party morass must be seared with a red-hot iron; our theory, our line of principle must be genuinely put into practice.[3]

Does all this not sound very topical today? Comment is superfluous: the picture looks very familiar ...

Here is an excerpt from a speech by Rakovsky, who at the time was Chairman of the Council of People's Commissars, and who, as I mentioned earlier, did not suffer from ukrainophilism:

I must admit to you: for some time on the eve of the Congress we cherished the hope that the nationalities question, as Il'ich had supposed, would become the central theme of our Congress, and here it has become its tailpiece. Our comrades endure the dispute on the nationalities question with impatience ... I don't want to blame anyone, since in this respect we are all guilty, and in Ukraine, when I see what a bad time we have forcing our organizations which work there in the conditions of a nationalities struggle, what a bad time we have forcing them to understand the significance of the nationalities question, I begin to be concerned about Soviet rule ...

In regard to the nationalities question we have a prejudice, a deep prejudice and one that is all the more dangerous because it is a communist prejudice, because its appearance is communist, because it has roots in our programme, and because this prejudice conceals our ignorance on the nationalities question. I remember a very characteristic remark of Comrade Stalin. When I returned from abroad after the adoption of the programme about the Union, Comrade Stalin told me: 'You know, many people have asked me: is this long-range, is this not a diplomatic move?' Yes, Comrades, the whole nationalities policy, our whole Soviet government in its intra-Union relations have been understood by the majority in Ukraine, and here in Russia even more, to be a certain strategic game of diplomacy: 'For goodness' sake, we solved the nationalities question way back in the October Revolution, our country is communist, we all *do* stand for internationalism.' Tell me, Comrades, how many of you can explain in what way the October Revolution solved the nationalities question? Don't forget that in 1919 authoritative comrades declared at the Party Congress that the nationalities question no longer existed ... What is the rank and file to do? And here we have a multitude of responsible comrades who regard the nationalities question with a smile, with a sneer: 'But we are a country that has gone beyond the stage of nationalities,' as one comrade expressed himself, 'we are a country where material and economic culture opposes national culture. National culture is for backward countries on the other side of the barricade, for capitalist countries, and we are a communist country.' [4]

Against the background of all this it becomes clear that there was reason to doubt the adequacy of the guarantees of rights for nationalities that had been proposed earlier. Yakovlev, in particular, said of them:

More about the guarantees proposed by Comrade Stalin. Does a second CEC[5] constitute a guarantee? I ask you to think this out calmly. Can the first CEC guarantee anything in practice, does it decide basic questions of principle independently? And if to the first CEC you add a second with the same rights, will the two CECs really make a joint contribution to the solution of the nationalities question? Let us look squarely at this. At the Party Congress we can demand a guarantee as to how steadfastly this will be pursued – not only paper guarantees ... How should the question be formulated? We have to seek other guarantees, and one of the most essential of them is the widest propagation of the ideas and thoughts developed in Lenin's last letters. This is what can make the whole Party shake itself and reflect. Without any doubt, this guarantee must be implemented, as the question is formulated in them with unusual precision and clarity, and the whole party must be made very conscious of it.[6]

And here we must state the most infamous part: the latter was not done, 'the ideas and thoughts developed in Lenin's last letters' never became the property of the Party and the people. These letters remained sealed in Stalin's safes until 1956, when they were published. But even since then they are not too readily quoted and, to put it mildly, not too willingly disseminated. This is understandable: Lenin's thoughts contrast too much with what is being done in the nationalities sphere today.

Let us look more specifically at some aspects and 'lines' of merciless revision of Lenin's nationalities policy. We shall then see the flowering and the triumph of the anti-Leninist, anti-communist tendencies and sentiments noted above in the Party workers' speeches; we shall see ignorance and irresponsibility regarding the nationalities question, indifference and contempt, Great Russian nationalism and Great-Power chauvinism, the gap between theory and practice, between words and deeds, bureaucratic centralization and levelling, etc., etc.

1 XII *s'yezd* RKP(B), pp. 502–5.
2 Apropos, the same point was raised at the X Congress in Comrade Safarov's joint report on the nationalities question: 'These simultaneous blows lead to nothing but a denial of nationalities' rights under the Soviet banner' (X *s'yezd* RKP(B), p. 196).
3 XII *s'yezd* RKP(B), pp. 571–3.
4 XII *s'yezd* RKP(B), pp. 577–8.
5 Stalin's proposed Chamber of Nationalities within the CEC (Central Executive Committee).
6 Ibid., pp. 597–8.

4
The future of nations; nations under communism

Our practical attitude towards a certain social phenomenon or the social weal depends decisively on our vision of its future fate and destiny. If we inform a houseowner more or less officially that in the immediate or near future his house will be razed to the ground and his garden turned into a building site for other structures, it is unlikely that he will start to improve his house and cultivate his garden; it is even less likely that his friends and guests would greet such an intention with enthusiasm. What probably would develop in such conditions would be something akin to that 'weekend cottagers' psychology, not unlike that which Maxim Gor'ky exposed in his day.

Something similar is happening among us on the matter of nationalities. Among the overwhelming mass of the population the notion prevails that the next, perhaps even the immediate, task of communists is the creation of a nationless society, an 'amalgamation of nations', and that therefore national languages and cultures are something moribund, backward, second-rate and even reactionary, at any rate something suspect and pitiable.

What is the source of this odd view, and why does it pass for 'Marxist'? Why is it linked with the idea of communism? In any case it has nothing in common with Marxism and communism and is their exact opposite.

Marx always ridiculed this kind of shady political machination or ignorance. Thus, for instance, informing Engels about a session of the Council of the International, Marx wrote sarcastically:

> ... The representatives of *'Young France'* *(non-workers)* came out with the announcement that all nationalities and even nations were 'antiquated prejudices' ... Anyhow, whoever encumbers the 'social' question with the 'superstitions' of the old world is a 'reactionary'.
>
> The English laughed very much when I began my speech by saying that our friend Lafargue and others, who had done away with nationalities, had spoken *'French'* to us ... I also suggested that by the negation of nationalities he appeared, quite unconsciously, to understand their absorption by the model French nation.[1]

Marx mocked this scheming, calling it 'Proudhonized Stirnerism' and Fourier's 'model phalansterianism', and pointed out its imperialist essence. But those who today preach similar views - the absorption of many nations by the 'model Russian nation' – call it ... Marxism and communism. What a bitter and absurd paradox! You will say that today nobody preaches the 'absorption' of nations, only their 'rapprochement' and 'amalgamation'. Yes, officially the press calls it 'rapprochement' and 'amalgamation' of nations. But should you ask how 99 per cent of the public interprets this 'rapprochement', you will see that for them it is a matter of that same 'absorption'. Even the figures of the last census are very eloquent on this. In 1914 Lenin wrote:

> In Russia, even according to official, i.e. palpably exaggerated statistics, which are faked to suit the 'government's plans', the Great Russians constitute no more than 43 per cent of the entire population of the country. The Great Russians

in Russia constitute less than half the population ... The 'subject peoples' in Russia constitute 57 per cent of the population, i.e. the majority of the population, almost three-fifths, in all probability actually more than three-fifths.[2]

Now, in the forty-ninth year of Soviet power, Great Russians, according to official data, account for *considerably more than half* of the population, and if we add the Russified non-Russians (in the census figures they are officially listed as people who consider Russian their native language), their number will be much higher. The relative numbers of Ukrainians and other 'nationals' have correspondingly decreased. What is responsible for this sharp change in ratio? Is this a result of the normal coexistence of nations? It can hardly be considered a success of communist nation-building; if any fully formed nation of the world were concerned, its communists would certainly think otherwise. We would have to search for analogies in quite a different, non-communist age and sphere of history. And this can hardly be linked with the 'Leninist nationalities policy' – Lenin is known to have described similar phenomena in such terms as 'Great Russian imperialism' and 'Russian GreatPower chauvinism'. Not a single document of Lenin's RSDWP(B) (Russian Social Democratic Workers' Party (Bolsheviks)) approved of the russification or assimilation of nations, especially the assimilation of smaller nations by a large nation, and nothing was said about the amalgamation of nations as an immediate task of the proletarian movement. But what is the source of this 'current opinion' which invariably and automatically links the concept of the proletarian revolutionary movement and the building of a future communist society with the concept of the 'amalgamation of nations' and 'nationlessness' (that is to say, in practice, the concept of both russification and assimilation)? Obviously, it is not the theory of scientific communism.

When the documents of the RSDWP speak about the 'amalgamation of the workers of all nations', they mean – and this is made very clear – their organizational union in single class organizations for the purpose of a common revolutionary struggle. 'The interests of the working class demand the amalgamation of the workers of all nationalities of a given state into single proletarian organizations – political, professional, cooperative-educational, etc.', while guaranteeing 'the full equality of all nations and languages'.³ As for the nations themselves, Soviet power has unequivocally declared it to be its task to foster their all-round development, especially the development of nations which were formerly oppressed and disenfranchised. In the joint report on the nationalities question at the X Party Congress it was proposed: 'Soviet power, the Communist Party, must become the paramount factor in the national cultural development of the toiling masses of oppressed nationalities.'⁴

The idea of the assimilation of nations, the idea of a future nationless society is not an idea of scientific communism, but of that kind which Marx and Engels called 'barracks communism'. This is also the idea of revisionists, social-democrats of the Second International. Kautsky, in particular, made much of it. As a relic of Kautskyism it had percolated into the communist movement at the beginning of the century but was quickly overcome, being pulled to pieces by Lenin and other communists.

You can often hear Lenin quoted as not only not condemning but, on the contrary, welcoming the assimilation of nations. But this is a brutal distortion of the Leninist spirit. First of all, Lenin defended not assimilation but the political union of proletarians of all countries, and *in this context* rejected opposition to such a union that was based on the fear of assimilation. Secondly, spontaneous assimilation was meant, and not a 'programme' assimilation, essentially different from the former and purposefully and systematically carried on by the state – *such* artificial assimilation was always criminal in his eyes; try only to imagine such a planned design in the Party documents of Lenin's time. Thirdly and finally, *non-condemnation* of assimilation in the sense and context that we are discussing is found *only* in Lenin's *pre-revolutionary* works; after the Revolution, having taken up the practical task of nation-building, Lenin substantially shifted his emphasis and did not say *one more word* about the benefit of any kind of assimilation, but directed the whole force of the struggle against russification, Great Russian chauvinism and Great-Power ideology, that is to say, in fact, *against assimilationism*. And this is quite comprehensible: in practice, national movements and the building of nations have shown that communism benefits from the maximum development of nations, and not from their diminishing and assimilation; any trend toward assimilation in the policy of a *ruling* party in a multi-national state with an imperialist past would unfailingly bring about a whole series of deep injustices towards the nationalities of that state and the rebirth, in new forms, of the old imperialist relations within that state, and would greatly harm the cause of communism and freedom in the whole world. This is what Lenin opposed.

This is why since 1917 Lenin did not say *a single word* in favour of any sort of assimilation; this is why he did not say *a single word* about the desirability of assimilation in the Soviet land; this is why, quite to the contrary, in the last years of his life he directed the full force of his struggle against Great Russian chauvinism and Great-Power ideology, the essence of which is assimilationism.

It is not by chance that in an address to the XVI Congress of the CPSU(B) the social-assimilationist position of Kautsky was contrasted with the internationalist position of Lenin:

> ... Lenin never said that national differences must disappear and that national languages must merge into one common language within

the borders of *a single* state *before the victory of socialism on a world scale*. On the contrary, Lenin said something that was the very opposite of this, namely, that 'national and state *differences* among peoples and countries ... will continue to exist *for a very, very long time* even *after* the dictatorship of the proletariat has been established on a *world* scale' (Vol. XVII, p. 178).

How can anyone refer to Lenin and forget about this fundamental statement of his?

True, Mr Kautsky, an ex-Marxist and now a renegade and reformist, asserts something that is the very opposite of what Lenin teaches us. Despite Lenin, he asserts that the victory of the proletarian revolution in the Austro-German federal state in the middle of the last century would have led to the formation of *a single, common* German language and to the *Germanization* of the Czechs, because 'the mere force of unshackled intercourse, the mere force of modern culture of which the Germans were the vehicles, without any forcible Germanization, *would have converted into Germans the backward Czech petty bourgeois, peasants and proletarians who had nothing to gain from their decayed nationality*' (see Preface to the German edition of *Revolution and Counter-Revolution*).[5]

It goes without saying that such a 'conception' is in full accord with Kautsky's social-chauvinism ... But can this anti-Marxist chatter of an arrogant German social-chauvinist have any positive significance for us Marxists, who want to remain consistent internationalists?[6]

This is how Stalin criticized chauvinism when this chauvinism was German.

However, as is well known, Stalin could talk well, but do the very opposite. In his time there began, and in Khrushchev's time there were developed, political practices on the nationalities question which corresponded more to Kautsky's conception, although they were concealed in 'Leninist' phraseology. And now we, completely forgetful of Lenin's 'fundamental statement' that nationalities and national languages will continue to exist '*for a very, very long time* even *after* the dictatorship of the proletariat has been established on a *world* scale', set ourselves instead the task of the amalgamation of nations. (The facts do not change if sometimes in place of 'amalgamation' some other formula is used, such as 'an even closer rapprochement': in practice this always means the absorption of other nations by the Russian nation, and not the other way round; let someone say in what way the Russian nation is drawing closer to the Armenian or the Estonian nation, for instance.) In effect, we are already setting ourselves the task of amalgamating nations *within a single country* now, long before the victory of socialism on a world scale, and long before the victory of communism in that very same single country.

Besides all the other inevitable negative consequences, this cannot fail to induce profound resentment, disillusionment and dissatisfaction among the nations that are, in fact, condemned to a slow disappearance, to a reduction to a common denominator represented by the other, 'leading' nation.

There is an enormous political and psychological difference between the general unification of all the peoples of mankind into 'universal humanity', that is to say between an assimilation of nations on a *universal human* basis, and assimilation of one nation by another, the absorption by one nation of others, the assimilation of several nations on the basis of *a single national culture*.

The first can still be envisaged as a fruitful perspective and a positive factor, as progress (although many outstanding thinkers, among them also Marxists, consider that even this would be a great backsliding for humanity; this well-argued thought Potebnya in his day briefly expressed in these words: 'Even if the unification of humanity in respect of language and of nationality generally were possible, it would be the ruin of human thought, like the replacement of our many senses by one.') Altogether the postulate of the future 'inevitable' amalgamation of nations is a very problematical, scientifically unproven notion, and 'Marxists' should follow the example of Marx who left such problems to the judgement of future generations, when there was no historical experience on the basis of which to solve them. How much more so should they when this historical experience attests to the inevitably reactionary nature of such notions.

As for the second kind of assimilation (on the basis of a single national culture or in some other way except on the basis of universal culture) it is identical with colonialism (since it deprives other peoples in advance of the essential condition of equality – the right to an equal contribution to universal culture, and condemns them to cultural dependence with all its consequences for the psychological nature of individuals belonging to this nation and for their resulting status in society).

'Assimilation' of the first kind cannot strictly speaking be called assimilation, but rather a universal union of humanity; here, at least, no nation will be wronged, for all stand to gain or lose equally. Assimilation of the second kind is assimilation proper; it is inevitably a grave historic injustice for the assimilated nations and leaves indelible marks of bitterness in them. But also to the assimilating nation it brings not good, but harm – a gradual internal decay of its culture and the burden of having committed injustice, even though unconsciously. At no time has it anywhere become, nor will it ever become, a sound foundation for the friendship of nations, as it can only divide them and produce distrust and hostility.

This is why Maxim Gor'ky wrote:

> Each tribe is the source of innumerable possibilities for the enriching of life with the energy of the spirit, and it is indispensable for the sake of a faster growth of world culture that this energy should develop normally, flow into life – to our happiness and joy – in conditions of maximum freedom.
> Democracy can recognize only one kind of assimilation as legitimate and natural – assimilation on the basis of universal culture ...[7]

Instead, the anti-Marxist and anti-socialist 'theory' is being vigorously implanted now, purporting that in the USSR, instead of many peoples and nations, one single 'Soviet nation' (?!), one single 'Soviet people' is taking shape, not in the sense of the sum total of all Soviet peoples and nations, not as a collective concept, but as some supposedly mono-national or nationless synthesis which did not exist, let us say, in the 1920s or 1930s and is being formed just now. This 'theory' pervades politics, propaganda, the press and education. As for culture, our whole press is full of phrases describing how a supposedly 'international (?!) culture' is developing among us even now. ('In the Baltic region, as everywhere else in our country, an international culture common to all Soviet nations is developing'; 'In our country an international culture; common to all Soviet nations, is developing fast.') This, however, is an absurdity, not only from the point of view of Marxism, but also of elementary terminology: only that which is characteristic of, or appertaining to, *all* nations, or *all* humanity, can be called international. Thus and only thus did Lenin understand this concept when he spoke about the international culture of democracy, about the international culture, interests, etc., of the proletariat.

The meaning given today to this confused concept, as well as the 'theory' of a single 'Soviet nation' (no matter how it is formulated) or 'Soviet people', not in the sense of a commonwealth but of an identity – is intended to prove and justify 'theoretically' the extensive process of russification. A purposeful encouragement and 'catalysis' of this development will cause enormous, incalculable, irredeemable losses to universal culture and to the whole spiritual life of the communist world.

To this we can add the question of our widespread practice of giving a negative qualification to nationalities and to everything national. The attribute 'national' is stubbornly applied only to such subjects as 'survivals' (to be eradicated), 'barriers' (to be broken), 'one-sidedness' (to be overcome), etc., etc., whilst at the same time the positive sense of the concept 'national' is played down, passed over and evaded in all ways. This is 'one-sidedness' indeed! Obviously, this does not promote the understanding of the vast historic, cultural and spiritual content, of the vast *positive* wealth of the concept 'nationality – national', an understanding which has inspired the great promoters of human history and culture, which has inspired the founders of scientific communism and all true Marxists and communists. (For instance, one of the most outstanding communist Marxist philosophers, Antonio Gramsci, wrote: 'The concept of the "national" is the result of an "original", unique combination (in a certain sense) which must be understood and conceived of in this originality and uniqueness if one wants to master it and guide it.' He also qualified 'the non-national conceptions' as 'mistaken' and as a 'modern form of old mechanicalism'.[8])

Still before the revolution A.V. Lunacharsky summed up the Marxist attitude towards the problem of nationality and criticized 'consistent cosmopolitans who think that the future will bring a complete unification of the human race, a single common language, and a single common culture'. He wrote that from the point of view of Marxism he attached 'enormous and vital cultural importance to nationalities' and hailed:

> ... such a broad development of the process
> of their rebirth to independent life of almost

forgotten and, as it were, decapitated nationalities ... Unity is only then a principle of beauty and high organization when its flexible framework embraces as rich a variety as possible. National variety, I would say, is a great human heritage, which, we hope, will be preserved to give us as yet unknown delights of the upsurge of life ...

Addressing myself specifically to the Ukrainian movement ... I must say at once that not a single national rebirth, subjectively speaking, arouses within me such ardent sympathy ...

We can expect the most gratifying results from the independent cultural development of the Ukrainian people,[9] for there is no doubt that it is one of the most gifted branches of the Slavic tree.[10]

As for communism, and the future communist society, Lunacharsky spoke quite clearly, and this is undoubtedly one of the elementary, fundamental truths of communism:

> Triply wrong are those who speak of a 'socialist levelling' or the triumph of some colourless cosmopolitanism in the case of the victory of the proletariat. No, the new society will give scope for the infinite colour and variety of each people's nature in its spontaneous current. It will destroy the deadening, mechanistic force of the state, it will kill the bestial, cannibalistic instincts which prompt the forced depersonalization of individuals and of nations. And just as the individual has never achieved such freedom and originality as he will achieve in the socialist future, nations have never raised their own voices in the chorus of mankind with such force and independence as they will do then.[11]

This is what true communists should strive for. It is in this spirit, in the spirit of a communist internationalist world-view, in the spirit of comprehension of the unique value of each national life and of its inexhaustible possibilities, and not in the spirit of a disdainful and thoughtless neglect of these values in the name of bureaucratic 'uniformity' and the 'leading Russian culture', that the youth of our country should be brought up. This and only this can guarantee genuine friendship between equal peoples, can guarantee the preservation and the increase of the immense national values fortunately united in our Union, and guarantee incomparable variety in the future spiritual life of the communist world.

But try to write this today in your own name, and the editors will strike it out as 'vague hints'.

The opposite tendency leads only to overt or covert, conscious or unconscious, intentional or unintentional grossness and brutishness on the nationalities question. Even if this does not appear nakedly, but in the form of indifference to the nationalities question, it is the same in essence. Indifference (that is today's fashion on this question) is the beginning of grossness, its potential, its source. Indifference, far from being the contrary of obtuse nationalism, is its obverse side and its potential ally.

> I do not think that nationalists can be conquered by the argument 'What is a nation to me? What can I buy with it?' The nation is a product of thousands of years of development. For centuries the national struggle inspired the most ardent passions. Thousands perished in this struggle. It was at times the source of life, at times the cause of death of great revolutions. Can you liberate the masses from this great ideology by means of a shopkeeper's 'What can I buy with it?'[12]

The only alternative to nationalism (both the defensive nationalism of small nations and the aggressive nationalism of large nations) is the instilling of a genuine national-internationalist feeling, of dedication to one's own nation, of love and esteem towards all other nations, of a desire to see your own nation contribute as much as possible to humanity, doing its utmost for it. Hence a genuine internationalist has a great sense of responsibility for his own nation, has the desire, in the words of Academician O. Bilets'ky, to gain for it a 'patent of nobility' before humanity.

The highest duty of man is to belong to humanity. But you can belong to humanity only through your own nation, through your own people. In the entire history of humanity, you can find only occasional exceptions to this general rule, confirmed both by grandiose mass movements and by the biographies of great men. As we say, occasional examples can be found when a man has left his own nation to join another, benefiting both it and humanity. But this is so only when his mother nation has already consolidated itself within the universal family, has secreted its national existence and does not suffer greatly through the loss of a few individuals. But if your nation is in a critical situation, when its very national existence and its future are at stake, it is shameful to abandon it.

1   Marx and Engels, SC, pp. 216–17.
2   Lenin, CW, XX, pp. 218–19.
3   KPSS v rezolyutsiyakh, I, p. 315.
4   X s'yezd RKP(B), p. 199.
5   K. Kautsky's foreword to K. Marx, *Revolution und Kontre-Revolution in Deutschland*, Stuttgart, 1896, p. xxii.
6   XVI s'yezd VKP(B). *Stenograficheskiy otchot*, Moscow-Leningrad, 1930, p. 54; English translation in J.V. Stalin, *Works*, XII, Moscow, 1955, pp. 374–5. All italics (including those in the quotations from Lenin and Kautsky) are Stalin's. The Lenin quotation comes from the first edition, N. Lenin (V. Ul'yanov), *Sobraniye sochineniy*, Moscow-Leningrad, 1925; cf. his CW, XXXI, p. 92.
7   V. Desnitsky (ed.), M. Gor'ky, *materiay i issledovaniya*, I, Leningrad, 1934, pp. 70–71.
8   A. Gramsci, *Note sul Machiavelli sulla politica, sullo Stato moderno*, Turin, 1949, pp. 114–15.
9   Take note: not from an 'international' Ukrainian-Russian-Tartar-etc. culture 'x' and not from a 'further rapprochement', but from an 'independent cultural development'!
10 A.V. Lunacharsky, 'O natsionalizme voobshcbe i ukrainskom dvizhenii vlastnosti', *Ukrainskaya zhizn'*, No. 10, 1912, pp. 10–11, 15, 19.
11 A.V. Lunacharsky, *Stat'i o literature*, Moscow, 1957, p. 429.
12 The Marxist Otto Braun as quoted by Lunacharsky in the above-mentioned article 'O natsionalizme ... '.

5
National sentiment, national consciousness, national duties

In our country these concepts are considered odious; at any rate, if anyone in Ukraine were to attempt to speak today about the national sentiment, national consciousness or national duties of the present-day Ukrainian, he would immediately and without hesitation be labelled a 'Ukrainian bourgeois nationalist'.

And yet, Marxism and scientific communism attach immense constructive importance to them. Marx and Engels used them frequently and particularly stressed the national duties and national mission of the working class (the German working class, for instance). They spoke about the necessity for the working class to wage a struggle for the 'national existence' of their people, about the 'national organization' of the working class and so forth.

This is how the outstanding Czech communist theoretician, Zdenek Nejedlý, sums up the attitude of Marxism-Leninism, the attitude of true communists towards this matter:

> From the very beginning the communists have differed from the old pre-war social-democrats not only by not underestimating the importance of the people's national sentiments and national culture (as was often done by those who interpreted internationalism as anti-nationalism), but, on the

contrary, by stressing its national consciousness as a great and important social force, and therefore they have formulated their attitude towards the nation quite differently. As Lenin excellently said, the communist inherits all the best that has been done and created before him, therefore also all the beautiful traditions of his nation and of its culture.

In their speeches the communists have constantly pointed out that the old social-democrats before the First World War were profoundly mistaken in underrating the national factor and the role of nationality, national sentiment and national culture for the working class.[1]

Perhaps this is relevant only to the communist movement of the 1920s–40s and has lost its force today? Perhaps this is important only for parties that struggle for power and loses its significance after they attain it? No, as recently as 1964 Palmiro Togliatti declared:

> National sentiment remains a constant value in the labour and socialist movement for a long period even after the attainment of power. Economic achievements do not stifle, but sustain it.[2]

Analogous statements can also be heard from other prominent communists throughout the world. The Communist Parties of the socialist countries of Europe (Poland, Hungary, Czechoslovakia, Romania and others) are leaders, in the correct national (which is also internationalist) education of their peoples.

As is well known, during the 1920s in Ukraine the CP(B)U conducted – according to the resolutions of the Comintern, the VIII, X, XII and other Congresses of the RCP(B), CPSU(B), and the Congresses of the CP(B)U – enormous national-educational work which went down in the history of the Party and of Ukraine under the name of 'ukrainization' (or 'de-russification').

The Ukrainian language was introduced into all spheres of social, civic and industrial life, knowledge of Ukrainian history and culture was fostered, there developed a sense of national belonging and of the national duties of a Ukrainian communist; in literature and journalism extensive discussion of nationality problems was permitted, and particularly the satirizing of such shameful phenomena as hatred of one's native language and culture, national nihilism and betrayal.

Preparatory work was being done for the ukrainization of the proletariat, of the large cities and industrial centres. At the same time the need was stressed for the 'distinguishing of russified workers, who use a mixed Ukrainian language, from Russian workers'. Regarding the latter, as a national minority in Ukraine, 'careful treatment ... and protection of their interests' was recommended; for the former, explanation of their national membership and their national duties.

In the theses of the Central Committee of the CP(B)U (1927) just quoted, this observation is made:

> The Party must persistently, systematically and patiently explain to the working class of Ukraine its responsibility for the strengthening of the alliance with the Ukrainian village; it must persuade the working class to take an active part in the ukrainization by means of studying Ukrainian, etc. The Party must ensure the creation of favourable conditions for the ukrainization of the proletariat in the industrial centres of Ukraine.[3]

This was a truly internationalist Leninist policy which safeguarded the interests and the full development of the socialist Ukrainian nation. But after only a few years this policy came to an end and the men who had been implementing it were removed. This was done by Stalin notwithstanding the resolutions of the Comintern and the Party Congresses, it was done silently, 'quietly', without any justification, theoretical or political. The resolutions were not carried out, they were not revised or repealed, but were simply put aside and replaced by quite opposite decisions. Even today the concept of 'ukrainization' is considered odious, and people are 'ashamed' or afraid to mention it, although, we repeat, it was a Leninist policy, elaborated at Party Congresses and approved by the Comintern. There began a policy of destroying the achievements of the previous period, a policy of physically destroying the Ukrainian nation, especially its intelligentsia. This reversal was indeed one of the greatest tragedies of the Ukrainian people in its entire history.

Besides everything else, this Stalinist policy was calculated to knock out of the Ukrainian people any trace of national sentiment and national consciousness. A taboo has weighed upon them for some thirty-five years, so it is not at all surprising that they are so little developed among a considerable mass of the Ukrainian population, to the point that some Ukrainians, just as in pre-revolutionary days, know nothing of their national membership, and for a fair number the concept of 'Ukraine' is nothing but an administrative-geographical term. Just as in pre-revolutionary days, a good number of Ukrainians are ashamed of their nationality and their language, and consider it rustic, 'uncultured' and third-rate. They are not aware of even their most elementary duties towards their native country and their people: to know and cherish Ukrainian history, culture and language, to read Ukrainian books, to support the Ukrainian theatre and so forth. Even worse, how many Ukrainians have given up their native language and their national self-knowledge as proof of their 'loyalty', so as 'not to stand out', 'not to be different'? How many of them shy away from national-cultural questions as if these were some sort of sedition, these questions towards which no self-respecting citizen should remain indifferent? How much contempt do we observe towards everything Ukrainian, simply because it is Ukrainian, on the part of the Ukrainians themselves?

The government of any country would be ashamed of such citizens. Why is there no feeling of shame in the government of the Ukrainian Soviet Socialist Republic, which is, strictly speaking, responsible for this situation?! Why is nothing done to teach a sense of national dignity, national consciousness and national duty to the citizens of socialist Ukraine, why is nothing said about this in the press, in literature or in public life? If the official circles have not the time, inclination or training for this, why should it not be permitted to that part of the intelligentsia (particularly the literary intelligentsia) which is willing and able to carry out the appropriate work?

Why should the leadership of the Ukrainian Soviet Socialist Republic not take at least that minimum of national education upon itself which is assumed, for instance, by Czechoslovakia in relation to its Ukrainian minority? Here is a small but eloquent example.

In 1952 the Central Committee of the Communist Party of Slovakia adopted a resolution to change over schools in territories with a Ukrainian ('Ruthenian') population from the Russian to the Ukrainian language. The implementation of this decision met with serious difficulties. Some parents stopped sending their children to school. The KSUT (Cultural Association of Ukrainian Workers) registered the reasons for such a state of affairs:

> The administrative introduction of Ukrainian as the language of instruction without any explanation for this historic change in national orientation, without any preparation of the parents or teachers for such changes, and also without any further broad explanatory work in this political sphere;

The low level of national consciousness and the national indifference of the Ukrainian working people, even a complete national disorientation of the Ukrainian population by previous regimes; and finally, a lack of qualified Ukrainian teachers and Ukrainian textbooks. To overcome this situation, the Central Committee of the Communist Party of Slovakia resolved first and foremost to develop 'political-educational work aimed at raising the level of national consciousness of the working people'.[4]

We do not do even that, although we have incomparably greater possibilities.

A national inferiority complex – contempt for one's own nationality, culture and language – is a fairly well-known phenomenon in history. It has been the experience of all peoples who have had to live under a foreign yoke, under national oppression. The Ukrainian people was under such oppression for 300 years. This could not fail to leave its marks. But have these marks not survived for somewhat too long? For a country with a constitutionally guaranteed state sovereignty and its own national political life this is more than strange. It becomes even stranger when one is not even permitted to speak about these marks and when nothing is done to instil a sense of national dignity, national sentiment and national consciousness into the citizens of the Ukrainian Socialist Republic.

---

1 Z. Nejedly, 'Kommunisty i natsiya', in his *Izbrannyye trudy*, Moscow, 1960, p. 344.
2 'Il Promemoria di Togliatti', *l'Unita*, 5 September 1964, p. 2.
3 V. Koryak (ed.), *Shlyakhy rozvytku ukrains'koyi proletars'koyi literatury*, Kharkiv, 1928, pp. 346–7.
4 'Krok do alahodzhennya', *Drudmo vpered* (Presov), xiv, No. 5, May 1964, p. 20.

6
The socialist republics and the forms of their cooperation

Today's popular conception of the essence and form of the Union of Soviet Socialist Republics has moved a long way from the idea of Lenin and the Party of his time, that is, from the idea of a free union of independent national states with a common social order. More than that, the very notion of independence, as applied to the republics, has long since been made a weapon of intimidation. A man has only to express dissatisfaction with even some small detail of Ukraine's position in the Union today (and this in itself is an unspeakable mortal sin) to be represented as a separatist; this is to intimidate him and to turn others against him. I personally have often heard such a rebuke directed against me, and more recently it has even resounded from official rostrums, for instance, at seminars within the network of party education. Is it not time to clarify certain things?

First of all, nobody in Ukraine advances the slogan of 'independence' today. At least I have not myself heard it. The 'nationalists' who are now under arrest were also far removed from it.

Secondly, even if someone advanced such a slogan, it would be un-Leninist and un-Soviet to accuse him on those grounds. After all, the Constitution of the USSR guarantees the Republics the right to secede from the Union,[1] which means that it recognizes every citizen's right to advance the idea of such a secession and to argue the case for it. As for the Leninist view on these matters, it must be recalled that Lenin, far from considering all 'separatists' as agents of imperialism, even recognized Bolsheviks among them: 'Among the Bolsheviks there are advocates of complete independence for Ukraine, advocates of a more or less close federal tie, and advocates of the complete amalgamation of Ukraine with Russia.'[2]

According to Lenin the watershed between revolutionaries and counter-revolutionaries does not lie here, but in their social class tendencies; in the All-Ukrainian Revolutionary Committee,

> Besides the Ukrainian Bolshevik Communists, there are Ukrainian Borot'bist Communists[3] working as members of the government. One of the things distinguishing the Borot'bists from the Bolsheviks is that they insist upon the unconditional independence of Ukraine. The Bolsheviks will not make this a subject of difference and disunity, they do not regard this as an obstacle to concerted proletarian effort. There must be unity in the struggle against the yoke of capital and for the dictatorship of the proletariat, and there should be no parting of the ways among Communists on the question of national frontiers, or whether there should be a federal or some other tie between the states.[4]

From other works of Lenin, it can be seen (as we shall do later) that on these questions he demanded the maximum renunciation and self-sacrifice from the communists of a 'large, dominant' nation in favour of smaller nations.

Unfortunately, these theses of Lenin were later violated, and in particular the Borot'bist Communists, who had met with a positive attitude from him, were removed from the leadership of Soviet Ukraine and later exterminated almost to a man. The same fate befell those forces in the CP(B)U who, headed by Skrypnyk, championed the Republic's Ukrainian national personality, although nobody could cast any doubts on their proletarian class position.

In this way Stalin kept destroying the communist essence in the name of the Great-Power form, in the name 'of the prejudices of the old Great Russian nationalism'.[5]

And today even the enemy of communism V. Shul'gin is welcomed, because he has expressed his Great-Power sympathies for the existing boundaries, while the communist Khvyl'ovy (who remained a communist in spite of his mistakes) is being reviled, because he was against Great-Power pressure in Ukraine, against that petty-bourgeois 'Great Russian riff-raff' which Lenin attacked so violently, and he used these precise words.[6] And today a GreatPower supporter is forgiven his non-communism (as long as he is a 'Russian patriot', of no matter which hue), while a Ukrainian communist is not forgiven the slightest trace of concern for his nation (which would immediately be branded as a 'deviation').

The most recent example of this is the well-known story of Assistant Professor M. Shestopal, a lecturer at Kyiv University, whom all commissions were forced to acknowledge as a highly qualified specialist, a fertile researcher and a model communist, but who was all the same dismissed from his post because in conversation he had allegedly questioned some aspects of the nationalities policy. And it ought to be known with what cruelty and stubbornness the authorities demanded his punishment, in spite of the protests of the whole student body, while in the same University there are dozens of lecturers who are unqualified, unproductive in scholarship, and, likely as not, not too well imbued with the ideals of communism. But this is no one's concern: the present-day bureaucrat and grandee knows only one object of hatred, the 'nationalist', although that 'nationalist' may be a thousand times better and purer as a man and communist than anyone else, even the bureaucrat and grandee himself. Judge for yourselves how far we have moved away from Lenin's formulation of this question:

> As internationalists it is our duty, first, to combat very vigorously the survivals (sometimes unconscious) of Great Russian imperialism and chauvinism among 'Russian' Communists; and secondly, it is our duty, precisely on the national question, which is a relatively minor one (for an internationalist the question of state frontiers is a secondary, if not a tenth-rate, question), to make concessions. There are other questions – the fundamental interests of the proletarian dictatorship; ... the leading role of the proletariat in relation to the peasantry – that are more important; the question whether Ukraine will be a separate state is far less important. We must not be in the least surprised, or frightened, even by the prospect of the Ukrainian workers and peasants trying out different systems, and in the course of, say, several years, testing by practice union with the RSFSR, or seceding from the latter and forming an independent Ukrainian SSR, or various forms of their close alliance, and so on, and so forth.
>
> To attempt to settle this question in advance, once and for all, 'firmly' and 'irrevocably', would be narrow-mindedness or sheer stupidity ...[7]

If anyone said these words today himself and not as a quotation from Lenin, the appropriate 'department' would immediately concern itself with him. That he would be driven out of the Party is beyond any doubt.

Can one even conceive of the possibility of Soviet Ukrainian citizens taking any initiative in the question of improving and changing the forms of the coexistence of the Socialist Republics, and the possibility of public discussion of such questions, or the possibility of their theoretical elaboration? There is not a trace of this in our life today.

In this respect we have completely rejected Lenin's teaching. Contrary to his direct, repeated and categorical instructions about the necessity for a persistent struggle against Russian Great-Power chauvinism as the main obstacle to socialist national construction and for maximum concessions towards nationals on questions of their national interest – contrary to all this, for several decades now, we have not only failed to struggle against Russian chauvinism and Great-Power ideology, but have withdrawn these very concepts from circulation. Instead, 'local nationalism' is proclaimed to be the principal enemy, under which heading have often been placed the most innocuous and elementary manifestations of national life, national dignity and honour. The struggle against this 'nationalism' has been waged with the weapons of terror.

1   Article 17.
2   Lenin, CW, xxx, p. 295.
3   Borot'bists: Ukrainian 'National Communist' party, active from 1918–20, its name derived from the title of their newspaper Borot'ba ('Struggle'). Most of its former members, many of whom after its dissolution joined the Bolsheviks, perished in the purges of the 1930s. Lenin, CW, has 'Borot'ba Communists' in place of 'Borot'bist Communists'.
4   Ibid., pp. 294–5.
5   Ibid., p. 295.
6   'velikorusskaya shval' (Lenin, CW, xxxvi, p. 606).
7   Lenin, CW, xxx, pp. 270–71.

7
The phantom of 'Ukrainian bourgeois nationalism' and the reality of Russian Great-Power chauvinism as the principal obstacle to national construction in the USSR

As is well known, during the discussion of the nationalities question in the Party there was a struggle for a long time between those who considered Russian Great-Power chauvinism to be the principal obstacle to the building of a genuinely international union of republics and those who instead expressed their antagonism towards 'local nationalism' in the Republics. Among the latter was Stalin who coined the special term 'social-chauvinism' with which he used to brand 'nationalists'. As is known, at the climax of Stalin's action against the 'social-chauvinists' Lenin intervened in this matter in December 1922,[1] resolutely putting an end to this campaign and calling upon the Party to launch a merciless drive against Russian Great-Power chauvinism as a mortal danger to the cause of proletarian internationalism and the building of a union of republics.

There are many today who do not like to remember these Leninist instructions, which makes it all the more necessary to recall them to mind. This is how Lenin formulated the question of two nationalisms:

> In my writings on the national question, I have already said that an abstract presentation of the question of nationalism in general is of no use at all. A distinction must necessarily be made between the nationalism of an oppressor nation and that of an oppressed nation, the nationalism of a big nation and that of a small nation.
>
> In respect of the second kind of nationalism we, nationals of a big nation, have nearly always been guilty, in historic practice, of an infinite number of cases of violence; furthermore, we commit violence and insult an infinite number of times without noticing it ...
>
> That is why internationalism on the part of oppressors or 'great' nations, as they are called (though they are great only in their violence, only great as bullies), must consist not only in the observance of the formal equality of nations but even in an inequality of the oppressor nation, the great nation, that must make up for the inequality which obtains in actual practice. Anybody who does not understand this has not grasped the real proletarian attitude to the national question, he is still essentially petty bourgeois in his point of view and is, therefore, sure to descend to the bourgeois point of view.[2]

And further on:

> ... The fundamental interest of proletarian solidarity, and consequently of the proletarian class struggle, requires that we never adopt a formal attitude to the national question, but always

take into account the specific attitude of the proletarian of the oppressed (or small) nation towards the oppressor (or great) nation.³

This was already being said during the Soviet period apropos of Soviet problems and on the basis of the experience of Soviet construction. After analysing this experience, Lenin said: 'I declare war to the death on Great Russian chauvinism.'⁴

In accordance with Lenin's directions, the XII Congress of the RCP(B) resolved: 'A resolute struggle against the survivals of Great Russian chauvinism is a top priority task of our Party.'⁵

In connection with the quite exceptional importance attached by Lenin to the struggle against Russian Great-Power chauvinism the need arises to consider at least briefly the following questions: what are the sources of this chauvinism, how does it manifest itself, in what way is it so dangerous, what safeguards are there against it, how did Lenin propose to fight it, and has his last testament in this respect been executed in regard to this, has this struggle been waged and is it still being waged today?

1 RUSSIAN CHAUVINISM AS A HERITAGE OF HISTORY

The XII Congress of the RCP(B) qualified Russian chauvinism as 'a reflection of the former privileged position of Great Russians'. Even earlier Lenin had noted: '... the Great Russians, under the yoke of the landowners and capitalists, had for centuries imbibed the shameful and disgusting prejudices of Great Russian chauvinism'; 'Accursed tsarism made the Great Russians executioners of the Ukrainian people.'⁶

Much was said about the same subject at the VIII, X, XII and other Party Congresses up to and including the XVI.

> ... The colonization of the borderlands is not simply the work of a few months, but of whole decades. For whole decades Russian imperialism colonized these borderlands. If we admit that economic development is reflected and manifested in various spheres of social and economic life, we must admit that the colonization of the borderlands by Russian imperialism created a colonialist ideology and a definite colonialist attitude of mind among the Russian elements living in these borderlands ... And until we rid ourselves of this ideology ... we will not achieve anything. We must launch a struggle against colonialism as such ...[7]

Have we today, in the forty-ninth year of Soviet power, totally dislodged this colonialist heritage and these colonialist attitudes?

Far from it. Today, especially in the large cities, there is a very considerable stratum of the Russian petty bourgeoisie which is hopelessly far from being a carrier of communist internationalism and is instead the spiritual heir of 'ten generations of colonizers'. This Russian petty bourgeoisie does not feel like a friendly guest or a good friend of the peoples among which it happens to live, but like the master of the situation and a superior element. It shows contempt towards these peoples and their culture, and instead of taking an interest in them, studying and absorbing their culture, language and history – as any good visitor, guest or friend who has been called upon to help always does – this petty bourgeoisie not only fails to study and absorb these things, but does not even show any interest in them. Moreover, they do not miss a single opportunity of slighting, mocking and ridiculing them. 'Well, they know Ukrainian borshch, they know Ukrainian bacon,' Mayakovsky wrote about them forty years ago.[8] But even now they do not know any more.

The attitude of this petty bourgeoisie to the Ukrainian people has crystallized and keeps on crystallizing in such 'pearls of folklore' of sad repute as 'Khokhlandia',[9] 'Hapkenstrasse',[10] and the like.

They are not more favourably disposed towards other peoples of the Union. 'Those Georgians are such loafers, such boors ... and such terrible nationalists'; 'those Azerbaijani are so dirty, such boors, and such nationalists'; 'those Latvians are such nationalists', etc., etc. In short, the whole world is made up of boors and nationalists, and only they, the Russian Philistines, are shining lights of culture and good genii of internationalism.

This stratum of the Russian petty bourgeoisie in the non-Russian Republics is a powerful, constantly active, politically reactionary, culturally and morally degrading factor, which does much to poison the cause of the friendship of nations in the USSR.

However, strange though it may seem, it is semi-officially considered to be the true carrier of correct ideas, the reliable prop of government, and a counterbalance to the 'local' people. The 'local' people are something the petty bourgeois still has to tackle ...

This is how this stratum was characterized in the Party resolutions of the 1920s, this is how it remains to this day. The difference – a vital one – is that then a determined and extensive struggle was waged against it, whilst now there is no struggle or even educational work in this direction. It is not even advisable to speak about this petty bourgeoisie, thus has its permanent intoxication with power become even more dangerous.

2   RUSSIAN CHAUVINISM AS THE CONFUSION OF THE UNION OF REPUBLICS WITH 'RUSSIA, ONE AND INDIVISIBLE'

At the X Congress of the RCP(B) the well-known Party worker Zatons'ky said:

... A kind of Red Russian patriotism has sprung up. And now we can observe how our comrades consider themselves with pride, and not without cause, as Russians and sometimes even look upon themselves primarily as Russians. They not so much cherish Soviet power and the Soviet federation, as lean towards a 'Russia, one and indivisible'. The necessity of genuine centralism is confused in some comrades' minds with the habitual notion of a 'Russia, one and indivisible'. There is an enormous confusion of concepts arising.

It is self-evident that under Soviet power centralism is necessary, this is natural ... But we must draw a firm distinction between what is actually called forth by necessity, by the nature of Soviet power, by the necessity of revolutionary struggle, and what is a survival of old national ideology among the Russian comrades. We must separate genuinely necessary centralization from primitive Russophilism [*rusopetstvo*] – the term is not mine, but Comrade Lenin's, who used it, unfortunately when it was already late in the day, only at the end of 1919, and even then, only at the Party Conference. But now it has acquired a wide currency and has started to circulate far and wide. This Russophilism exists everywhere, it exists above all in the depths of our Party masses. It is found not only among those colonizers who had to adapt to communism in the remote borderlands, like Turkestan; this Russophilism can also be observed here, in Moscow, and in our central institutions. Everywhere you will find, alongside a revolutionary attitude in other directions, a certain inertia, a certain sluggishness in that one and a certain confusion of the concept of Soviet

> unity with a leaning towards a 'Russia, one and indivisible'.[11]

And further on:

> ... They [the broad Party masses] should not adhere to that primitive Russian line to which a considerable part of our comrades adhere, to the detriment of Soviet power and to the detriment of the Soviet federation.[12]

Somewhat later Stalin spoke about this in his address to the XII Congress of the RCP(B):

> ... the *Smena Vekh*[13] idea has come into being, and one can discern the desire to accomplish by peaceful means what Denikin failed to accomplish, i.e., to create the so-called 'Russia, one and indivisible'.[14]
>
> It is by no means accidental, Comrades, that the *Smena Vekh* men have recruited a large number of supporters among Soviet officials. That is by no means accidental. Nor is it accidental that the *Smena Vekh* gentlemen are singing the praises of the Bolshevik Communists, as much as to say: You may talk about Bolshevism as much as you like, you may prate as much as you like about your internationalist tendencies, but we know that you will achieve what Denikin failed to achieve, that you Bolsheviks have resurrected, or at all events will resurrect, the great idea of a Great Russia. All this is not accidental. Nor is it accidental that this idea has even penetrated some of our Party institutions ... Great-Power chauvinism and the most hidebound nationalism is growing in our

> country by leaps and bounds, striving to obliterate all that is not Russian, to gather all the threads of government into the hands of Russians and to stifle everything that is not Russian.[15]

Thus spoke Stalin in 1923 during Lenin's lifetime and under his 'searching gaze'. But in time, having changed from party functionary to ruler, he himself swung right round and expended considerable effort 'to gather all the threads of government into the hands of Russians'. This new volte-face found its concentrated formulation in the ideas expressed by Stalin in his famous toast – 'To the great Russian people' (where other peoples of the Soviet Union appeared in a clearly secondary role and where the victory over fascism was attributed not so much to the socialist order as to inborn 'Russian endurance' and the equally inborn ability to unite everything 'around the Russian principle').[16]

Everybody still remembers the notorious orgy of 'Russian priority' which began subsequently and lasted for several years. Today many of its elements appear tragicomic and incredible, but it did take place and left an indelible imprint on all our social and spiritual life. Its visible and invisible consequences are active even today.

The intentional or unintentional confusion of the USSR with 'Russia, one and indivisible', that 'certain confusion of the concept of Soviet unity with a leaning towards a "Russia, one and indivisible"' which Zatons'ky sarcastically spoke of in 1921, have today been absorbed into the bloodstream of many people and manifest themselves in a variety of ways.

Not so long ago our press publicized with considerable relish and satisfaction the letters of V. Shul'gin to the Russian White Guard émigrés, in which he called upon them to be reconciled with Soviet power, because it not only had not destroyed Russia, but on the contrary had saved and extended it. Which Russia Shul'gin had in mind is clear. Obviously not Lenin's but the one that he himself dreamed of in 1922:

'The International will pass, but the boundaries will remain.' A bitter paradox of history: these latter words were said at the very time when Lenin proclaimed 'war to the death on Great Russian chauvinism' and when Stalin took up arms against the *Smena Vekh* men. And today, forty-three years later, we somehow do not hear any voices raised against Great-Power ideology, the strictures against 'Russia, one and indivisible' have also died down, and instead we hear the elegiac voice of V. Sbul'gin, who, wandering across Little Russia, which is so close to his heart, is happy to see that in spite of its new industrial landscape it has remained Little Russia, and philosophizes amiably on the eternal theme that Ukraine is one of the provinces, one of the 'borderlands' of Russia ...

It would have been possible not to speak ill of this old man who has had a difficult life and has returned home to spend the rest of his days here, if it had not turned out historically that even in prerevolutionary days his name became – not without cause – a symbol of antisemitism and ukrainophobia, and if his voice were today only a fact of his personal biography and not the evidence of something larger: a certain reassessment of values.

This reassessment has gone somewhat far and is being conducted on a rather broad front. During the last ten or twenty years, for example, a thorough revision of the history of Russia and the contiguous peoples has been accomplished with the aim of justifying Russian imperialism.

What Marxism-Leninism considered as colonial banditry and campaigns of conquest (which they really were) are now being glorified as 'the valour of the Russian arms'. What MarxismLeninism considered the rapacity, perfidy and shameless trickery of Russian tsardom (which it really was) is now being represented to the people as 'the brilliant successes of Russian diplomacy', as its 'great traditions'. Not to waste space on things that are widely known I refrain from citing hundreds of pertinent examples; however, if necessary, I am prepared to cite them at any time.

The 'rehabilitation' of the colonial heritage of the Russian Empire as the 'ancestor' of the USSR is entering more and more widely into contemporary Russian literature, criticism and journalism. (A recent, but by no means unique, example is V. Firsov's poem 'Russia from the Dew Drop to the Star' – it was printed in part in *Pravda* – in which the road to communism leads 'through Poltava' and other exploits of the Russian autocrats.)[17]

Reading certain books, articles and speeches you cannot but be amazed: when was this written? In the fifth decade of the Union of Soviet Republics or in the nineteenth century, at the height of yet another campaign aimed at the Bosporus or some other such place? Why do the authors handle notions that are far removed from communism and are as like the notions and phraseology of the 'faithful servants of the Fatherland' from the nineteenth century as are two peas in a pod?

I will take the liberty of quoting a passage from an article by the Admiral of the Fleet of the Soviet Union, I.S. Isakov, 'Sixteen point turn', with which *Nedelya* opened its 'Nautical club' this year.

The author proposes:

> to recall how our enemies continue in their attempts to this very day ... to cut Russia off from the sea, like Shchedrin's hero who tried to 'undiscover America'. With the same success attempts were made through the centuries to close for the Russian people all exits to the sea.
>
> In the remote past these attempts were made by force. Let us recall the Astrakhan kingdom, blocking the exit to the Caspian Sea. Let us recall the double lock, in Azov and in Yenikal, closing the exit into the Black Sea from the delta of the Don. The exit from the Dnieper was likewise locked with a double turn of the key

– in Karacharov and in Ochakov. In the Baltic the role of Cerberus was played in turn by the Livonian Knights, the Hanseatic League, and later Sweden. The fortress 'Oreshek' [little nut] [!], or 'Schlisselburg' (key fortress), has remained in the mouth of the Neva to this very day.[18]

Seemingly natural things. But how frightening that they seem natural to us. This means that we have become used to them. But try to reflect on them. Where is the communist class approach? The author completely identifies the present-day USSR with the Russian Empire, that 'detainer of an immense amount of stolen property'. He heartily approves 'someone else's property'. He repeats what was written by the propagandists of tsarist times and in their falsified history textbooks which looked at the whole surrounding world from one point of view: whether it was 'in the way' of Russia or not, whether it satisfied the appetites of tsarism or not. And woe to the people which found itself 'on the way to the sea'. Later they moved even beyond the sea with patriotic ditties:

> How beyond the ocean blue
> In the steppe the weeds grow wild:
> How beyond the ocean blue
> Infidels have multiplied.

This is how the Russian slaves were trained to look upon other peoples.

'How good that the Russian peasant from the provinces of the interior, without waiting for the Englishmen to finish speaking, climbed down from his stove-bench and went to conquer the oceans,' Admiral Isakov exclaims beautifully.

Forgive me, Admiral, but we know about 'the Russian peasant from the provinces of the interior' from more authoritative sources: Turgenev, Grigorovich, Nekrasov, Herzen,

Chernyshevsky, Reshetnikov, Sleptsov, Bunin ... Somehow, they are silent about how this peasant got off his stove-bench and without batting an eyelid went on conquering the lands and the ocean blue, and liberating peoples. They do, however, tell us how this peasant was driven by famine and poverty, by corvée and recruitment, how this peasant was flayed and, to make him even more of a slave and at the same time to acquire new slaves, was sent for even longer to neighbouring countries and beyond the ocean blue ... And these great Russians – Herzen, Chernyshevsky, whole generations of revolutionaries in the 1860s–80s, up to the Bolsheviks, up to Lenin – dreamed that the Russian peasant, having climbed down from his stove-bench, would not go beyond the ocean and would go nowhere that tsarism sent him, but would remain at home and put things in order there ... And this, let us take note, is the crux of the matter: tsarism taught the seeking of enemies outside, 'on the way to the sea', whilst the revolutionaries explained that the enemy was not to be found there, in Schlisselburg ('Oreshek', as the Admiral touchingly immortalizes the tsar's wellknown joke), and not in Astrakhan, not on the Baltic and not in the Hausa, but first and foremost at home, whither all energies should be directed.

The Admiral and scholar, I.S. lsakov, cannot fail to know this ... Why then does he repeat the sacramental cliches from the semiofficial press of the last century about 'the Russian peasant from the provinces of the interior' and his mystical yearning to reach beyond the oceans? Why does he confuse the Dnieper Cossacks with this peasant? Why does he forget elementary geography and history? Why does he forget that all the lands and peoples he mentioned never belonged to Russia, but were seized by the Russian tsars (and not by the 'peasant from the provinces of the interior' 'on the road to the sea')? (Thus the whole 'guilt' of these lands and peoples in the eyes of tsardom was the guilt of the lamb before the wolf: 'You are guilty if only because I'm hungry.')[19] Why does he identify the imperialistic conflict of tsarist Russia, the clashes of one imperialist with others, with the revolutionary conflict of 1917? 'This "tradition"[20] was continued also during the civil war: what a pitiable Shul'gin-type interpretation of the grandiose class battle of the proletariat, of the grandiose drama of universal history!

Such pearls result from forgetting the Marxist, class viewpoint for the sake of Great-Power ambitions; this is how thought accommodates itself in an atmosphere of Great-Power patriotism!

Similar examples, no longer of 'a certain', but of quite a handsome 'confusion of the concept of Soviet unity with a leaning towards a "Russia, one and indivisible"' can be quoted at length ... oh, at what length!

The clear and precise understanding of the imperialist, colonialist essence of tsarist Russia has been lost, and the past is beginning to be redesigned on the pattern of the present, according to present needs.

Recently one of our foremost leaders (out of esteem for his years and merit I shall not mention his name), while delivering an official address in Tallinn, at the twenty-fifth anniversary celebrations of the Estonian SSR, said among other things (I quote from *Pravda*):

> It should be noted that also under the tsar the general cultural level of the Estonian people was relatively high, while the city of Tartu was an ancient and important centre of higher education not only for Estonian youth but also for other peoples of Russia.

What a moving idyll, what 'friendship of nations' and 'mutual aid', simply an 'exchange of cadres'! That the Estonian people was and is a people of high culture and that Tartu was a traditional centre of education is a fact. But it is equally a fact that 'under the tsar' everything was done to strip the Estonian people of its culture and in particular to transform Tartu (Derpt) University into an instrument of colonial oppression and russification. ('We do not wish [it] to be a spiritual hotbed of disinclination ... towards the ruling nation.')[21] It is typical of tsarism that it stole Derpt University from the Estonian people and stripped it of its national character under the very pretext that it was needed 'by all the peoples of Russia'! It could not have been without good reason that the Marxists used to assure us that Russia was not a friendly family but a prison of nations, turning them against each other and depriving the non-Russians of access to culture and education (if a certain people did preserve a 'relatively high' culture, it was only because it did not have time to lose it completely 'under the wings of the twin-headed eagle'), and that all the official 'smooth talk' on the theme of a 'common Fatherland' was nothing but out-and-out hypocrisy.

Engels (surely a Marxist) wrote once: 'No spoliation, no violence, no oppression on the part of Tsardom, but has been perpetrated under pretext of "progress", "enlightenment", "liberalism", "the deliverance of the oppressed".'[22]

And now it turns out that, after all, it was just like that: 'enlightenment, liberalism and the deliverance of the oppressed'. There were especially a multitude of 'voluntary unions', 'reunions' and 'annexations', perfectly voluntary, of course, the first, the second and the hundredth time. (The Russian tsars were known to be ashamed of coercion, in which respect they differed from all other sovereigns in world history, and – not being Marxists! – did not recognize the use of violence.) And for such a radical reshuffle of the philosophy of history there is no need to create new theories, to construct conceptions, to negate ageold attainments of learning, or to reject memorable facts there is no need for this bother, all that is needed is to replace the word 'tsarism' by 'Russia' (still better, by 'the Russian people') and to say everything the other way round. As if the 'subjugation of the Crimea', the 'pacification of the Caucasus' ('as well as other rebellious tribes'), the 'liberation of Warsaw' and similar heroics 'from Finland's frosty rocks to Colchis' fiery shore'[23] were the initiative of 'the Russian people' or of 'the Russian peasant from the provinces of the interior', and as if all those generals, those Yermolovs, Paskeviches, and Murav'yovs, 'the hangmen', together with the Terrible ones, the Great ones, the Big Sticks, and the Liberators,[24] were the representatives of that very same 'Russian peasant'.

Not so long ago works of history, literary scholarship and folklore dealt objectively and truthfully with the history of Russia's relations with surrounding peoples, with the history of Russian colonization. People wrote quite naturally, as of well-known things, about all the 'charms' of colonization, about the annihilation of entire peoples 'on the road to' the next sea or ocean. It was not strange for such things as this to be read and written:

> The first people fated to receive the blow of the Russian conquerors moving towards Siberia were the Voguls ... As Russian settlements drew closer to the Urals, the Voguls put up a great resistance against the newcomers and even later, at the end of the sixteenth century, surrounded on all sides by stockaded forts, continued to fight against the Russians ...
>
> The main body of the Voguls ... changed after the Russian conquest into semi-nomadic trappers, fishermen and reindeer herdsmen ... Oppressed by the Russian conquerors, the Vogul people, which had been vigorous and warlike, which had known mining, the blacksmith's craft and agriculture, which had conducted trade and waged war, now declined, lost its former skills and, hemmed in on all sides, withdrew into impenetrable thickets ... The Russian conquest concentrated the thoughts and desires of the Vogul people upon

the struggle for its national liberation. But the years pass, the power of the conquerors is consolidated, the hopes of liberation dwindle more and more, and from the depths of the people a new image emerges, the image of a warrior from the common people ... a hero, who shall perform feats of valour and shall rid the Voguls of Russian overlordship. This type of hero is also known to us from the epics of other oppressed Siberian peoples ... Yanyy Keib [the epic hero] enumerates the acts of violence and cruelty committed by the Russians after their victory:

Then they took away our country,
And our rivers, and our forests.
They imposed a heavy tribute
On the hearth of every homestead,
Took our wives, and we, like bondsmen,
Started serving them with meekness.

With the arrival of the Russians

Silent death came swiftly flying,
Bringing sickness to our people,
Bringing pestilence to reindeer ...

These words of Yanyy Kelb are the words of all Siberian peoples ...

Day by day they (the Russians) were increasing,
Day by day our people dwindled,

remarks Yanyy Kelb.

The mournful mood of the Vogul people in the face of threatened destruction takes the form

> of a lament; not only do people weep, but also
> birds, fish, animals, the forest, and all nature ...
> There followed one of those insurrections of the
> oppressed northern peoples, which are so frequent
> in Siberian history from the beginning of the
> seventeenth up to the nineteenth century.[25]

Such historic truth was commonplace and natural. It was widely represented in the works of historians, sociologists, publicists, demographers, men of letters, and, in general, in the social sciences of the 1920s–30s as well as in progressive thought of pre-revolutionary times and – especially in its documentary aspect – in the majority of pre-revolutionary scholarly publications.

Nowadays we do not find anything of the sort. Balancing on the brink of the tone and phraseology of the pre-revolutionary semi-official press and Katkov-style propaganda (and actually sliding into them), everywhere there is presented a bright picture of the 'benefits' brought by Russia to the conquered peoples (probably, those are meant who managed to survive under the paternal hand of the autocrats; it is still uncertain how best to account for those who were magnanimously 'wiped from the face of the earth'; it seems to be easiest with those whose names have not been preserved: they did not exist and that is that). Among those 'benefits' are the rescue of their national existence from predatory neighbours, peace, tranquillity, friendship, the development of crafts and commerce, culture, etc., etc. Khrushchev, speaking in the capitals of the Central Asian republics, particularly liked to hammer home two points: Russia brought these peoples peace and tranquillity, put an end to domestic feuds (through firm rule) and to 'feudal splintering'; also, it brought them a higher culture (this to peoples with a culture that goes back a thousand years, before the existence of Russia!) ... Reading these generous 'revelations' of Khrushchev's you keep hearing a familiar note ... Until, finally, you remember:

well, well, isn't this the same 'pacification' or 'liberation' of peoples 'from their inner falsehood' and 'instability', so much talked about 150, 200 and 300 years ago by unpleasant people, from Catherine II to Pobedonostsev? As to culture, we can find analogies in history from Pizarro's time to our own day (although nowadays even the colonizers of Africa are ashamed to speak openly of it). This is the end result of naked political expediency, of ignoring the spirit of Marxism and of only a formal utilization of its phraseology.

True, a little correction is being made in this respect: it is being said that these blessings were not brought to these peoples by tsardom, or even Russia in general, but by the great Russian people. But, if I may say so, policy in general and colonial policy in particular was nevertheless shaped by the Russian tsardom, and not by the Russian people. In short, this 'correction' is of the kind that would allow us to justify the conquest of India by saying that the English people is a great people and it will not do to offend it by reminding it of its colonies.

What an unusual people – unique in the whole world – which could make others happy while being itself one of the most unhappy, and which bestowed on others what it did not possess itself! How could it, for example, bring culture, if, as we know, for 95 per cent of the Russian population this culture was inaccessible and, according to Lenin's words, within the tsarist Empire 'the development of capitalism and the general level of culture [were] often higher in the non-Russian border regions than in the centre'.[26]

It is obvious that all questions are far more complex and it is false, anti-historic and anti-Marxist to boil them down to pseudopatriotic stories and propagandist commonplaces about the great Russian people extending the fraternal hand of magnanimous aid first to one and then to another neighbouring people, ad infinitum. Here the historical and Marxist class approach with its regard for facts is replaced by a primitive propagandist, nationalistic, GreatPower attitude.

And yet this same un-Marxist view is being put about everywhere and, in particular, inculcated into generations of schoolchildren.

Try to imagine what a foundation for morality and civic virtues our youth derives from this propaganda thoroughly resembling that against which the true sons of Russia, from the revolutionary democrats of the 1860s to Lenin, fought with all their might.

And what about the 'nationwide celebrations' of the 300th, 400th, 200th, 150th and other anniversaries of 'voluntary reunions', annexations, 'entries' and other territorial 'accessions', as they were more honestly called in olden times? Recently, I think, even the 450th anniversary of the 'voluntary annexation' of Kazan was celebrated, that same Kazan which Ivan the Terrible butchered to a man ... What is next: a celebration of the voluntary reunion of the Crimea and the voluntary resettlement of the Crimean Tartars from the southern shore to Siberia? For the taste for nationwide masquerades has not yet been lost, it seems ...

At the same time, no attention is paid to generally known historical facts, to the evidence of Russian and other national literatures, to the voices of progressive public figures, to the traditions of revolutionary thought, or to the fundamental documents of Marxism-Leninism, which, both separately and taken together, say:

First: not a single one of these 'annexations' and 'reunions' was 'voluntary', neither in essence nor even in form. Even Ukraine did not 'reunite', but entered into a treaty of alliance,[27] which later was perfidiously broken by tsardom. Compare, for instance, Herzen's words:

> Khmel'nyts'ky committed himself to the
> tsar not out of sympathy for Moscow,
> but out of antipathy for Poland. Moscow,
> or rather Petersburg, deceived Ukraine
> and made it hate the Muscovites.

> Joining Great Russia, Little Russia [Ukraine] reserved considerable rights for herself. Tsar Alexis swore to respect them. Peter I, on the pretext of Mazeppa's betrayal, left only a vestige of these privileges. Elizabeth and Catherine introduced serfdom there. The unfortunate country protested, but could it withstand that fateful avalanche rolling from the North to the Black Sea and covering everything ... with a uniform icy shroud of slavery?[28]

A number of other peoples and territories were gained by fraud, bribery and intrigues with other rulers. There are more than enough apposite facts and documents, for example, in many volumes of Solov'yov's *History of Russia*.[29] Concerning the 'voluntary' annexation of Georgia, a contemporary attests the following:

> The original impetus for occupying Georgia came from the suggestion of Count Pushkin, who, prompted by ambition and perhaps also by zeal for the Fatherland, thought he perceived in the accomplishment of this undertaking the means of crowning with success his intentions, both personal ones and also those useful for his service generally.

The same document mentions the motives for subjugating other Caucasian territories: 'A territory will be annexed, which abounds in metals, crops and cattle ...'[30] As we can see, the matter was explained simply and clearly. Finally, the peoples of the North, Siberia and Central Asia the tsardom conquered and, whenever possible, destroyed, on the grounds of their being 'savages' and 'robbers'.

Secondly: conquest did not and could not bring any economic or cultural improvement to any of these conquered peoples, who, on the contrary, declined or even became extinct. How many peoples and tribes died, out in Siberia, how many were there whose names have not even come down to us! It is known what impoverishment tsardom brought to Asia; it is known that in Ukraine it established serfdom, brought ravages, deprived the nation of its intelligentsia, and extinguished all the centres of cultural life. Concerning Ukraine, the contemporary scholar and public figure V.N. Karazin said: '*Ne pouvant, sans douleur, la voir, malgré ses richesses et les talents qui s'y offrent en foule, abandonnée a la chicane et au mépris ...*' And about the fate of the Crimea he wrote: '... *la Crimée, changée en desert du pays délicieux et trés peuplé qu'elle était sous les Turcs*'.³¹ In Ye. Markov's book *Sketches of the Crimea*³² we may find factual data attesting that while the education of children in the Crimean Khanate was compulsory, after the Russian conquest total illiteracy gradually triumphed. There are also similar documentary data about Ukraine, where in Khmel'nyts'ky's time and during the first decades of the Hetmanate there were schools in almost every village, whilst at the beginning of the nineteenth century, that is to say some hundred years later, there were ten times fewer, according to the data of an official census. This is why Academician Bahaliy expressed what was generally known when he said in the Council of State:

> For everybody the fact is more or less beyond question that the Little Russian [Ukrainian] population in the nineteenth century was culturally backward in comparison with the Great Russian or non-Russian population, and one of the chief reasons for this backwardness was precisely the above-mentioned difficulty³³ ... while in the seventeenth century the Little Russians were famous for their education and, as is well known, carried it even into Muscovite Russia.³⁴

H. Petrovs'ky spoke in similar vein at the session of the Fourth State Duma on 4 June 1913 (his speech was written by Lenin):

> I must tell you that Archdeacon Paul of Aleppo says in his study of literacy in Ukraine in 1652 that almost all domestic personnel, and not only the males, but also their wives and daughters, could read. The censuses of 1740 and 1748 say that in seven regiments of the Hetmanate, in the Poltava and Chernihov provinces, there were 866 schools with Ukrainian as the language of instruction for a total of 1,904 villages. That is, one school for every 746 persons. In 1804 an ukaz was issued forbidding instruction in the Ukrainian language. The consequences of national oppression have continued to be felt. The 1897 census showed that the least literate people in Russia were the Ukrainians. They were on the lowest level. That was in 1897, and at that time 13 per cent of the population were literate.[35]

Thirdly: a phenomenon cannot be considered progressive if it is characterized by violence, colonialism, the decay of civic virtues and culture of the subjugated nations, and even their physical annihilation or biological extermination (classical genocide), if it intensifies national enmity (and not friendship, as is shamelessly claimed now, notwithstanding Lenin's: 'Accursed tsarism made the Great Russians into the executioners of the Ukrainian people'[36]), if it intensifies reaction, and if it bleeds white the revolutionary forces within the ruling nation itself. 'The long, centuries-old history of the suppression of the movements of the oppressed nations, and the systematic propaganda in favour of such suppression coming from the "upper" classes have created enormous obstacles to the cause of [the] freedom of the Great Russian people itself, in the form of prejudices, etc.'[37] All the more reason then that Marxism-Leninism did not and could not consider all this progressive.

Let us think logically. Was tsarist Russia a despotic empire, or not? If it was, how can a Marxist-Leninist admit even the possibility of a genuine (and not merely formal) voluntary annexation or reunion as a part of that process which went down in history as a classical example of a colonial offensive? Let him who can explain this: how could a process of colonization and imperial plundering compose a long chain of 'voluntary' reunions and annexations? Or the other way round: how did a series of such reunions and annexations add up to imperialism? Is this dialectics? No, sophistry and absurdity.

But let us suppose that tsarist Russia was not a despotic empire and that Russian colonialism is an invention of Russophobe nationalists. Let us suppose that such a chimera as voluntary annexations and reunions really did take place as regards Russia, so as to set it specially apart from other countries of the world, in which such heavenly manna never did nor will rain down in the course of all human history.

Then we will raise another question: does Marxism applaud the loss of national sovereignty, its renunciation under conditions of capitalism or, what is more, of feudalism? With profound and heartfelt sympathy for those who love celebrating 300th and 450th anniversaries, we must admit: it does not. Quite the contrary. Marxism, if you allow me to say so, considers it 'unadvisable', both for those who are annexed ('As long as it lacks national independence,' Engels writes, 'a ... people is historically unable even simply to discuss in earnest any domestic questions'),[38] and for those who annex ('No nation can be free if it oppresses other nations').[39]

Here is one more opinion from Engels: 'Irish history shows one how disastrous it is for a nation when it has subjugated another nation. All the abominations of the English have their origin in the Irish Pale.'[40]

On the whole, it is interesting to analyse the fecund ideas of Marx and Engels on the relations of England and Ireland: on many questions they link up with the history of Russian-Ukrainian relations ... More than that, Marx and Engels even directly advise 'to separate' (sic!). '... *It is in the direct and absolute interest of the English working class to get rid of their present connection with Ireland.*'[41]

Quoting this letter, Lenin adds:

> Marx advocated the *separation* of Ireland from England ...
>
> The economic ties between Ireland and England in the 1860s were, of course, even closer than Russia's present ties with Poland, Ukraine, etc. The 'unpracticality' and 'impracticability' of the separation of Ireland (if only owing to geographical conditions and England's immense colonial power) were quite obvious ...
>
> The policy of Marx and Engels on the Irish question serves as a splendid example of the attitude the proletariat of the oppressor nations should adopt towards national movements, an example which has lost none of its immense *practical* importance. It serves as a warning against that 'servile haste' with which the philistines of all countries, colours and languages hurry to label as 'utopian' the idea of altering the frontiers of states that were established by the violence and privileges of the landlords and bourgeoisie of one nation.[42]

But all the same, perhaps all this does not apply to Russia, for, as the Russians have been assured since time immemorial, 'What is death to the German is healthy for the Russian.' Alas, there is something about Russia too, especially about those voluntary reunions.

In the article 'On the National Pride of the Great Russians' Lenin writes: 'The economic prosperity and rapid development of Great Russia ... require that the country be liberated from Great Russian oppression of other nations ... '[43] This is almost literally what Herzen never tired of writing in his day, that Russia should rather let her parts go than draw them in.[44] 'We should be very sorry if Little Russia [Ukraine], for instance, being called upon to express her thought freely, could not preserve her total independence.'[45]

H. Petrovs'ky's speech in the State Duma, which we have quoted earlier (and which, as we have mentioned, was written by Lenin), deals thus with the same question:

> Our landlords and official circles try to instil the thought in the people that the self-determination of nations will have a disastrous effect on the state. But look at Sweden and Norway: there you have civilized countries. You know that law and order, civilization and education are a hundred times higher there than here. In 1905 Norway wanted to separate from Sweden, and what happened? It separated peacefully and freely, in spite of the fact that Sweden has twice as many inhabitants. They did not start hounding Norway, they did not start inciting their people against the Norwegians, to fight Norway and impose the Swedish yoke upon it.[46]

In the work 'The Discussion on Self-determination Summed up' Lenin approvingly cites these words of Engels about the Russian Empire:

> 'And as to Russia,' says Engels, 'she could only be mentioned as the detainer of an immense amount of stolen property [i.e., oppressed

nations],[47] which would have to be disgorged on the day of reckoning.'[48]

Here you have your 'voluntary reunions', here you have your nationwide celebrations, here you have Russia's mission as the saviour of the surrounding peoples!

To satisfy the most absurd tendency of identifying the USSR with the heritage of the former Russian Empire and of 'rehabilitating' the latter, today's historian does not interpret the 'history of the Fatherland' as the history of the Russians, Ukrainians, Georgians, Latvians, etc., respectively, but as the history of the Russian Empire, the master of that 'immense amount of stolen property', failing to distinguish its lawful owners[49] and in fact defending the rights of the robber: 'It is very important for us to disclose how their[50] natural and just protest against tsarist oppression flowed into the most pernicious channel of a *struggle* against annexation to Russia, a struggle advantageous only to the local feudal lords and, at times, the foreign enemies of our peoples.'[51] Obviously, the words about the protest against national oppression being 'natural' and 'just' pay mere lip-service to 'public decency', for the sole actual manifestation of a struggle against national oppression, of a struggle against annexation by tsarism is immediately qualified as a supreme evil and, quite in the spirit of official tsarist propaganda, linked with the plots of 'foreign enemies'. As an historian, A.M. Sakharov must know that all Russian tsars, from Peter I and Catherine II to Nicholas II, attributed all revolutionary and especially national movements in their Empire to intrigues by foreign powers, and tried to represent the leaders of these movements, from Radishchev to Lenin, from Hordiyenko to Drahomanov and Hrushevs'ky, from Shamil to Kenesary and Arnangeldy Imanov, to the Russian Philistine as the paid agents of foreign powers. As an historian, A.M. Sakharov must know, has no right not to know, that for the conquered peoples the greatest 'foreign enemy' was precisely the Russian Empire, just as it was the greatest enemy for all the true sons of Russia, from Radishchev to Chaadayev, and from Herzen to Lenin. They did not worry about the unity of the Russian Empire, oh no! quite the contrary! But the present-day historian, the 'Marxist' A.M. Sakharov and others of that ilk (whose name is legion) do worry! They worry about the unity and 'inviolability' of 'Russia, one and indivisible', of the Russia of Peter I, Catherine II, all the Alexanders and Nicholases!

But some historians and theoreticians go even further. Thus V.V. Timoshenko in his article 'Was Byelorussia under Tsarism a Colony in the Economic Sense?' arrives at the conclusion: 'Belorussia was not a colonial appendage of the Russian Empire'; 'Belorussia was in the economic sense neither a colony nor a semicolony.'[52]

So that one is left wondering why did Yanka Kupala write his famous poem about Byelorussians ...

Among Timoshenko's arguments there is, for instance, this one: 'In legal status the Belorussian provinces differed in no way from the neighbouring Russian provinces.' There is no proof that 'the tsarist government took measures that were purposely designed to hold back the economic development of the North-Western Region'. It is really touching how uncritical and naive our learned historians are ready to become when the spirit of the age demands it! 'In legal status...' ! As if V.V. Timoshenko did not know that legally and formally everybody was 'equal' in the Russian Empire (that is to say, equal slaves). The learned historian believes what official Russia said and wrote about this matter. But then he will also have to believe that tsarist Russia was the most progressive and most democratic country in the world, the bearer of progress and prosperity, and the shining light of civilization, as was claimed by official propaganda and by the learned 'servants of the Fatherland', as was believed by the Russian Philistine and by part of the foreign public. (The French philosopher Helvetius, for instance, praised Catherine II as the servant of truth and an enlightener of humanity at the very moment that this defender of truth and freethinking condemned the *Russian* philosopher Radishchev to penal servitude in Siberia, while commenting spitefully: 'They will send a couple more from France,' meaning that they will send French spies to replace the one liquidated!)

The learned historian is touched that the tsarist government did not take any measures to hold back the economic development of Byelorussia. Forgive me for asking, but why should they hold it back? To weaken the strength of their Empire? The Russian tsars and 'servants of the Fatherland' were not such fools. They developed the economies of the conquered territories, but in a way that was useful to them, harnessing these economies to their own. And they were so well alerted to the need for the development of these economies that the necessity for regulation and intensification in the economic field was advanced as the main reason for abolishing the vestiges of Ukrainian home-rule in the times of Catherine II. (Compare Teplov's well-known 'Memorandum on Little Russia'.[53])

Some present-day historians and theoreticians do not know, or pretend not to know, what Machiavelli knew and what was already known in Roman Imperial times, namely: that the nature of foreign government in conquered territories can vary, just as types of colonialism vary. It is one thing when an economically backward country has been conquered and is colonized, and a different thing when the country is a developed one. It is one thing when a nation with an already developed political self-consciousness and a tradition of statehood is being oppressed, and a different thing when the subjected population has not yet changed from an ethnographic mass into a fully-fledged nation. It is one thing when the colonized territories are overseas, and another when they are adjacent, one thing when the victim is a foreign race, and another when it is related.

> The colonization of a country does not always take place by the simple process of direct and violent conquest and annexation. In the case of a major developed country, with an old civilization – often older than its invaders – and strongly entrenched traditional political institutions, the process of penetration and eventual subjugation is often more subtle and gradual.[54]

Russian colonialism has developed in peculiar circumstances and has its own aberrant characteristics and its own peculiarities.

Compared to the 'classic' colonialism of the great European powers, Russian tsarist colonialism had a number of distinctive features. For instance, since its expansion was not directed towards overseas territories but towards neighbouring lands, the whole matter was not limited to the imposition of a colonial administration and to economic exploitation but developed into full assimilation, into a social digestion of the conquered countries. What is more, the colonizers relied on 'peaceful' means, using force of arms only 'in the case of necessity' against 'restive' natives. It is interesting to note that tsarism, faithful to its lofty Christian mission and fraternal love, never treated the neighbouring peoples which it subjugated, or anticipated subjugating, as inferiors or as a lower race. On the contrary, it first recognized them generously as equal citizens of the Empire and bestowed all 'rights' on them, and only then went to war against them to affix to them by any means whatsoever this equality and these rights. One result of this unique approach was that any resistance against the conquerors was designated in advance as 'treason to the Fatherland'.

The whole history of the Russian tsars is full of complaints about 'treason', punishments for 'treason', searches for 'treason' and anticipation of possible 'treason' ... Where is the secret of this phenomenon, unparalleled in world history?

Probably in the bizarre meaning itself given to this concept by Russian tsardom and its strategists and moralists.

But then, they spoke of 'treason' in order to intimidate while knowing full well on whose toes they were treading ...

A high dignitary wrote about this:

> When the state contains within its bounds conquered lands inhabited by diverse tribes which have not yet morally merged with the conquerors, such a merging can and must eventually be brought about by legislative and governmental measures through the wise formulation of statutes and their strict execution, but as long as the elements which are openly or secretly hostile to such a moral merging of all parts of the body politic to which they belong are not fully imbued with a feeling of attachment to the common, indivisible Fatherland, the Government must necessarily base its authority in the semi-subjected provinces on the solid organization of military establishments.

And to encourage a speedy 'moral merging' within 'the common, indivisible Fatherland', a cunning, complex and flexible strategy of suppressing, corrupting and denationalizing the oppressed peoples was developed.

Here we find the hypnotic power of the universal and invincible mission of Russian tsardom (the Third Rome), which it is hopeless to resist. Here we find the myths about Russian tsardom as the support and liberator of Slav peoples either from the Turks, or from someone else, linked with a cunning exploitation of the political and psychological situation. Here we find the consistent eradication of 'antiquity' and the 'conceptions of former times' (formulas of Catherine II).

Here we find the age-old policy of 'divide and rule', complemented by typically native nuances:

> For our security in Ukraine, it is necessary first of all to sow discord between the commanders and the hetman ... When the people find out that the hetman will not wield such power as Mazeppa, I hope they will come with denunciations. Then the informers should not be shown harshness. If two come with a lie, and no harshness is shown, the third may come with the truth, and the hetman and his officers will feel apprehensive ... It is necessary that in all border towns there should be commanders who disagree with the hetman; if they disagree, all their affairs will be open to us.[55]

The dialectics of 'Russianization' should be noted. 'Russianization', as we know, was the basic formula of the Russian tsarist nationalities policy; let us recall on the one hand the aim of Peter I 'to establish Russians in the country'[56] in the precise sense of Machiavelli's recommendation ('to hold them [the acquired states] ... one of the best, most effective expedients would be for the conqueror to go to live there in person');[57] and on the other hand the gradual extirpation of the national-cultural peculiarities of the conquered people ('As long as a people preserves its faith, language, customs and laws it cannot be considered subdued').[58] As a culmination of everything, to mask these processes and to break down inward resistance, theories about a 'common Fatherland', about 'consanguinity' and the like were developed and drummed into the people.

The feeling of 'consanguinity' and 'fraternity' went so far that when Dmitriy Sechenov, the Bishop of Nizhniy-Novgorod, in Elizabeth's reign, ordered a Mordvin heathen cemetery to be destroyed (in his attempts to convert the natives), thereby causing an insurrection of the Mordvins, he justified his actions with the argument that the Mordvins were not Mordvins at all, but slightly modified Russians, 'the old Russian idolaters who could not speak Mordvin but a Yaroslavl' dialect and differ from the Russian inhabitants of the Nizhniy-Novgorod province'.[59]

The very same men and institutions, inciting the peoples of the Russian Empire against each other and suppressing all, could speak beautifully about 'brotherhood': 'One should not stir up questions that divide brothers, one should not say that Ukrainians and Great Russians ... do not speak the same language',[60] appealed the 'liberal' Professor Kapustin in the Third Duma in 1909.

Such examples run into thousands. They bear eloquent testimony to the Jesuitical skill of tsarism which could pass off the basest and most treacherous things as the most noble and sacred. Not for nothing did the creators of Russian policy diligently study the experience of the Roman, German and Austro-Hungarian Empires particularly from the point of view of their colonizing methods.

From the Roman Empire the Russian tsars took over the basic principles of their policy: '... in every other province they invaded, the Romans were brought in by the inhabitants', states Machiavelli.[61] The Russian tsars did the same thing. They suppressed even the Polish revolutions, all three of them (1799, 1830–31 and 1863–4), at the request of the Poles themselves, as is recorded in the relevant historical documents. And all was done with the purpose of liberation: even the previously mentioned liberal Aksakov calls the 'action' of the Russian army in Poland 'a purely liberating action ... that is, liberating the Poles from their own inner falsehood'.[62]

In the case of Ukraine this was even more evident. Catherine abolished Ukrainian home rule with the sole purpose of liberating 'the people ... from the many petty tyrants that have taken to tormenting it'.[63]

The introduction of serfdom and other encroachments upon Ukraine were also accomplished with the purpose of 'liberation': 'for equalizing the liberties of the Little Russian people, likewise subject to Her Imperial Majesty'.⁶⁴

It is particularly interesting that even the russification of schools was introduced under the banner of progress and at the request of the Ukrainians themselves.

In the matter of 'unity' Catherine held high hopes of the so-called 'people's schools' which she planned with a special purpose: to replace the traditional national schools which still existed in a number of borderlands, among them Ukraine. The 'people's schools' were to be Russian, of course.

On 20 October 1782 her private secretary A.V. Khrapovitsky took down her words: 'Through the introduction of people's schools the diverse customs in Russia will be brought into harmony and *mores* corrected.' 'As soon as the people's schools are introduced and firmly established, ignorance⁶⁵ will be exterminated by itself: there is no need of violence here.'⁶⁶

This latter idea is particularly touching and characteristic of the Russian tsars who always condemned 'violence' and consistently adhered to the 'voluntary' principle so close to their hearts.

Catherine II intended to introduce the self-same Russian 'people's schools' in place of the Ukrainian ones specifically at the request of the parents, at the request of the Ukrainians themselves, and wrote therefore to Rumyantsev, her man in Ukraine: 'I wish you to persuade some of the so-called *pany* [gentlemen] in the region to present a petition in which they might ask for a better system of schools and seminaries and, if possible, to have a similar petition from clerics or secular men for the transfer of the clergy to civil status: then we would know how to make a beginning.'⁶⁷

One could say a great deal more about the artful contrivings of national oppression in tsarist Russia, concealed behind a very noble façade, so that not everybody saw it at the time. Many people, and not only Philistines, were probably made indignant and surprised by words like the following:

> At present there is probably no equal to our Great Russian nationalism and the landowners' patriotism in Europe, and not only in Europe, but even in Asia. In the whole world you can find nothing worse, nothing more infamous than what is being done here to the oppressed peoples ...
>
> But, beside the medieval persecutions of Jews in [this] barbarian and savage country, it seems to be the special task of the government to persecute the native languages of all nations. Slav nations, Byelorussians, Ukrainians and Poles are especially persecuted ... The 'Black Hundreds' and their lackeys call Russia a Great Slav state probably on the sole ground that this great state exercises the greatest oppression of the Slav peoples.[68]

Marx, Engels and Lenin considered Russian tsarist colonialism and oppression to be the most dreadful in the world, not least because it reached the peaks of hypocrisy and cynicism in using the noblest phraseology for the basest purposes and because it was so efficient at concealing the reality behind the outward appearances of things.

Returning now to our discussion about 'reunions', annexations and the like, we may say that all the above logically leads to an elementary conclusion: if it is worthwhile marking such dates (and probably it is, since after all they represent very important turningpoints in the histories of the nations concerned), their commemoration should be used for a broader elucidation of the forms and peculiarities of Russian imperialism, for an explanation of the vile and reactionary essence of militant Russian nationalism and Great-Power ideology (the Party aimed at precisely this kind of educational work in the 1920s), and for instilling an understanding of the fundamental *difference* between the present Union of Republics and the former Russian Empire, and not a sense of *heritage*.

But now it is the sense of heritage that is being inculcated. Heritage of territory, heritage of 'territorial integrity', heritage of 'sacred boundaries', *heritage* of the 'invincibility of Russian arms', heritage of the 'union around the Russian principle' (the very same which communist Marxists used to hate so much) and of Russian 'leadership', heritage of the 'elder brother', heritage of the notion of Russia's exceptional role and mission among the surrounding peoples, etc. – except that all this is expressed in pseudo-internationalist phrases. This is not the heritage that communists can be proud of. The great Lenin was ashamed of *this* heritage and took pride in quite a *different* Russian heritage, in the truly great Russian heritage of the revolutionaries.

> We are full of a sense of national pride, and for that very reason we *particularly* hate *our* slavish past (when the landed nobility led the peasants into war to stifle the freedom of Hungary, Poland, Persia and China), and our slavish present, when these self-same landed proprietors, aided by the capitalists, are leading us into a war in order to throttle Poland and Ukraine, crush the democratic movement in Persia and China, and strengthen the gang of Romanovs, Bobrinskys and Purishkeviches, who are a disgrace to our Great Russian national dignity. Nobody is to be blamed for being born a slave; but a slave who not only eschews a striving for freedom but justifies and eulogizes his slavery (e.g., calls the throttling of Poland and Ukraine, etc., a 'defence of the fatherland' of the Great Russians) – such a slave is a lickspittle and a boor, who arouses a legitimate feeling of indignation, contempt and loathing.[69]
>
> ... The Great Russians cannot 'defend the fatherland' otherwise than by desiring the defeat of tsarism in any war, this as the lesser

evil to nine-tenths of the inhabitants of Great Russia. For tsarism not only oppresses those nine-tenths economically and politically, but also demoralizes, degrades, dishonours and prostitutes them by teaching them to oppress other nations and to cover up this shame with hypocritical and quasi-patriotic phrases.[70]

These words should be seared with a red-hot iron (may it for once do some good) on the wooden foreheads of today's lickspittles and boors who cover up the infamy of the past with hypocritical, pseudopatriotic phrases and stage costly 'nationwide celebrations' on the sites of national tragedies. Do they not understand that by repeating today what are essentially the fictions of the tsarist semi-official press, both as regards the treatment of Russian history and the treatment of Russia's relations with surrounding peoples, they perforce set themselves up as the successors to those semi-official organs and identify the USSR with the former Russian Empire? Do they not understand that they are betraying Leninism – no more, no less – and substituting a Great-Power approach for a class revolutionary approach?

All this is done supposedly in the name of the glorification of the Russian people and its mission. But the Russian people's undoubted greatness lies not in this, and altogether one should not use the term 'people' in such an unscrupulous, demagogic way when it is a question of complex historic, economic and social developments. Marxists analyse them concretely, and where Great-Power enthusiasts and 'patriots' want to conceal all kinds of unsavoury practices by use of the terms 'people' and 'Russian people', Marxists find the concrete Russian landlord, merchant, factory-owner, official and kulak. Here is one more example of how the communists in revolutionary years formulated the question about the relations between Russians and the indigenous populations of territories subjugated by tsarist Russia. This is a fragment from the joint report on the nationalities question at the x Party Congress (Comrade Safarov):

> ... Since 1916 in the Semirech'ye region alone, 35 per cent of the Kirghiz rural population have died out ... The second figure is the loss of 70 per cent of their cattle by those same Kirghiz ... Mistrust of the Russian town has been imbibed by the natives with their mother's milk. The Kirghiz even have proverbs which are still frequently used. The Kirghiz says: 'Kill a Russian's father and give him money'; 'If you have a Russian friend, keep a stone behind your shirt.' In olden times the Russian was to the Kirghiz an official, a policeman, an oppressor and a robber. Obviously, a special approach is needed here so as to join up the non-exploiting element of the borderlands with Soviet power ... Well, who succeeded in penetrating into the Party there? ... The old Russian official. Formerly he had relied upon the imperialists, but when that stay collapsed, when he saw that he could not expect direct assistance from the bourgeoisie and landlords in Moscow and Petersburg, he understood that in the Turkestani situation of national enmity an authority of some kind had to be established, just so long as this authority was Russian. Thus the Party became soiled there, because we did not succeed straight away in attracting into it native proletarian and semi-proletarian elements. But there are such elements, and if we succeed in attracting them, they will honestly and selflessly fight under our banners. But who actually got into our ranks were the communist parson, the Russian policeman, and the kulak from Semirech'ye, who to this day keeps

dozens of hired labourers, has hundreds of cattle, and hunts the Kirghiz like game.

During the revolution such horrors took place there, about which it is time to speak openly in order to rid ourselves finally of the Russian colonialist tendencies which are still alive in our ranks, so that the resolutions of the Comintern should not be merely empty words for us.

... The Russian Great-Power kulaks, who were ordained to become the 'bearers' of proletarian dictatorship in the borderlands, thrust the native masses back into the camp of the counter-revolution.

... Naturally in the industrially undeveloped borderlands the number of Russian proletarians was infinitesimal, and at the same time, since authority had to be constituted exclusively of Russians, kulaks and others followed suit.

And now, by virtue of every Russian in the borderlands having the privilege of being a 'proletarian', authority was constituted from the most infamous crowd of hangers-on, who both with the aid of Soviet authority, and by themselves being in the ranks of Soviet authority, brought about all sorts of counter-revolution.

... This is the situation, Comrades, which we have not yet fully reversed, this is the heritage of imperialist colonial relations. It is the automatic continuation of the old colonial relations behind a Soviet façade ...

... According to statistics from the Semirech'ye region, during the time of the revolution Russian kulak landownership increased from 53 per cent to 70 per cent. Take note, Comrades, during the time of the revolution, during the time of Soviet power! And at the same time the number of Kirghiz who died out in the Semirech'ye region rose to 35 per cent.

Here, Comrades, we have to say quite definitely that without the restoration to the indigenous borderland populations of their right to till the land, to the populations that are literally dying out, there can be no question of any Soviet nationalities policy in the borderlands. In particular this concerns the Kirghiz, Bashkirs and a whole series of mountain tribes in the Caucasus, where the tsarist government in former times gave the best pieces of land near the sources of water to the privileged Russian population. These kulaks, Comrades, number hundreds of thousands. Hundreds of thousands of kulaks in the borderlands, who have constituted the living force of imperialism, have lived and continue to live, enjoying a whole series of privileges by virtue of their economic supremacy, by virtue of owning an enormous quantity of land.[71]

How does this earnest and honest, responsible and internationalist talk contrast with today's sweetly sentimental 'patriotic' falsifications about 'the assistance of the fraternal Russian people' – in conditions of tsarist colonialism!

And let us note: precisely those Russian revolutionary communists who at the dawning of Soviet power really extended the hand of fraternal assistance to the 'national minorities' by declaring a merciless war on Russian Great-Power chauvinism, by dispossessing the Russian kulak of his lands and grounds and giving them to the dwindling local population, by showing concern about Soviet national home rule, cadres, culture and education – precisely those Russian revolutionary communists did not make a great song and dance about their assistance and their mission, though they may well have had good grounds for doing so. On the contrary, they stressed Russia's historic guilt towards these peoples and regarded their action of decolonizing, among other things, as a reparation for this historic guilt. This is a perfect (and beautiful!) parallel to the way in which Marx and Engels formulated the question of the historic debt of the English working class to Ireland.

This was a truly internationalist, revolutionary proletarian outlook. Today it is being replaced by a Russian 'integralist', messianic Great-Power, Imperial Roman attitude.

The constant stress, laid now on the leading role of the Russian people, now on its special mission in the history of neighbouring peoples, now on its constant selfless (unilateral!) assistance, etc., etc. – all this is very remote from a Marxist-Leninist understanding of the real historic process, remote from a revolutionary proletarian world view. This is a revival in different forms of the conception of 'union around the Russian principle' which is hateful to Marxists, and it cannot fail to promote the development among a certain section of Russians – by no means the best – of a conscious or unconscious feeling of national superiority, and in the other peoples of the Union a complex of national inferiority.

The accompanying broad 'reshuffle' and undisguised rewriting of the past, of well-known facts of history – in the direction of falsification to fit the demands of the day – develops a disregard for truth, unscrupulousness and cynicism, which is also incompatible with the principles of communist education.

Finally, the persistent 'correcting' of Russian pre-revolutionary history, the history of the Russian Empire, in the interests of current politics, the desire to trace present statehood from the traditions of past statehood,[72] and in this connection the curious 'rehabilitation' and whitewashing of that landowning bureaucratic statehood with its 'victories', its 'reunions', its 'military glory', and its 'liberations' – all this must provoke the suspicion: isn't this where the rub is coming?

The question arises, who needs all this and what for? Would it not be better and more creditable to educate youth in the spirit of the Leninist concept of national dignity and internationalism; to impart to them an understanding of the antithesis between Russian Great-Power ideology and Russian patriotism, Russian Great-Power ideology and internationalism; to give them an honest presentation of history and understanding of the tragedy of those phenomena and developments which the stronger side interpreted too much to its own advantage and finally 'ratified' by first law in its own version? Should not youth be educated in the spirit of esteem, respect, love and concern for all nations – not a merely verbal profession of these, for the sake of 'form', but real and active, to be cherished in the heart as a vital force, and should not youth be directed towards a profound and noble understanding and feeling for our mutual responsibility, as representatives of the various nations, for the fate, the future, the cultures, the languages – for the genuine flowering – of all the nations that are historically united in the Union of Soviet Socialist Republics?

3   RUSSIAN CHAUVINISM AS THE PRACTICE OF ATTRIBUTING TO THE RUSSIANS WHAT HAS BEEN CREATED BY ALL THE PEOPLES OF THE USSR

One way of confusing the USSR with 'Russia, one and indivisible' consists in attributing to the Russians what has been created by the common efforts of all the peoples of the USSR. Numerous Ukrainian scholars, scientists and artists of the remote and recent past are rather unceremoniously, without any reference to their nationality, labelled as Russian scholars, etc., simply because colonial conditions under tsarism in Ukraine or their personal circumstances forced them to work beyond the boundaries of Ukraine. So much for the past. But similar tendencies to credit the Russians with everything also exist in the present context. Formulas like 'Russians

Orbit Sputnik'; 'Russians Build Aswan'; 'Russians Help Peoples of Africa and Asia' come from the bourgeois press and from foreign political phraseology – where the USSR is consistently identified with Russia and no need is felt to know other Soviet nations – into the Soviet press, and from there become imprinted on the mind of the public. Nothing, however, is heard, for instance, about the assistance given to those nations by such a member of the United Nations as the Ukrainian Soviet Socialist Republic, nothing is heard about the participation of Ukrainians in all these undertakings. Neither have Ukrainians received a single word of thanks from those Asian and African peoples, and what is more, the latter do not even know of the existence of such a nation although its share in that 'Russian aid' is considerable. Many young people from the AfroAsian countries study in Ukrainian universities, but the majority of them do not even suspect that they are enjoying the hospitality and assistance of the *Ukrainian* nation, a nation with its own culture, language and statehood. Of course, the fault is not theirs ... Apropos of this, in recent times a new 'proof' has been adduced for the contention that in the Ukrainian universities it is not feasible to lecture in the Ukrainian language: you cannot do it, for there are foreigners studying there ...

Innumerable facts, some of them rather curious, show how readily and even zealously our press and our public men encourage this identification of the USSR with Russia and this non-recognition of other nations which originates abroad. At the International Film Festival in Mar del Plata the Ukrainian film from the Kyiv Dovzhenko Studio *Shadows of Forgotten Ancestors* was awarded the second prize and was warmly acclaimed by the public. But, naturally, the 'renown' of the UN member, Ukraine, in the world is such that the Argentinian public knows nothing of the existence of such a sovereign state or of such a people. Since the name Kyiv means nothing to them, they shouted: 'Viva

Rusia! Viva Moscu!' You might think there was nothing else to do but flush with shame that the name of one's people is unknown and that the credit for a triumph of its art should go once more to the Russians. But one sees the head of the State Committee of Cinematography of the Ukrainian SSR, S.P. Ivanov, describing all this in the newspaper *Vechirniy Kyiv* [Evening Kyiv] without a trace of awkwardness, quite unaware of the bitter irony of fate ...

I am sure that such phenomena do not benefit anyone... The Russian nation – one of the greatest and most glorious in the world does not need this for its fame and grandeur. On the contrary, to a cultured Russian this can only be offensive.

4 RUSSIAN CHAUVINISM AS NATIONAL NIHILISM, PSEUDO-INTERNATIONALISM AND PSEUDO-BROTHERHOOD

Lenin repeatedly stressed the danger of not only conscious, but also unconscious, Russian Great-Power attitudes and chauvinism which may be quite imperceptible to their exponents but are none the less very dangerous. These often take the form of national nihilism and a superficial and false understanding of internationalism. We have discussed this already in Chapters 2 and 3.

Psychologically it is not difficult to understand their origin: since the time of the Mongolian invasion the Russians have not known *national* enslavement; for centuries they have enjoyed statehood and domination. They have never faced the tragic question of national being or non-being; as the saying had it, they have been 'nationally sated', and not always could they all understand those who were 'nationally hungry'. They could not understand all the injury inflicted by, and the hidden workings of, national oppression. It is not surprising that amongst them (although, naturally, not only amongst them) one finds many people who tend to overlook national injustice, to underestimate the national question, to consider it an idle folly or a notion that does not merit the attention of a high-minded person, and is something that prevents one from devoting all one's energies to more important matters and to the service of humanity. These people are congenitally incapable of understanding the profound interaction of the universal and the national, as between the whole and its part, they are insensible to the irreparable losses suffered by the 'universal' when its sources – the nations – are weakened or bleed to death. (And yet they would quickly feel any encroachment upon their own nation.)

There are a good many people who assure us that they are internationalists, that they love Ukraine, Georgia, Latvia, etc., even that they love them fraternally, and that they are therefore all the more outraged when a Ukrainian, Georgian, Latvian, and so on, stresses his own nation's distinctness and separateness from Russia. 'Why should we make national distinctions, we are all brothers,' such comrades complain sincerely. Indeed, there is a grievance here. But let us consider calmly its origin. We do not doubt the sincerity of their love. But love is not everything. Even the sincerest and strongest love can offend and can even be a menace to its object. This may happen, for instance, when something is loved *possessively*, as something inseparable and indistinguishable from oneself, when one does not realize the distinctness, independence and self-sufficiency of the object of one's love. Genuine love differs from this naively selfish feeling by realizing the full distinctness, individuality and sovereignty, the full existence 'beyond oneself' and 'without oneself' of the object of one's love; it differs not only in this realization but also in holding this object in the highest esteem and from this drawing its inspiration. Such a love therefore will not be offended when its object intimates its separateness.

Let us explain this by an historical example which ought to be pondered by some of those comrades who sincerely love Ukraine. Generally speaking, everybody loved Ukraine, though, naturally, each for his own reasons and in his own way. The Russian tsars, for example, loved her very much. I am saying this without irony, for it was really so; they loved her, and sincerely at that. Thus, Empress Elizabeth prayed to God: 'Love it as I have come to love this winning and gentle people.' Catherine II even regretted that the capital had not been built on the banks of the Dnipro, so much was she pleased by 'the excellent air and the warmth of the climate' (this touching admission can be read in her diary, kept by her secretary, Khrapovitsky).[73] All official Russian patriots greatly loved 'the blessed South' – Little Russia – and so did all the landowning and bureaucratic leeches and all the shopkeeping and administrative locusts. But, and this is most touching, those ukrainophobe on principle and the militant Russian nationalists loved her most of all – fiercely, indivisibly, to the death, fraternally.

Here, for instance, speaks one of the ideologists of the Slavophile – pan-Russianist variant of the 'common Fatherland', Ivan S. Aksakov (son of the well-known writer), branded in his time by Shevchenko as a serf-owner and a 'champion of the rod', writing in his newspaper *Den*':

> In regard to the ancient Russian provinces inhabited by our brethren in blood and religion, the Little Russians, the Red Russians and the Byelorussians, Russia bases herself on the most unquestionable of all rights – the moral right, or to be more exact, the moral duty of brotherhood.[74]

This 'moral duty of brotherhood', it turns out, did not permit Aksakov to accord the Byelorussians and Ukrainians the national rights which he two-facedly proclaimed. This 'morality' obliged him to appropriate foreign property:

> We stand for the full *freedom* of life and development of every people...

But:

> We consider the Byelorussians our brethren in blood and spirit and think that Russians of all appellations [!] ought to form one common, compact family.
>
> ... The Little Russian question does not exist at all for Little Russia.
>
> The Little Russian question does not exist for the simple reason that this is an all-Russian, territorial question for the people, for the entire Russian land, concerning equally closely the inhabitant of Penza and Volhynia. Trans-Dnieper Ukraine and Byelorussia are not a conquered land which can be argued about, but a part of the living body of Russia: question or argument has no place here.[75]

As we see, colonialism can appear not only in the form of open discrimination, but also in the form of 'brotherhood', and this is very characteristic of Russian colonialism. (We have already cited above an official appeal to brotherhood in the State Duma.)

Is there anyone who does not know, at least from the works of Lenin, the name of M.N. Katkov, the faithful Cerberus of absolutism, the hater of revolution and of the liberation of peoples, the fierce and tireless ukrainophobe? This name is the symbol of the 'prison of nations'. It was Katkov who negated not only the self-determination of nations, but even the slightest national autonomy, on the grounds of 'brotherhood' and 'internationalism': 'They want to impose an order based precisely on national differences.'[76] Again this self-same Katkov loved Ukraine more than anyone else – intensely and sincerely.

> We love Ukraine, we love her as a part of our Fatherland, as a living, beloved part of our people,

as a part of ourselves, and this is why any attempt to introduce a feeling of mine and thine into the relationship of Ukraine towards Russia is so odious to us. We love Ukraine with all her peculiarities [!] in which we see the token of future riches and variety in the common development of the life of our people.[77] We do not understand, we cannot recognize any rivalry between Ukrainian and Russian. We see in this a most false and harmful concept. We love Ukraine, the distinctive character of her children, the poetry of her legends and melodies: her airs are as close and akin to us as the songs that rise above the Volga. We are very far from condemning those Ukrainians who feel a passion for their native land. *Le patriotisme du clocher* is a highly commendable feeling, but it must not exclude a broader patriotism; the interests of the *native country* should not be opposed to the interests of the *Fatherland*.[78]

Almost everything seems to be 'correct' and even 'high-minded' here. Why then did all progressive Russia consider Katkov a herald of despotism, an especial enemy of nationalities, and a ukrainophobe in particular? Why did Lenin brand him as such? Perhaps there was a mistake here, or perhaps his judgement applied not to these, but to other views of Katkov's? No, precisely to these, there can be no mistake about it. Such ideas were being expressed by all official Russia. *All official* Russia loved Ukraine in this manner, as long as there was no division into 'mine' and 'thine' (you see, they were against 'selfishness' and 'national divisions'!). In the case of necessity, under the pressure of circumstances, they were ready to accord anything to Ukraine, except one thing: 'the right of opposing the interests of the *native country* to the interests of the Fatherland', that is to say, the right of being herself. It was at that time that the theory was being developed about the Russian Empire being the 'common homeland' of dozens of nationalities. After the uncovering of the Brotherhood of Cyril and Methodius,[79] for instance, the Chief of the Gendarmes Count Orlov gave instructions to watch closely

> that the teachers and writers act in accordance with the spirit and aims of the government ..., without giving preference to love of their native country over love of the Fatherland, the Empire, omit everything that could harm this latter love so that all the conclusions of scholars and writers should lead to the advancement not of Little Russia [Ukraine], Poland, and other countries separately, but of the Russian Empire in the totality of the peoples comprising it.

People should also be led away from 'conjectures about the independence and former freedom of the subject peoples of Russia'.[80]

As we can see, for the chieftains of the Russian Empire and for the ideologists of Great Russian chauvinism it was not difficult to be 'internationalists'. But their 'internationalism' is the 'international-ism' of the robber who has seized the choice morsels and does not want to hand them back. Instead, he appeals to the conscience of the victim: what a shame and what backwardness to separate 'mine' and 'thine', how ignoble, how unfraternal; would it not be better to continue together and to look after our 'common' property ...

This is why *progressive* Russia considered Katkov a symbol of oppression and deceit, this is why Lenin scourged 'Katkovism', this is why Katkovism is a loving ukrainophobia – the 'internationalism' of an extreme Russian Great-Power chauvinist. This is why the fact that today certain people begin to repeat the phraseology of Katkov and other 'all-Russians' cannot fail to be disturbing.

May this historic episode (and there are thousands of them) be a lesson: not everything is internationalism that looks like internationalism, that calls itself internationalism, and that seeks to commend itself to us as internationalism. Not everything is nationalism which the opposite side declares to be nationalism or 'separatism'. Not everything is brotherhood that claims to be brotherhood.

Not everything is love that calls itself love. We shall not search for analogies. But if someone speaks about love, let us take a closer look: does this love think about itself or about its object? True love for another people or peoples means that we want that people to be itself and not similar to us; we want to see it independent and equal outside and beside ourselves, not as a part of ourselves; we are ready to aid its self-establishment, and not assimilate it to ourselves. The existence of man requires the existence of other men of equal worth, the existence of nations requires the existence of other nations of equal worth.

When an 'internationalist' complains that a certain 'national' does not throw himself into his embrace, 'fences himself off', 'clings' to his separateness and 'conserves' his culture and language, we must see that his 'internationalism' is the 'internationalism' of a Russian Great-Power chauvinist, his love is the greed to appropriate and to swallow.

As Lenin said:

> If a Great Russian communist insists upon the amalgamation of Ukraine with Russia, Ukrainians might easily suspect him of advocating this policy not from the motive of uniting the proletarians in the fight against capital, but because of the prejudices of the old Great Russian nationalism, of imperialism.[81]

For Lenin there was one criterion of internationalist sincerity in this question: the recognition or non-recognition of

Ukraine's unconditional right to total separation, to full national independence. Lenin recognized this right without reservation, while the serfowners, 'progressives', federalists and similar supporters of 'Russia, one and indivisible' either did not recognize it or recognized it 'with certain reservations'. This lies at the heart of the matter.

The expediency or possibility of such a separation at any given moment is quite a different matter. Lenin gave a warning that the formulation of *this* question would depend on how fully the national interests of the Republics were satisfied in the future Union. It is this that connects both questions. Only on the condition of the total recognition and deep understanding of Ukraine's right to separation and independence will it be possible to carry out a programme of national construction that will fully satisfy national needs. Then the question of formal separation will not be raised even rhetorically.

5 UKRAINOPHOBIA

Does ukrainophobia exist in Ukraine today? Many people will be taken aback by this question. But not everybody. I am sure one can find many Ukrainians and even non-Ukrainians who will not only confirm this but even cite examples from their own experience. Let us agree beforehand that ukrainophobia does not necessarily mean the desire to wring every Ukrainian's neck (although such feelings do exist: Stalin himself, as is known from the reports of the xx Party Congress, was greatly grieved that it was physically impossible to send all Ukrainians to Siberia). There can be a liberal and even highly cultured ukrainophobia. We have already seen that there can be a ukrainophobia that springs from a great love of Ukraine as the 'pearl' of Russia, or from an all too extraordinary understanding of brotherhood. It is possible to love Ukraine as an ethnographic concept and simultaneously to hate it as a nationalpolitical concept. This is how all sworn enemies of Ukrainian 'separatism' loved it, from Catherine II (cf. her famous philippics against 'the silly little Cherkassians'[82] for their 'depraved opinion according to which they consider themselves a people distinct from the Russians' and for their 'false and adventitious republican notions') to the well-known 'progressive' P.B. Struve who formulated the idea thus: for Ukraine, against 'Ukrainism' ('nationalism'!):

> I ... dare say that, being traditionally ukrainophile, progressive Russian public opinion must energetically, without any ambiguities or indulgences, enter into an *ideological* struggle with 'ukrainism' as a tendency to weaken and partly even abolish that great acquisition of our history, all-Russian culture.[83]

How Lenin appraised this highly civilized ukrainophobia is well known.

What a nationally and morally ill-bred, backward person one must be to repeat something similar today, only expressed in different terms! And there are a great many 'cultured' people like this whose credo is: 'I love Ukraine, but hate the nationalists.' The slightest clarification will show that by 'nationalists' they mean any Ukrainian who has preserved the least trace of his nationality. ('Why do they cling to that "language" of theirs?')

But there is also a ukrainophobia of an openly cannibalistic nature. During the incident of the Shevchenko evening in the Gor'ky Machine Tool Factory, mentioned earlier, the head of the factory committee Glazyrin interrupted the poetry reading by shouting: 'Translate that into human language, we don't understand Banderist language!'[84]

And was it not a mark of special confidence in the sincerity and correctness of Glazyrin's political line that he was sent to the VI World Congress of Trade Unions in Warsaw as a member of the Ukrainian delegation? What fine people represent Ukraine in international organizations! When in 1963 the Young Writers' and Artists' Club decided to honour the memory of Ivan Franko and organized a torchlight procession to his monument you could hear Russian interjections from the crowd along Kyiv's main street: 'Look! Banderists! What a lot of them!' Everybody heard this and knows this, just as everybody knows about the lecturer from the Medical Institute, Assistant Professor (!) Tel'nova, who desecrated the Shevchenko monument, an incredible act, unheard of in any civilized country. Naturally, Tel'nova not only went unpunished, but on the contrary, everything was done to neutralize the consequences of the unforeseen initiative of chance witnesses and to hush up the affair. This, after all, is understandable. As the events of 22 May 1964 and 27 April 1965 have shown, quite a different type of person is being rounded up at the Shevchenko monument ...

Similar examples could be multiplied. And how many times has anyone in Kyiv who has dared to speak Ukrainian in the street, on the tram or elsewhere, not sensed a glance of mockery, contempt or hatred, or heard muffled or loud abuse directed at him. Here is an ordinary Russian conversation in a cinema near a poster announcing the film *Son* (Dream):[85]

> 'You should see how the Banderists come in gangs to this movie ... '
> 'And do you know who Banderists are?'
> 'Of course I do. I don't need any telling. I'd finish those reptiles off like this (*an expressive gesture*) ... all of them.'

And here is one mother telling another: 'My son hasn't gone to school because of this Ukrainian language. He hates the Ukrainian teacher so much. He calls her "a Banderist".' (*Satisfied laughter of the two mothers*.)

And here a schoolboy in his second year declares: 'Oh, how I hate that Ukrainian language.' He has no convictions as yet, but this much he knows already. And he asks:

'Mummy, was Bohdan Khmel'nyts'ky brave?'
'How can I put it ...'
'Was he a Russian?'
'A Ukrainian.'
'Ukrainian?!' (*The disappointed child pulls a wry face.*)[86]

The child goes to a 'Ukrainian' school,[87] in the capital of Ukraine '... And this child is far from being an exception: in his school the majority are of that way of thinking ... Can you imagine how hellish it must be to work in such a school as a teacher of Ukrainian! How difficult, how practically impossible, to communicate the spirit of Ukrainian literature. And how ridiculous, feeble and boring this literature must appear even to the teacher himself, emasculated as it is, trimmed and put before such an audience in textbooks of cast-iron orthodoxy.

How does all this arise? Have those people who occupy themselves particularly with the sources of 'Ukrainian nationalism' ever put themselves this question?

Similar examples could be quoted by the hundred. Whenever you happen to mention this subject, 'responsible comrades' answer with a disgusted snort: You have certainly found a subject! Marketplace gossip!

Dear 'responsible comrades', your disdainful and impatient snorts prove only how profoundly incapable you are of adopting a Leninist approach to the matter. Lenin taught us that any policy manifested itself *visibly* in the *everyday life* of millions. Not everyone reads newspapers and not everyone believes them. But everyday life is real for everyone and influences everyone. The facts quoted and others like them are the visible everyday consequences of a policy of tacit (conscious or unconscious) conniving at Russian Great-Power chauvinism. Influenced by similar facts, Lenin spoke about the 'Great Russian riff-raff' and about the necessity of fighting Russian chauvinism to the death.[88] Meanwhile you say that these are bagatelles, nonsense and hostile inventions, that everything is all right, and that perfect internationalism reigns everywhere, if only one could finally eradicate Ukrainian, Georgian, Latvian and other 'nationalisms' ...

Until recently the existence of antisemitism in the USSR has been denied in the same way. Heavens, what a mortal sin and tactlessness, what political illiteracy it was to mention antisemitism! Khrushchev was foaming at the mouth trying to prove that such questions were paid for in American dollars. He untiringly and very knowledgeably kept enumerating the flames of Jewish scholars, scientists, artists (he liked particularly to stress that even in the government there was a Jew – Minister Dymshits – and that there were even Jews among the Sputnik constructors). As if this was the point, as if this were enough to drive out antisemitism (or ukrainophobia) from conscious politics and to make it disappear everywhere, even in the decisive sphere of practical everyday life.

And now, after so many Ciceroniads, Jeremiads, Lazariads and Nikitiads,[89] it has seemingly been decided to return to Lenin: *Pravda* in its leading article of 5 September 1965 calls, in Lenin's words, for a 'tireless "struggle against antisemitism".'[90] Well, it is good that this has been said at least belatedly, though it could have been said much earlier! They said it and ... filed the newspaper. But when and how will this 'tireless struggle' begin?

6 RUSSIAN CHAUVINISM AS ULTRA-CENTRALISM

Not so long ago, in the last years of Khrushchev, much was said about the national Republics having become outdated in many ways in their present form and it was suggested that their status should be revised with a view to further amalgamation. These non-official talks were linked with the question of a new constitution, and echoes of them could be heard on the pages of periodicals. Meanwhile more was being done in practice. For instance, an economic regionalization was established that did not take into account the boundaries of the national Republics. Inter-Republican Councils of National Economy were introduced, practically making a fiction of the sovereignty of the Central Asian Republics in particular. Further 'redivisions' and 'mergers' were also talked of. All this reflected a general tendency towards an even greater disregard, not only practical, but also formal, of the sovereignty and the economic, geographic, political and legal integral status of the national Republics. At present the offensive against the vestiges of the Republics' economic sovereignty and other rights is masked in the form of the 'struggle' against so-called 'localism' as well as the form of theories about the Republics' boundaries having lost their significance.

Such measures and such tendencies are not new. Lenin gave a warning against them at the beginnings of Soviet rule. The Party condemned them in its resolutions in the 1920s, in the times of the Leninist nationalities policy.

Here is one such decision:

> It must be considered one of the striking manifestations of the heritage of the old order that a considerable number of Soviet officials, both at the central and at the local level, regard the Union of Republics not as a union of equal state entities required to safeguard the free development of the national Republics, but as one move towards the liquidation of these Republics, as a start on the formation of a so-called 'union, one and indivisible' ...
> Condemning such an interpretation as anti-proletarian and reactionary, and proclaiming the absolute necessity of the existence and further development of the national Republics,

> the Congress calls on Party members to be on the alert so that the uniting of the Republics and the merging of Commissariats may not be utilized by Soviet officials of a chauvinist tendency to cover up their attempts to ignore the economic and cultural needs of the national Republics. The merger of Commissariats is a test for the Soviet state machinery: if this experiment were to acquire a GreatPower orientation, the Party would be forced to counteract such a perversion by the most energetic measures, including initiating the reconsideration of the merging of certain Commissariats.'[91]

It was also considered necessary that 'the Republics should be granted sufficiently wide financial, more specifically, budgetary, powers ensuring them the opportunity of displaying their own stateadministrative, cultural and economic initiative'.[92]

At the same XII Congress of the RCP(B) speakers kept stressing how important it was for the correct progress of national construction to guarantee the national Republics wide economic powers and opportunities and to safeguard their economic sovereignty.

Here, for instance, is a fragment from the speech of the Georgian delegate, Mdivani:

> Comrades, we assert that the nationalities question by no means consists, as is unfortunately often held by many comrades in the highest positions of authority, just of the questions of language or of cultural and national autonomy.
>
> For Soviet power, for communists, for Marxists, it is first and foremost economic activity which is everything and determines everything.
>
> We assert that the economic factor should

in no way be excluded from the nationalities problem. On the contrary, this economic factor must be the content of the nationalities question, otherwise we have no particular reason for learning this or that language if it is not to be given a real chance, and there is no point in creating this or that culture if it will not have an economic basis. This is the most important thing which we must understand and firmly establish here.

We can speak about the maximum and minimum of this economic activity that can be apportioned to the various nationalities, but first of all we must firmly establish here that in the economic factor lies the starting point of the solution of the nationalities question. This must be our point of departure, everything else will follow of itself.[93]

Such thoughts were being expressed and such decisions made under the influence of the ideas developed by Lenin in his last speeches, letters and instructions. Lenin considered centralization for its own sake 'no matter what, no matter how' to be very harmful and dangerous to the cause of communist national construction, and to be one of the most real manifestations of Russian Great-Power ideology. Lenin constantly stressed that centralization and unification are not absolutes, that they are necessary not in themselves but only as a form of mutual assistance in the face of capitalist encirclement, and that they are permissible only to the extent that they do not encroach upon the sovereignty and independence of the Republics and their governing bodies (their 'separate People's Commissariats'). Otherwise 'centralization' and 'unification' ought to give way to republican sovereignty. Here are some of Lenin's ideas regarding this:

> ... We cannot be sure in advance that as a result of this work we shall not take a step backward at our next Congress of Soviets, i.e., retain the union of Soviet socialist republics only for military and diplomatic affairs, and in all other respects restore full independence to the individual People's Commissariats.[94]
>
> ... The need to rally against the imperialists of the West, who are defending the capitalist world, is one thing ... It is another thing when we ourselves lapse, even if only in trifles, into imperialist attitudes towards oppressed nationalities, thus undermining all our principled sincerity, all our principled defence of the struggle against imperialism. But the morrow of world history will be a day when the awakening peoples oppressed by imperialism are finally aroused and the decisive long and hard struggle for their liberation begins.
>
> It must be borne in mind that the decentralization of the People's Commissariats and the lack of coordination in their work as far as Moscow and other centres are concerned can be compensated sufficiently by Party authority, if it is exercised with sufficient prudence and impartiality; the harm that can result to our state from a lack of unification between the national apparatuses and the Russian apparatus is infinitely less than that which will be done not only to us[95] but to the whole International from the slightest deviation to 'imperialist attitudes' 'towards our own non-Russian nationalities'.[96]

These clear-cut instructions of Lenin were disregarded and consigned to oblivion, and a course was set for the complete and automatic subordination of the Republics to the centre, and for the abolition of republican sovereignty. Who would dare today to formulate the question as Lenin had formulated it?

Even a cursory observation of the economy of the Soviet Republics shows what damage economic over-centralization inflicts and how it fetters the existing possibilities of development of a number of Republics, Ukraine in particular. It is possible to analyse only a few general data, because in our country detailed economic statistics are for some reason kept behind triple lock and key or not calculated at all. How can you, for example, speak of the sovereignty of Ukraine, when for thirty years, till 1958, the Ukrainian SSR did not compute its national income or national product – that is to say, those indices without which no idea can be formed about the economy of a country. In any case, it is not easy to compute economic indices in a Republic which in fact has no economy of its own. Thus in 1958 the gross production of industrial enterprises under Union jurisdiction in the USSR amounted to 69 per cent of the total industrial output, while capital investment in the enterprises and organizations subordinated to the Councils of Ministers of the individual Republics amounted to only 3 per cent of the total.[97]

These are verily 'sovereign' governments in the Republics without their native language in the administration, without international contacts, and without even the right to intervene in the economy on their own territory!

The situation changed with the introduction of the Councils of National Economy. Thus, in the Ukrainian SSR 97 per cent of industry was subordinated to the government of the Republic. At that time there was much fine talk about broadening the powers of the Union Republics.

The Councils of National Economy did not prove their worth. It would have been logical to subordinate industry directly to the republican Ministries, whilst simultaneously broadening the powers of industrial enterprises and associations. After all, it is easier to see on the spot all the hidden possibilities: resources of raw materials, reserves of manpower, etc. In Moscow one could have created not directing, but consultative and coordinating inter-republican bodies. It was done otherwise, according to the formula: the enterprise is linked to Moscow. Having somewhat broadened the powers of the *managers* of enterprises, there was a return in the key branches of industry to the system of Union and Union-Republican Ministries and Committees. Nobody spoke at this point about the sharp limitation of the powers of the Union Republics.

What ultra-centralism brings to Ukraine it is impossible to calculate in detail because of that same secrecy or neglect regarding statistics. To such 'uncharted areas' belongs the production achieved in Ukraine by enterprises under Union jurisdiction. It is also impossible to determine exactly how much of the revenue which the Republic hands over to the Union budget (and much more is handed over than is left) returns through redistribution and how much is spent on centralized organizations, establishments and enterprises.

Nevertheless, economists have tried to determine the financial position of the Ukrainian SSR in relation to the Union budget. After making dozens of reservations saying 'that the revenue from a number of branches' (for instance, transport) is unknown to them, they offer the following data (we suppose they did not wish to portray a worse situation for Ukraine than really exists; rather the reverse):

> In 1960 the total turnover tax in the territory of the Republic amounted to 5,442 million roubles. From this sum 1,509.4 million roubles, or 27.7 per cent, were allotted to the state budget of the Ukrainian SSR, and 3,932.6 million roubles, or 72.3 per cent, to the Union budget.

But, perhaps, this revenue is refunded to the Republic? The book *National Income of the Ukrainian SSR* gives the following answer. In 1960 Ukraine handed over to the Union budget the said 3,932.6 million roubles plus other deductions, giving a grand total of 5,288.8 million. At the same time, she received 1,113.0 million through redistribution from the budget. This leaves a balance in favour of the Union budget of 4,175.8 million. In 1959 this balance amounted to 3,886.7 million, in 1961 to 3,664.8 million, etc. There are still additional expenditures, since 'Ukraine delivers to other Union Republics products the price of which has been set below cost.'[98]

Ukrainian industry is far from developing at its full potential rate. During the last decades in the Russian SFSR, due to an active stimulation of industrial development, the urban population has increased sharply, reaching 52 per cent at the time of the 1959 census. At the same time 'industrial' Ukraine had 46 per cent urban and 54 per cent rural population, that is to say a much lower urban population than in the developed countries of the West and in a number of European socialist countries. And this happens in a Republic generously endowed by nature with the resources necessary for industrial development!

Ukrainian industry's contribution to the total industrial income of the Union for 1960 amounted to 17 per cent, while in agriculture the corresponding figure was 22.9 per cent. Moreover, the agricultural contribution is growing steadily: in 1961 it rose to 25.5 per cent (that is to say, from Ukraine was derived a quarter of the total agricultural income of the Union).

From the data on the structure of the aggregate social product of the Ukrainian SSR in 1960 it can be seen that the most noticeable deviations from the all-Union structure occur precisely in the sectors of industry (5 per cent *reduction*) and agriculture (25 per cent *increase*). A comparison of the structures of national income in Ukraine and in the Russian SFSR for 1960 gives the following picture: in Russia industry accounted for 56.7 per cent of the total income of the Republic, in Ukraine for 47.9 per cent. The corresponding figures for agriculture are 15.9 per cent for Russia and 26 per cent for Ukraine.

In the same publication the scholars from the Institute of Economics of the Academy of Sciences of the Ukrainian SSR modestly hint at the necessity of 'equalizing the economic development of the great economic regions of the country'. For the time being, however, the economy of Ukraine is kept lagging behind. The long-range plans for 1961–80 envisage a fivefold increase in the aggregate product of the USSR, while the social product of Ukraine is to increase by a factor of 4.5 to 5. From the report of the Chairman of the State Planning Committee of the USSR at the December Session of the Supreme Soviet we learn that in 1966 the gross industrial production of Ukraine will increase less than that of any other Republic: by 5.5 per cent (in the Russian SFSR: by 6.5 per cent; in the Kazakh SSR: by 7.2 per cent, etc.) [99]

Economic over-centralization, which, as has been pointed out above, inhibits the development or causes the one-sided development of a number of regions in the USSR, also brings with it the spiritually ravaging displacement of large masses of the population, often without any economic justification.

For a long time, we have been speaking proudly of the absence of unemployment in our country. But in reality, it exists, only in a concealed form. For instance, all of Western Ukraine is in the grip of such concealed unemployment. After so many resounding words had been said about the flowering of the economy of these provinces, A.N. Kosygin stated at the September Plenum of the Central Committee of the CPSU that 'considerable manpower reserves exist in small towns, especially in the Western regions of Ukraine, Byelorussia, a number of districts in Transcaucasia ...'[100] Let us add that in Western Ukraine they exist not only in towns, but even more so in the villages. What are these 'manpower reserves' but another name for great numbers of semi-unemployed who struggle along on casual earnings or are forced to abandon their ancestral homesteads to seek work, at best in southern Ukraine and the Crimea, at worst thousands of miles away in Siberia and northern Kazakhstan, where industrial development is stimulated (to a large degree at the expense of Ukraine).

A few years ago, the directors of the L'viv Council of National Economy (by virtue of their nationality, innocent of any 'nationalism') were pointing out the great economic effect which metallurgy, machine building, light industry and the food industry would produce in the western territories which are so rich in raw materials and power resources. However, in Western Ukraine to this day only the exploitation of the mineral wealth (sulphur, coal, gas, oil and potassic salts) is being intensified. The industry of that region resembles a monster with elephantine feet, a stunted body and a microcephalic head. Thus, it is understandable why thousands of Ukrainians have to leave their native country (today this emigration is called *orgnabor*).

What awaits the Ukrainians who leave to render fraternal assistance to Siberia is well known. This, after all, is not Czechoslovakia, where national-educational work is conducted among the Ukrainians and it is explained to them that they should teach their children their own language. Neither is it Poland, where besides the provision of Ukrainian primary and secondary schools, Ukrainian language groups are formed in those Polish schools in which the numbers of Ukrainian children do not warrant the setting up of separate forms. This is the Russian Federation, which has solid districts of long-established Ukrainian settlement in the regions of Kursk, Voronezh, Kuban', the Urals, Siberia and the Far East, which has hundreds of thousands, millions of Ukrainians in the Virgin Lands and in the Siberian cities, but *not a single* Ukrainian school, *not a single* newspaper or book published there, *not a single* Ukrainian radio programme or cultural-educational establishment. Denationalization, a forced one by its nature, is in store for those people who have come to render fraternal assistance.

Concealed unemployment which causes emigration is also a characteristic of a number of other industrially underdeveloped regions of Ukraine. Compare, for instance, the present populations of the towns in the province of Chernihiv – Korop, Baturin, Novhorod-Siverskiy – with what they were a hundred years ago. They were higher then ...

Emigration undermines the strength of a nation. The well-known specialist in demography, a Doctor of Economic Sciences, Professor B.Ts. Urlanis writes:

> Direct losses from emigration, frequently representing a considerable proportion of the natural increase in the country's population, are augmented by indirect losses. A decrease in the number of young people affects not only the process of reproduction of the population but the entire economy of the country.[101]

From the report of a Doctor of Economic Sciences, V. Bondarenko, at the General Meeting of the Department of Economics, History, Philosophy and Laws of the Academy of Sciences of the Ukrainian SSR, 22–23 February 1965, data were quoted indicating that the natural increase of Ukrainians is one of the lowest in Europe and that 23–24 per cent of the girls in Ukrainian villages have no opportunity to marry because of the emigration of young men.

As we all know, the most important branches of industry and construction in the USSR are centralized. The Union and UnionRepublican Ministries completely neglect such an important matter, which Lenin had stressed, as the training of permanent cadres of specialists in the territories of the various Republics. (This, after all, would also be economically more profitable.) This is why specialists (not only engineers and technicians but also skilled workers) are being sent en masse from Russia to Ukraine, while Ukrainians are sent to other Republics. The constant inflow of this Russian element in the present conditions in Ukraine is a powerful encouragement to growing russification. To be specific, this element amounts already to over 17 per cent of the population. Meanwhile, Ukrainian workers, engineers and technicians are invariably denationalized outside the Republic due to the circumstances noted above.

Let us take as an example one of the great Ukrainian construction projects, the building of the Kyiv hydroelectric power station. The project is under the authority of the All-Union Committee for the Construction of Power Stations (although many large and small power plants and hydroelectric stations are being built in Ukraine, which could have its own ministry). At the end of 1963, when the number of workers on the project almost reached its maximum, the labour force was made up of 70–75 per cent Ukrainians, 2 per cent Byelorussians, 20 per cent Russians, and smaller numbers of several other nationalities. We have even more exact data about the management division of the main installations, which occupied the key position in the project, There the personnel consisted of 446 Ukrainians (73.6 per cent), 127 Russians (nearly 21 per cent), 16 Byelorussians, 6 Poles, 3 Latvians, 2 Georgians, 2 Bulgarians, 1 Chuvash, 1 Jew, 1 Gypsy and 1 Gagauzi.

The power station seems to have been built mainly by Ukrainians. And yet almost all the top posts on the job (construction chief, chief engineer, most sectional and divisional managers) were occupied by Russians. They also constitute the majority among the rank-and-file engineers and technicians. Among the Russian workers a much higher percentage are highly skilled than among the Ukrainians. Many of the latter were dismissed when the construction was nearing completion. Of the 127 Russian members of the management division of the main installations, only 11 were born in Ukraine, the rest came from Russia.

On the other hand, a great number of Ukrainians have been working on Siberian construction projects, in particular the Bratsk hydroelectric power station, not only as labourers, but also as foremen, superintendents, and sectional and divisional managers.

What advantage does such an 'exchange of cadres' at the Kyiv hydroelectric station offer? When the managers and highly skilled workers do not understand Ukrainian and do not feel any need of it ('What do we need it for? We're here today, somewhere in the Baltic region or in Azerbaijan tomorrow'), or even mock the 'khokhol language' (not to mention the fact that here, as everywhere else in Ukraine, all business and technical documentation is exclusively in Russian), the Ukrainian worker cannot help losing the desire to use his language anywhere outside his own dwelling or hostel room. That privileged 20 per cent group imposes its will in a lordly manner on all the rest, and so day schools, evening schools and semicorrespondence courses are conducted in Russian; kindergartens and nurseries likewise use Russian; all cultural and service establishments are Russified, except for the construction site newspaper, which is printed in a kind of jargon and in a miserably small edition.

Such an anti-Leninist policy is not the work of short-sighted economic managers. It is sanctioned from above and argued theoretically. *Pravda* on 5 September 1965 in its leading article 'The Leninist Friendship of Nations' writes rather transparently (in spite of the phraseological smokescreen): 'The growing scale of communist construction demands a constant exchange of cadres between peoples. Therefore, any display of national separateness in the training and use of workers of various nationalities in the Soviet Republics is inadmissible.'[102] As practice and the above example show, 'workers of various nationalities' means primarily Russians, while the 'display of national separateness' means the employing of national cadres and the national language of one or other of the 'sovereign' Republics. This state of affairs is diametrically opposed to Lenin's directions which were carefully to cultivate national cadres in the Republics and, in particular, to ukrainize gradually the whole government and economic administration of the Ukrainian SSR.

How marvellously we are executing Lenin's will, if in the fortyninth year of Soviet power a Republic with a population of 45 million, with numerous universities, technical schools, and scientific research institutes cannot provide itself with national cadres ...

To sum up this discussion of Russian Great-Power chauvinism in Soviet conditions and in 'communist' forms, let us quote, for the sake of a final clarification, how the Central Committee of the Communist Party of Ukraine (Bolsheviks) characterized it in its theses of 1927:

> The XII Congress of our Party in April 1923 established that the chief obstacle to the solution of the nationalities question and to the removing of national inequality consists in the survivals of Russian chauvinism ...[103]
>
> Russian chauvinism in Ukraine is deeply rooted in the mass of the Russian petty bourgeoisie and the intellectual professional stratum. Here it should be stressed that Russian chauvinism in Ukraine finds powerful support among the masses of the Russian petty bourgeoisie outside Ukraine. It is backed by old, and as yet far from dislodged, prejudices about the 'Ukrainian dialect', about the superiority of Russian culture, etc....
>
> The chauvinistically minded workers of our Soviet administration have thousands of links with the specialists serving the Union administration, and they still attempt everywhere to utilize centralization – which is absolutely necessary for the cause of the proletarian revolution – in their struggle against the economic and cultural development of the national Republics. The Party will struggle

resolutely against Great-Power and bureaucratic chauvinism, under whose influence even Party members sometimes fall. Beside the influence of Russian petty-bourgeois Great-Power forces on workers and even on Party members, we still find to be fairly widely spread, both among the proletariat and among Party members of Russian extraction, a kind of national nihilism, an indifferent and sometimes even contemptuous attitude towards the nationalities question, and the use of phrases about internationalism merely as a smokescreen.

The Party is obliged to struggle resolutely, within its own ranks as well as among the proletarian masses, with the prejudices of the Russian and Russified part of the proletariat, with the perversion of internationalism, with pseudo-internationalism, Russophilism and chauvinism. The Party must fully expose to the proletariat the reactionary nature of Russian chauvinism, laying bare its roots, its historic origin, etc.[104]

It is not hard to see that this analysis still holds good today, that the tasks set out in this document have not been accomplished, that the document itself, like many others of a similar kind, was quietly 'buried' and that the Leninist policy therein outlined was quietly and fraudulently revised and replaced by its opposite.

1   Lenin, 'The Question of Nationalities or "Autonomization"', *CW*, XXXVI, pp. 605–11.
2   Ibid., pp. 607–8.
3   Ibid., p. 609.
4   Lenin, *CW*, XXXIII, p. 372.
5   KPSS v rezolyutsiyakh, I, p. 713.
6   Lenin, *CW*, XXX, p. 295; XXV, p. 91.
7   X *s'yezd RKP(B)*, p. 209.
8   Mayakovsky's lines are from 'Dolg Ukraine' (1926).
9   'Khokhlandia': 'Land of the Khokhols', Khokhol being the derogatory Russian term for Ukrainians.
10 'Hapkenstrasse': 'Hapkas' Street', from Hapka (Agatha), a 'lowclass' Ukrainian Christian name; a derogatory name for a Ukrainian district.
11 X *s'yezd RKP(B)*, pp. 203–4.
12 Ibid., p. 206.
13 *Smena Vekh* ('Change of Landmarks'): a Russian émigré journal, published in 1921–2 in Paris, which propounded the idea that the introduction of the New Economic Policy in Russia suggested that the Soviet state was beginning to move towards a bourgeois order; this initiated the *Smena Vekh* trend amongst the, mainly émigré, Russian intelligentsia at first opposed to the Soviet regime towards cooperation with the Soviet government.
14 Stalin, *Works*, V, Moscow, 1953, pp. 243–4.
15 Ibid., pp. 249–50.
16 Stalin's toast: pronounced on 24 May 1945.
17 V. Firsov, 'Rossiya ot rosinki - do zvezdy', *Pravda*, 9 August 1964, p. 6; published in full in *Oktyabr'*, No. 10, 1964, pp. 3–10.
18 I. S. Isakov, 'Povorot na 16 rumbov', *Nedelya*, No. 4, 17–23 January 1965, p.11.
19 'You are guilty ...': from I. Krylov's fable, 'The Wolf and the Lamb'.
20 'To suppress the maritime undertakings of the Russians.'
21 O. Bodyansky, 'Zamechaniya na proyekt obshchego ustava Imperatorskikh rossiyskikh universitetov', *Chteniya*, 1862, II (April–June), Section 5, p. 218.

22 F. Engels, 'The Foreign Policy of Russian Tsardom', *Times* (n.s,), I, 4, London, April 1890, p. 362.
23 'From Finland's frosty rocks ...': from Pushkin's *Klevetnikam Rossii* (To Russia's Slanderers) (1831).
24 'The Terrible': Ivan IV; 'the Great ones': Peter I, Catherine II; 'the Big Stick': Nicholas I ('Palkin'); 'the Liberator': Alexander II.
25 M.A. Plotnikov, *Yangaal-Maa. Vogul'skaya poema*, Moscow-Leningrad, 1933, pp. 9–11, 39–40.
26 Lenin, *CW*, XX, p. 408.
27 'Treaty of alliance': soyuz of the original can mean either 'alliance' or 'union'.
28 Iskander [Herzen], 'Rossiya i Pol'sha. (Pis'mo vtoroye)', *Kolokol*, No. 34, 15 January 1859, p. 274; A. I. Herzen, *Sobraniye sochineniy*, VII, Moscow, 1956, p. 227.
29 S.M. Solov'yov, *Istoriya Rossii* (29 vols, St Petersburg, 1851–79, and subsequent edns; the latest, 15 vols, Moscow, 1959–61).
30 'Rassuzhdeniye o pol'zakh i nevygodakh priobreteniya Gruzii, Imeretii i Odishi, so vsemi prilezhashchimi narodami', *Chteniya*, 1862, II, Section 5, p. 87.
31 V.N. Karazin, 'Pis'mo k knyazyu Adamu Chartoryskomu', *Russkaya starina*, III, 1871, pp. 703–4, 707. ['Not being able, without pain, to see it, in spite of its riches and the talents which are offered there in abundance, abandoned to chicanery and contempt ...' And about the fate of the Crimea he wrote: '... the Crimea, turned into a desert from the delightful and densely populated country it was under the Tures'.
32 Ye. Markov, *Ocherki Kryma*, St Petersburg, 1872; 2nd edn., 1902.
33 Instruction not in the mother-tongue.
34 *Gosudarstvenny Souet. Stenogr. otchoty. 1911–12 g.*, St Petersburg, 1912, c. 3045.
35 V.I. Lenin, *Sochineniya*, 3rd edn, XVI, Moscow-Leningrad, 1931, p. 689.

36   Lenin, CW, XXV, p. 91.
37   Lenin, CW, XX, p. 413.
38   K. Kautsky, *Aus der Friihzeit des Marxismus. Engels' Briifwechsel mit Kautsky*, Prague, 1935, p. 67.
39   K. Marx and F. Engels, Sochineniya, XV, Moscow, 1935, p. 223 (originally published in *Der Volksstaat*, No. 45, 1875).
40   F. Engels's letter to K. Marx, 24 October 1869, in K. Marx and F. Engels, *Selected Correspondence*, London, 1943, p. 264.
41   Marx and Engels, SC, pp. 279-80.
42   Lenin, CW, XX, pp. 440-42.
43   Ibid., XXI, p. 105.
44   I-r [Herzen], 'Russkiye ofitsery v ryadakh insurgentov', *Kolokol*, No. 161, 15 April 1863, p. 1326.
45   Editorial, 'Russkim ofitseram v Pol'she', *Kolokol*, No. 147, 15 October 1862, p. 1214.
46   Lenin, *Sochinenjya*, 3rd edn, XVI, p. 692.
47   Lenin's interpolation.
48   Lenin, CW, XXII, p. 342 (cf. also note 3, p. 67 above).
49   Cf. A. M. Sakharov, 'O znachenii otechestvennoy istorii', *Istoriya SSSR*, No. 4, July-August 1965, pp. 3-12.
50   the oppressed peoples'
51   Ibid., p. 10.
52   V.V. Timoshenko, 'Byla li Belorussiya pri tsarizme koloniyey v ekonomiches kom smysle?' *Istoriya sssr*, No. 1, January-February 1965, pp. 40, 50.
53   G.N. Teplov, 'O neporyadkakh, kotoryye proiskhodyat nyne ot zloupotrebleniya prav i obyknoveniy, gramotami podtverzhdennykh Malorossii', in P. Kulish, *Zapiski o ruzhnoy Rusi*, II, St Petersburg, 1857, pp. 175-96.
54   R. Palme Dutt, *The Crisis of Britain and the British Empire*, London, 1957, pp. 456-7.
55   Solov'yov, *Istoriya*, VIII, pp. 349-50.
56   'Ocherki Livonii', *Chteniya*, 1865, II (April-June), Section 5, p. 99.
57   N. Machiavelli, *The Prince*, Harmondsworth, 1961, p. 36.
58   Montesquieu quoted in 'O neobkhodimosti vvesti vo vsekh guberniyakh i oblastyakh lmperii russkiye organicheskiye zakony', *Chteniya*, 1865, III (July September), Section 5, p. 181.
59   Solov'yov, *Istoriya*, XI, p. 206.
60   *Gosudarstvennqya Duma, iii, sess. 3, ch I*, St Petersburg, 1910, c. 3022.
61   Machiavelli, op. cit., p. 38
62   I.S. Aksakov, 'Pol'skiy vopros i zapadno-russkoye delo', in his *Polnoye sobraniye sochineniy*, III, Moscow, 1886, p. 382.
63   Solov'yov, *Istoriya*, XIII, p. 347.
64   Ibid., XII, p. 200.
65   What is meant are those very same 'diverse customs' and 'depraved opinions' about national 'variance', that is, diversity.
66   A.V. Khrapovitsky, 'Pamyatnyye zapiski', *Chteniya*, 1862, II (April-June), Section 2, p. 4.
67   Solov'yov, *Istoriya*, XIII, p. 430.
68   Lenin, *Sochineniya*, 3rd edn, XVI, pp. 687-8.
69   Let today's ukrainophobes and eradicators of 'nationalism' ponder these words!
70   Lenin, CW, XXI, p. 104.
71   X *s'yezd RKP(B)*, pp. 190-94.
72   It is not for nothing that the school syllabus in the history of the USSR does not begin with our times, those of the USSR, but is in fact the history of the Russian Empire, which becomes the history of the USSR, whereas, logically, the history of the USSR should be really the history of the USSR itself, with the previous periods comprising the histories of the various nations which make up the USSR today being treated separately.
73   Khrapovitsky, 'Pamyatnyye zapiski', *Chteniya*, 1862, II, Section 2, p. 28.
74   I.S. Aksakov, 'Pol'skiy vopros i zapadno-russkoye delo', in his *Polnoye sobranrye sochineniy*, III, Moscow, 1886, p. 7.
75   Ibid., pp. 15, 16, 132-3.
76   Cf. M.N. Katkov, *Sobraniye peredovykh statey 'Moskovskikh vedomostey'. 1865 god*, Moscow, 1897, p. 805.

77 You see what an internationalist! Even greater than some of our present ones.
78 Ibid., 1864 god, p. 87.
79 The Brotherhood of Cyril and Methodius: a secret Ukrainian society (1845–7) with a programme advocating the federation of all the Slav nations, each to have self-government, religious and political equality, and in which serfdom was to be abolished. Its members were some of the outstanding Ukrainian intellectuals (T. Shevchenko, M. Kostomarov, P. Kulish and others), who were arrested when its existence was denounced to the authorities in 1847.
80 *Taras Shevchenko, Dokumenty i materialy*, Kyiv, 1963, p. 55.
81 Lenin, *CW*, XXX, p. 295.
82 Cherkassians: a synonym for 'Ukrainian Cossacks' in Russian documents of the late seventeenth century, it acquired derogatory connotation in the following century. (Cherkassy: at that period an important centre in Ukraine.)
83 P. Struve, 'Obshcherusskaya kul'tura i ukrainskiy partikulyarizm. Otvet Ukraintsu', *Russkaya mysl'*, Moscow, XXXIII, No. 1, January 1912, p. 86.
84 Banderist: here a synonym for 'Ukrainian' expressing hostility.
85 *Son* (Dream): based on Shevchenko's poem of this name (1844).
86 Both above conversations are in Russian.
87 A 'Ukrainian' school: here, a school subordinated to the Ukrainian SSR Ministry of Education, though with Russian as its medium of instruction.
88 Lenin, *CW*, XXXVI, p. 606, and XXXIII, p. 372.
89 Lazariads, Nikitiads: an allusion to the speeches of Lazar Kaganovich and Nikita Khrushchev respectively.
90 'Leninskaya druzhba narodov', *Pravda*, 5 September 1965, p. 1.
91 KPSS v rezolyutsryakh, I, p. 715.
92 Ibid., p. 716.
93 XII s'yezd RKP(B), pp. 497–8.
94 i.e., governments of the Republics.
95 But, as you see, also to us.
96 Lenin, *CW*, XXXVI, pp. 610–11.
97 These and the following data are taken from the book *Natsional'nyy dokhod Ukrains'koyi rsr v period rozhomutoho budivnytstva komunizmu*, ed. O.O. Nesterenko, Kyiv, 1963.
98 Ibid., table 33, p. 151; pp. 150, 152–3.
99 N. Baybakov, 'O gosudarstvennom plane razvitiya narodnogo khozyaystva SSSR na 1966 god', *Pravda*, 8 December 1965, p. 3.
100 A.N. Kosygin, 'Ob uluchshenii upravleniya promyshlennost'yu ... ', *Pravda*, 28 September 1965, p. 2.
101 B.Ts. Urlanis (ed.), *Naseleniy, mira; spravochnik*, Moscow, 1965, p. 78.
102 'Leninskaya druzhba narodov', *Pravda*, 5 September 1965, p. 1.
103 Thus we stress: as long as Russian chauvinism exists, there is no national equality.
104 V. Koryak (ed.), *Shlyakhy rozvytku ukrains'koyi proletars'koyi literatury*, Kharkiv, 1928, pp. 346–7.

8
Actual equality and formal equality

'In capitalist society, statistics were entirely a matter for "government servants", or for narrow specialists; we must carry statistics to the people and make them popular so that the working people themselves may gradually learn to understand and see ...'[1]

Before we begin this discussion let us define the subject more accurately. We must distinguish on principle between the equality of *nations* and the equality of the nationals, or *members*, of nations. Thus, for instance, in the Russian Empire a Russian serf or peasant, a Russian shopkeeper or landlord were in almost the same position as a Ukrainian serf, peasant, shopkeeper or landlord respectively. Taken separately, they were equal to each other in their rights (or in their lack of rights); a serf was a serf and a landlord was a landlord. Their *nations*, however, Russia and Ukraine, were not in a similar position and by no means enjoyed equal rights.

Here we shall speak about the equality of nations, and not of their members. Thus we reject as meaningless and hypocritical such questions as: 'Who prevents you from speaking Ukrainian?' Even the more intelligent tsarist ministers saw that a genuinely antiUkrainian policy lay not in forbidding the use of the Ukrainian language (which is impossible), but in causing the people to abandon it by themselves. 'And where do you see discrimination (or an encroachment)? Look how many Ukrainians (Jews, etc.) there are in government posts, in science, in the arts.' As if there had been few before the revolution! If we were to understand the matter in such a Philistine way, and not politically and socially, we should have to admit that the formula of tsarist Russia as a 'prison of nations'[2] is unjust: after all, they did not hang or imprison people for their nationality, they did not shorten your career for such a reason, whoever you were, as long as you served the tsar and the Fatherland faithfully. Tsarist ministers liked to stress 'internationalism' and the 'friendship of peoples': 'Under the wings of the twin-headed eagle there is enough room for all the nationalities inhabiting our Fatherland to live in tranquillity.'[3] And, as we have already seen, they especially pushed fraternity ('Why divide brothers?') ...

This sort of Philistine approach may perhaps be appropriate in a communal kitchen, but not in politics. Let us forget it and go on to discuss a serious political approach, most consistently and clearly formulated and advanced by Lenin.

Not by chance did Lenin frequently underline the necessity of real safeguards for the rights of the Republics and of real guarantees of national equality. The point is that he distinguished in principle between the formal equality of nations with which a bourgeois democrat or a pseudo-socialist is satisfied, and the real, actual equality of nations for which every communist should strive.

> The Communist International's national policy in the sphere of relations within the state cannot be restricted to the bare, formal, purely declaratory and actually non-committal recognition of the equality of nations[4] to which the bourgeois democrats confine themselves – both those who frankly admit being such, and those who assume the name of socialists (such as the socialists of the Second International).[5]

In the actual conditions of the USSR, in which history has endowed the Russian nation with a much stronger position than that of the others, no matter how many declarations of equality are made, this Russian preponderance will lead to inequality in real life. The only solution is to compensate for this actual inequality by measures which, taken formally and superficially, might appear to be an 'infringement' of the interests of the Russian nation. Because of the extreme importance of this question, we shall *quote for a second time* those words of Lenin's which we have already cited in connection with Lenin's analysis of Russian Great-Power chauvinism under Soviet conditions.

> That is why internationalism on the part of oppressors or 'great' nations, as they are called (though they are great only in their violence, only great as bullies), must consist not only in the observance of the formal equality of nations but even in an inequality of the oppressor nation, the great nation, that must make up for the inequality which obtains in actual practice. Anybody who does not understand this has not grasped the real proletarian attitude to the national question, he is still essentially petty bourgeois in his point of view and is, therefore, sure to descend to the bourgeois point of view.[6]

This profound precept of Lenin's has in actual fact remained unadopted and unassimilated. Skrypnyk complained about this state of affairs in his time, and there is all the more reason to speak about it today.

Everywhere the very opposite is being done. For instance, in Ukrainian universities lectures are given in Russian, on the grounds that many Russians study there (as if it were not their elementary civic duty to learn Ukrainian in such a case). Russian culture, Russian books and the Russian press are actually predominant in Ukraine. Out of every one hundred roubles' sales of book-trading organizations in Ukraine, barely five roubles come from Ukrainian books and ninety-five, if not more, from Russian books or foreign books in Russian translation. The percentage of Ukrainian books in the libraries of the Ukrainian SSR lies somewhere between one and five. At the XII Congress of the RCP(B), speakers discussed the importance of a just distribution of the press among the nations of the USSR:

> In Russia there are now approximately between 1,800,000 and two million copies of Russian newspapers. The remaining half of the population of Soviet Russia has roughly 70,000 copies. What is this? This is a display of actual inequality ... And for this reason, we must map out appropriate practical work here ... and not only formulate the question correctly in theory.[7]

Much was done after this, and there was a vast expansion in the circulation of the nationalities' press. But have we reached actual equality today? Are we even aware of such a task? Let us see. Enormous numbers of books, newspapers and magazines are being imported into Ukraine from the Russian SFSR (their quantity considerably exceeds the quantity of Ukrainian books, newspapers and magazines published in Ukraine), and this alone creates inequality, an unfavourable ratio for the Ukrainian printed word. Any bookstall can give us an idea of this: several dozen or hundreds of Russian books, newspapers and magazines and only somewhere in the corner two or three in Ukrainian and one in Yiddish. But besides that, almost every republican or provincial newspaper in Ukraine is published also in a similar Russian edition. Every republican or provincial publishing house brings out a considerable percentage of Russian books. Scientific and technical publishing houses in general bring out incomparably more in Russian than in Ukrainian. The republican radio not only devotes much time to the relaying of broadcasts from Moscow (and as everyone knows, Moscow radio does not broadcast in the national languages of the Republics), but also broadcasts many Russian programmes of its own. To justify this situation the argument is sometimes put forward that seven million Russians live on the territory of Ukraine. But this is not the point. First of all, the percentage of Russian publications in Ukraine is many times greater than the percentage of the Russian population; secondly, what does the equal number of Ukrainians in the Russian SFSR and in Kazakhstan have? At last, one Ukrainian newspaper, one Ukrainian school? Even the supply of the press from Ukraine is highly unsatisfactory.

In short, not only does the colossal power of central, all-Union production work for Russian culture and for the Russian printed word, but even the relatively miserable capacities of the republics are further split and, in some cases, give to Russian culture a considerable proportion, and in others the lion's share.

Let us quote some publishing data arrived at by calculations based on the official publications of the Book Chamber and other official statistics.

In 1950, 43,100 titles were published in the USSR in editions totalling 821 million copies. Of this number, 30,482 titles, totalling 640,391,000 copies, were printed in Russian, which amounts to 71 per cent of the titles and 78 per cent of copies printed. This leaves merely 29 per cent of the titles and 22 per cent of copies printed for the languages of the non-Russian nations, which compose nearly 50 per cent of the population! Are these not eloquent figures? But the most shameful thing is that in the following years this disproportion grew, so that in 1963 75 per cent of the titles (58,158 out of 77,600) and 81.4 per cent of the copies printed (1,026,934,000 out of 1,262,000,000) were in Russian, leaving merely 25 per cent of the titles and 18.6 per cent of the copies printed to the languages of all the non-Russian peoples![8] Is this not a fearful proof of the actual *inequality* of cultures?[9]

We have already said that book production in Ukraine constitutes a miserable part of the all-Union production (during the period 1950–63 it composed about one-tenth of the titles and numbers of copies, whilst the population of the Ukrainian SSR accounts for almost 20 per cent of the Union population, which means that Ukraine should contribute about one-fifth of the total book production, or twice as much as at present). Furthermore, this production hardly increased from 1958 and fell in 1963 to below the previous year's level, representing both in titles and copies printed less than one-tenth of the all-Union production (9.8 per cent of the titles and 9.2 per cent of copies printed).[10]

But even in this disproportionately small output of the Ukrainian publishing houses *more than half* the titles and one-third of the copies printed were in the Russian language. In the period from 1960 to 1963 printing in Ukrainian comprised *less than half* the titles and slightly more than two-thirds of the copies printed (and even that mainly because of *belles-lettres* and political mass editions). The percentage of Ukrainian books in the number of copies printed by Ukrainian publishers fell from 80 per cent in 1950 to 66 per cent in 1963. Thus, book production in the Ukrainian language in the USSR amounted in 1963 to 3,325 titles, or 4.3 per cent, while the Ukrainian population amounts to 17 per cent.[11] This output amounts to *only one quarter* of the fair proportion.

In the field of periodicals, the picture is even gloomier. Out of a total number of 1,408 with an annual circulation of 181,282,000 in 1950, only 274 (19 per cent) with an annual circulation of 19,277,000 (10.6 per cent) were printed in the national languages of the Republics. In 1963 their share of titles fell to 17.9 per cent (699 out of 3,912), although the circulation increased somewhat to 13 per cent. Ukraine's share in the all-Union output of titles fell from 11.4 per cent

(160 out of 1,408) in 1950 to 6.5 per cent (254 out of 3,912) in 1963. But even among these editions published in Ukraine only about half (130 in 1963) are printed in Ukrainian. This means that in 1963 Ukrainian-language periodical editions in the USSR constituted only 3.3 per cent of the titles (130 out of 3,912) and about 4 per cent of the circulation. With a Ukrainian population of more than 17 per cent in the USSR, this means an actual falling behind by a factor of 4 to 5.[12] The share of Ukrainian-language newspapers amounted in 1963 to 11 per cent of the titles (765 out of 6,791[13]) and just under 7 per cent of the circulation (1,243 million copies out of 18,311 million). It should be noted that while in 1950 a total of 1,192 newspapers was published in Ukraine, among them 972, or the majority, in the Ukrainian language, in 1963 the total number of newspapers rose to 2,366 of which only 765, or less than one-third, were printed in Ukrainian![14]

If we take the total number of scientific and scholarly books published in the USSR in the period from 1956 to 1960, Ukrainian language books amount to 3.9 per cent of the titles (compared to 77.0 per cent in Russian) and 2.9 per cent of the copies printed (compared to 85.5 per cent in Russian).

It is noteworthy that this disproportion has grown especially rapidly during the last few years. Compared to its 1956 level printing in the Russian language rose to 173.1 per cent in 1960, while printing in the languages of the non-Russian peoples of the USSR rose to only 117.4 per cent.

In 1956 the Academy of Sciences of the Ukrainian SSR published 9 journals in the Ukrainian language and 3 in Russian; in 1958-9, 14 in Ukrainian and 3 in Russian; in 1962-3, 13 in Ukrainian and 4 in Russian; in 1966 it is planned to have 13 in Ukrainian, 9 in Russian, and one bilingual; i.e., all new publications are launched in Russian. In 1962 the Academy of Sciences of the Ukrainian SSR published 183 book titles in Ukrainian (60 per cent) and 122 in Russian (40 per cent). In 1963 the corresponding figures were already 166 (49 per cent) and 169 (51 per cent). In 1964 Russian books amounted to 53.5 per cent (156 titles), while Ukrainian books dropped to 46.5 per cent (136 titles). Furthermore, the Ukrainian language editions are predominantly studies in literature, linguistics and political literature. Apart from works on the humanities the number of Ukrainian books is incomparably smaller, whilst in the physical, mathematical and applied sciences there are almost none, and that is the case from year to year. Likewise Ukrainian books comprise a paltry percentage from the Technical Publishing House of the Ukrainian SSR and from the specialized publishing houses. In 1963, according to the data of the Book Chamber of the Ukrainian SSR, the Technical Publishing House published 121 book titles in Russian and only 32 in Ukrainian (of the university textbooks included in this number, 11 were in Russian and 1 in Ukrainian, and this at a time when there is a total lack of Ukrainian university textbooks!); the State Publishing House of Building and Architectural Literature, 122 in Russian and 11 in Ukrainian; the Medical Publishing House, 188 in Russian and 54 in Ukrainian, with most of the Ukrainian items being simple pamphlet-type publications.

Four scientific and technical publishing houses in Ukraine (*Tekhnika, Zdorov'ya* [Health], the Agricultural Publishing House, and the Publishing House of Building Literature) plan to publish in 1966: 657 titles in Ukrainian and 709 in Russian. The total volume of the Ukrainian books is to be 5,334 printers' sheets, the volume of the Russian books, 9,314 sheets, the number of copies printed, 7,652,000 and 7,557,100 respectively. However, again the Ukrainian literature is predominantly on an elementary level, whilst nearly all the serious scientific and technical literature is in Russian. The publishing house *Tekhnika*, for instance, plans in its section on the physical and mathematical sciences 28 titles in Russian and only 1 in Ukrainian! Out of 102 republican interdepartmental collections of scholarly and scientific papers 86 are to be in Russian and only 16 in Ukrainian. It is noteworthy that even the Publishing House of Agricultural

Literature publishes almost all such interdepartmental collections in Russian.

Very telling material can be found in *Book Orders from the Composite Subject Plan of the Publishing Houses of Ukraine for 1965*[15] in the sections on engineering, chemistry, building, architecture and municipal economy. Here from 517 titles only 82 are in Ukrainian, that is to say 16 per cent of the total fewer than in Russian. Further breaking down of the figures shows that in technical literature, out of a total of 303 titles, 259 are in Russian and 44 in Ukrainian; in chemical literature, out of a total of 40 titles, 35 are in Russian and 5 in Ukrainian; in building and architectural literature, out of a total of 174 titles, 140 are in Russian and 34 in Ukrainian.

This plan does not indicate the sizes of books involved or the number of copies printed, which would have given an even more exact picture of the situation, since the Ukrainian items are chiefly editions of secondary importance or simple pamphlets. However, the prices are given, thereby permitting us to estimate the sizes and – what is no less important – the outlay on Ukrainian books. The total value of all the titles is 258.10 roubles. From this sum, the cost of the Russian books amount to 227.96 roubles, and that of the Ukrainian books, to 30.14 roubles, that is to say a mere 11.7 per cent of the total value, or seven times less than the value (and therefore the volume) of the Russian titles.

The situation in the provincial publishing houses is even more discouraging. The publishing house Donbas, for instance, plans, for 1966, 58 titles in Russian and 41 in Ukrainian; 366 printers' sheets in Russian and 125 in Ukrainian; 1,410,000 copies in Russian and 271,000 in Ukrainian.

In many respects Ukraine is in a much worse situation even than other non-Russian Republics, as can be seen from this table:

Republics	Plan for 1960 in printers' sheets	Therefrom in the language of the Republic	%
Lithuanian	1,174	1,057	90
Estonian	300	228	76
Tadzhik	126	88	70
Latvian	600	300	50
Turkmen	64	32	50
Azerbaidjan	386	124	32
Armenian	186	55	30
Kirghiz	333	67	20
Ukrainian	510	102	20

The relative production of technical information published in the languages of the Republics[16]

As we see, Ukraine shared last place where the publication of technical information in the native language was concerned. On a per capita basis the inferiority of her position is even more striking. In the Lithuanian SSR, where the population is about ten times smaller, over ten times more of such material was being published, that is to say over a hundred times more per capita!

And now, some data about textbooks. In 1960, 229.9 million copies were published for primary and secondary schools. Out of this number 65.9 million copies, or 28.7 per cent, were published in the languages of the non-Russian peoples, while these peoples comprise now 45.4 per cent of the total population of the USSR. In the same year 27.9 million copies were published for establishments of higher education. Out of this number only 2.1 million copies, or 7.5 per cent, were published in the languages of the non-Russian peoples. As we see, the disproportion is colossal.

Further food for thought is supplied by statistics on the ratios of nationalities among graduate specialists working in the national economy and university students in the USSR and the Ukrainian SSR. On 1 December 1960 there were in the Union 3,545,234 specialists with a higher education working in the national economy. Among them there were 517,729 Ukrainians, or 14.6 per cent, a proportion which is about 18 per cent lower than the ratio of Ukrainians in the population of the USSR taken overall. There were 2,070,333 Russians, or 58.4 per cent, which is 7 per cent higher than the corresponding ratio of Russians in the population of the USSR. Calculating per 10,000 of a given nationality's population, Ukrainians contributed 139 specialists with a higher education, Russians 182.[17]

As we see, the disparity is considerable, and obviously to the Ukrainians' disadvantage. This disparity has been produced not only by a heritage of inequality, but has also been *developing* in our times due to the fact that the preparation of Ukrainian cadres has been proceeding at a slower pace (since 1941 Ukrainian cadres have grown by a factor of 4, Russian cadres by a factor of 4.2).[18] In 1939, the number of persons with a higher education per 1,000 of the population in Ukraine was higher (7) than the all-Union average (6), while in 1959 it was lower (17) than the all-Union average (18) or the figure for the Russian SFSR (19).[19]

In the establishments of higher education of the Ukrainian SSR at the beginning of the academic year 1960–61 there were 417,748 students. Out of this total, 260,945 or 62.5 per cent were Ukrainians, which is much lower than the percentage of the Ukrainian population in the Ukrainian SSR (76.8 per cent). There were 125,464 Russian students, or 30 per cent of the total, which is a much higher percentage than that of the Russian population in the Ukrainian SSR (16.9 per cent). At the same time out of a total of 1,496,097 students in institutions of higher learning in the Russian SFSR, there were 67,793 or 4.5 per cent Ukrainians, which almost equals the percentage of the Ukrainian population on the territory of the Russian SFSR (3 to 4 per cent).[20] Thus a fine, necessary and indispensable thing – the exchange of cadres and of students

– is in this particular case organized incorrectly, to the disadvantage of the Ukrainian population, which remains by far the loser. In the Ukrainian SSR there are 8 students per 1,000 of the Ukrainian population and 18 per 1,000 of the Russian population – more than double the Ukrainian figure.

To some extent this can be explained by the fact that many Russians from the Russian SFSR study in Ukrainian universities, but only to some extent. For in the USSR as a whole the ratio is not favourable to Ukrainians. Thus, there were, in 1959–60, 482 students per 100,000 of the Ukrainian population and 732 per 100,000 of the Russian population. According to official data from 1927–8 the percentage of Russian students in the USSR was 56.1, that is to say 3.2 per cent higher than the proportion of the Russian population of the USSR. The corresponding figures for 1957–8 are 62.3 per cent and 7.4 per cent. In 1927–8 there were 14.6 per cent Ukrainian students; in 1957–8, in spite of the incorporation of the Western Ukrainian provinces, 13.8 per cent; in 1960–61, 13.4 per cent (although 17.8 per cent of the population of the USSR is Ukrainian).[21] The statistical handbook *The National Economy of the* USSR *in 1963* sets the percentage of Russian students in 1962–3 at 61 (1,803,800 out of a total of 2,943,700) and that of Ukrainian students at 14.5 (426,900 out of the same number).[22] [23]

Higher Education in the USSR calculates that for Ukraine in 1960 there were 46,657 scientists and scholars, wherefrom 22,523, or fewer than half of them, were Ukrainians. The number of postgraduate students in the USSR was 36,754, of which 4,081 or 11 per cent were Ukrainians.[24] This is much less than the proportion of Ukrainians in the USSR (17.8 per cent), and postgraduate students are the source of future scientific cadres.

According to data published in the journal *Problems of Philosophy* in 1957,[25] there were at that time 222,893 scientists and scholars in the USSR, amongst them 21,762 Ukrainians. This is one of the lowest ratios in the Union: 6 per 10,000 of

Ukrainian population. The number of Russian scientists and scholars was 144,285, that is to say, 12 to 13 per 10,000.

Naturally, it is not a question of Ukrainians being consciously barred from science and scholarship – we do not know of such instances. And the task is not to decree that the percentage of Ukrainian scholars be raised as a matter of urgency – this also is impossible. But we have to look into and analyse this serious situation, and the Ukrainian nation's striking failure to keep up in the key sphere of brainpower. What is the explanation of it?

Naturally, all this is no accident but springs from certain serious social and political causes. To disclose and eliminate these is the task of sociologists and of those who elaborate and direct the nationalities policy. Unfortunately, they are still silent, and no social research is being done in this sphere, at least not publicly. There are only isolated, single-handed amateur attempts.

Thus, a citizen of Odessa S. Karavans'ky established, on the basis of authentic documents of those entering the Odessa Polytechnic Institute in 1964–5, that only 43 per cent were Ukrainians, a number which does not correspond at all to the percentage of Ukrainians engaged in material production in the Ukrainian SSR or even in Odessa itself. After analysing the appropriate documentary material, S. Karavans'ky established that as a result of discriminatory admission procedures which make it more difficult for Ukrainian school-leavers to enter establishments of higher education (in such establishments in Ukraine, competitive entrance examinations include Russian language and literature, while Ukrainian language and literature appear only in examinations for the humanities, thus giving the advantage to Russians or to the school-leavers from Russian schools; entrance examinations in special subjects are also mostly conducted in Russian), the percentage of admissions in relation to applications is higher for Russians than for Ukrainians. Thus, in 1964 out of 1,126 Ukrainian applicants the Odessa Polytechnic Institute admitted 453, or 40 per cent; out of 1,042 Russian applicants it admitted 477, or 46 per cent.

On the basis of these and similar data, S. Karavans'ky requested the Public Prosecutor of the Ukrainian SSR to bring a criminal action against the Minister of Higher and Special Secondary Education of the Ukrainian SSR, Yu.M. Dadenkov, according to Article 66 of the Penal Code of the Ukrainian SSR, which provides for punishment for the infringement of the principle of national and racial equality. The consequences were not long in coming: S. Karavans'ky was himself arrested.

Actual inequality can be observed in many spheres of culture.

Teaching in establishments of higher and secondary technical education is conducted in Russian, unlike that in other Union Republics (the Baltic and Transcaucasian ones), despite numerous promises and deceitful gestures in the direction of ukrainization.

There are probably more Russian than Ukrainian theatres in Ukraine. Cinema, this 'most popular of the arts', is almost entirely Russian. Even films from Ukrainian studios are shown dubbed in Russian and not the other way round, as it was done in the 1920s. And so, wherever in social and cultural life we choose to take a cross-section, we see actual inequality appearing behind the trappings of formal equality. We see Ukrainian culture and language being pushed into a secondary, 'losing' position (after all, what equality of languages is there to speak of, when the Ukrainian language is virtually banished from the inner spheres of life, and those individuals who use it in the cities only become the butt of derision?).

In the succeeding chapters we shall discuss this in greater detail. Here we will add only that sometimes matters are taken to the point when even formal equality is infringed in certain ways. The Constitution of the USSR prohibits the preaching of national exclusiveness. Meanwhile it appears in the form of propaganda (which we discussed earlier) preaching the special, exclusive role of the great Russian people in the historic and in the present destiny of all other peoples of the USSR and of the former Russian Empire. (By the way, the real author of this 'theory' is none other than the 'Liberator', Emperor Alexander II, who liked to speak about his Empire as a family of peoples and especially about 'the special role of the Russian people in this family'.) We see equally open and intensive 'theorizing' about the special place of the Russian language as the 'language of international communication' and the 'second native language' of all the peoples of the USSR. Is this not an outrage upon Lenin's principle 'not [to] permit ... the overriding of any one nationality by another, either in any particular region or in any branch of public affairs'?[26]

It could be answered: but all these formulas with which we are dissatisfied reflect the real state of affairs. This is precisely the point! If they were simply wilful theorizing by the authorities nobody would pay any attention to them. But unfortunately they reflect (I would even say they reflect but weakly and faintly) the real state of affairs, and the tragic part is that this real state of affairs is remote from a just solution of the nationalities question, remote from what Lenin thought and outlined. And it is the duty of a communist, and all the more so if he is a leading communist, to consider how this real state of affairs might be changed in the direction of communism and not of Great-Power mania and 'the overriding of one nationality by another'.

In his time Lenin also encountered a 'real state of affairs'. After a lengthy absence from practical leadership due to illness, he encountered in December 1922 the 'real state of affairs' in the nationalities question and experienced a profound shock. In this turmoil, gravely ill, he dictated to his secretary the notes 'The Question of Nationalities ...', where he gave his own appraisal of the 'real state of affairs' and proposed changing it radically.

> It is quite natural that in such circumstances the 'freedom to secede from the union' by which we justify ourselves[27] will be a mere scrap of paper, unable to defend the non-Russians from the onslaught of that really Russian man, the Great Russian chauvinist, in substance a rascal and a tyrant, such as 'the typical Russian bureaucrat' is. There is no doubt that the infinitesimal percentage of Soviet and Sovietized workers will drown in that tide of chauvinistic Great Russian riff-raff like a fly in milk. It is said in defence of this measure[28] that the People's Commissariats directly concerned with national psychology and national education were set up as separate bodies.[29] But there the question arises: can these People's Commissariats be made quite independent? and secondly: were we careful enough to take measures to provide the non-Russians with a real safeguard against the truly Russian bully? I do not think we took such measures although we could and should have done so.[30]

And Lenin proposed changing the 'real state of affairs', since communists need the reality of justice, not the reality of brutishness.

---

1   Lenin, CW, XXVII, p. 261.
2   Ibid., XX, p. 219.
3   Cf. V.N. Kokovtsov's speech of 28 October 1911 in *Gosudarstvennaya duma. Stenograficheskiye otchoty. Tretiy sozyv. Sessiya 5, chast' I*, St Petersburg, 1911, cols 701, 758.
4   Is this not the kind of recognition with which we often content ourselves?
5   Lenin, CW, XX.XI, p. 147.
6   Lenin, CW, XXXVI, p. 608.
7   XII s'yezd RKP(B), p. 596.
8   *Narodnoye khozyaystvo SSSR v 1963 godu. Statisticheskiy yezhegodnik*, Moscow, 1965, pp. 612–13.
9   See Tables 1, 2 and 3 for the production of books and periodicals in Ukrainian for 1964–68.
10 Ibid., pp. 614–15.
11 Ibid., pp. 612–15.
12 bid., pp. 616–17.
13 See Table 4 for newspaper publishing statistics.
14 Ibid., pp. 618–19.

15 *Zamovlennya na literaturu po zvedenomu tematychnomu planu vydavnytstv Ukrainy na 1965 rik*, Kyiv, 1964.
16 *Voprosy organizatsii i metodiki nauchno-tekhnicheskoy informatsii i propagandy. Po materialam Seminara rabotnikov nauchno-tekhnicheskoy informatsii i propagandy, Moskva, 16 maya – 11 iyunya 1960 g.*, Moscow, 1960, p. 7.
17 *Vyssheye obrazovaniye v SSSR. Statisticheskiy sbornik*, Moscow, 1961, p. 67; *Narodnoye khozyaystvo SSSR v 1962 godu. Statisticheskiy yezhegodnik*, Moscow, 1963, p. 11.
18 *Vyssheye obrazovaniye v SSSR ...*, p. 69.
19 Ibid., pp. 30–31.
20 Ibid., pp. 128–31.
21 Ibid., p. 84; *Narodnoye khozyaystvo ... 1958 ...*, p. 841.
22 *Narodnoye khozyaystvo ... 1963 ...*, p. 579.
23 See Table 5 for student numbers in 1963–9.
24 *Vyssheye obrazovaniye v SSSR ...*, pp. 215, 223.
25 I.P. Tsameryan, 'Velikaya Oktyabr'skaya sotsialisticheskaya revolyutsiya i korennoye izmeneniye natsional'nykh otnosheniy v SSSR', *Voprosy filosofii*, No. 5, September-October 1957, p. 57.
26 Lenin, *CW*, XX, p. 224.
27 And to speak of which, if I may add, is tantamount to a political crime.
28 The subordination of the republican People's Commissariats to the centre, Moscow.
29 Incidentally, what has happened to these People's Commissariats?
30 Lenin, *CW*, XXXVI, p. 606.

9
Ukrainization and its repression

Lenin and other leading Party members repeatedly explained that while formal equality of nations had been won in the October Revolution, the safeguarding of the actual equality of nations required an extended period of purposeful national construction.

For a start, the X Congress of the RCP(B) in 1921 outlined the following immediate tasks to help the 'non-Great-Russian peoples':

1 to develop and consolidate their Soviet statehood in forms appropriate to the conditions of the national way of life of these peoples;
2 to develop and consolidate, in the native language, justice, administration, economic and governmental bodies composed of local people who know the way of life and psychology of the local population;
3 to develop a press, schools, the theatre, clubs, and culturaleducational establishments generally, in the native language;
4 to establish and develop a wide network of courses and schools, general as well as professional and technical, in the native language.[1]

Today we must state that not one of these four objectives (and these were only the immediate tasks) has ever been accomplished and now we are further than ever from accomplishing them.

1. Statehood is and has everywhere been built in an identical shape, to a standard pattern (contrary to what Lenin clearly said on this subject).
2. Administration, economic and governmental bodies functioning in the native language do not exist (in any case not in Ukraine).
3. The press, schools and the theatre are only partly Ukrainian, and even then, only formally. Furthermore, the Ukrainian share has lately been shrinking in favour of the Russian, especially in the schools. As regards clubs, cinemas, cultural-educational establishments and groups, lectures, etc., they hardly exist at all in the native language, but are conducted in Russian, especially in the cities.
4. Professional and technical education in the native language does not exist at all; it is conducted entirely in Russian.

It is not for us to say why these direct and clear resolutions have not been carried out and whether someone will be made to answer for this state of affairs. We simply state a fact.

But we must add that in Ukraine there was an honest and energetic attempt to carry out these resolutions, known by the name of ukrainization. People are ashamed to mention it now, and the word itself has been rendered odious. In reality, however, it was an attempt at a truly internationalist policy, outlined in Lenin's direct instructions and in the resolutions of the Congresses of the RCP(B) and the CP(B)U, supported and sanctioned by the Comintern. (Even earlier, for instance, when the UCP, Ukrainian Communist Party, was disbanded, the Comintern guaranteed the national development of Ukraine.)

Earlier we have already spoken briefly about ukrainization. Here it should only be added that this was a broad political concept which included:

1. The education of the working people of Ukraine in a revolutionary class spirit and towards an understanding of their national identity, their socialist national statehood, and their responsibility for the socialist national construction of Ukraine; the development of national consciousness and dignity and of an international attitude towards other peoples.
2. The education of the Russian population of Ukraine in a spirit of respect and considerate friendliness towards Ukrainian national life – national state construction, culture, language, traditions, etc. The encouragement of the Russian population to acquaint themselves with Ukrainian culture, history and language, and to take part in the creation of new national cultural values. The safeguarding of the national-cultural needs of Russians as a national minority in Ukraine.
3. The ukrainization of Party, Soviet and social activity in general.
4. The ukrainization of economic, scientific and technical activities.
5. The ukrainization of the large cities and industrial centres.
6. The acquisition of Ukrainian language and culture by the proletariat, the education of the proletariat in this language and culture, and the transformation of the proletariat into their active creator.
7. The ukrainization of the school system, and of technical, professional and higher education.
8. The ukrainization of cultural-educational institutions.
9. The active fostering of the maximum development of all branches of Ukrainian culture.
10. The safeguarding of an essential minimum of economic self-government and initiative for Ukraine.
11. The same in the political and diplomatic sphere.

12 The safeguarding of the national-cultural interests of several million Ukrainians living in other Republics, especially in the Russian Federation, with a view to incorporating adjacent territories with a predominantly Ukrainian population (in the Don, Kursk and other regions).

As we see, the question was formulated thoroughly and earnestly. This is just how it should have been formulated by the communists of the Ukrainian Soviet Republic, whose people had lived for 450 years under colonial oppression (Polish for over 150 years, Russian for about 300) and, having finally won their freedom, had to repossess themselves of their elementary rights.

If that political course had been followed, Ukraine – in addition to its present achievements in economics, science and, to some degree, the arts – would undoubtedly have achieved immeasurably more and would have gladdened all the nations of the Union and all the peoples of the socialist commonwealth by the originality of her socialist profile, the brilliance and dynamism of her national culture, and the all-round blossoming of her national life. She would have been not a propagandistic but a genuine, tangible, compelling example for all the young national states of Asia and Africa, and for all national liberation movements, of the fruitfulness of the Leninist approach to the national problem.

But this daring, constructive Leninist policy had its fierce enemies, both open and secret. The delegates to the XII Congress of the RCP(B) spoke about them in their speeches, which have already been quoted in part. In the first years after Lenin's death these enemies still tolerated the Leninist course, but then began to chafe against it more and more.

In 1927 the Central Committee of the CP(B)U addressed itself to the Executive Committee of the Comintern concerning the Russian nationalist deviation in the Party, which was obstructing ukrainization. The essence of this deviation was characterized in these terms:

This deviation consists in the ignoring and underrating of the importance of the nationalities question in Ukraine, often while hiding behind internationalist phrases. In particular it consists:

1 in the belittling of the importance of Ukraine as a part of the USSR and in an endeavour to interpret the creation of the USSR as a *de facto* liquidation of the national Republics;
2 in the preaching of a neutral Party attitude towards the development of Ukrainian culture and in its treatment as a backward and 'rustic' kind, as opposed to the Russian 'proletarian' culture;
3 in attempts to preserve at all costs the predominance of the Russian language in the internal state, civic and cultural life of Ukraine;
4 in a formalistic attitude towards the implementation of ukrainization, often paid lip-service only;
5 in the uncritical echoing of chauvinist Great-Power views about the so-called artificiality of ukrainization, about the 'Galician' language which is incomprehensible to the people, etc., and in the fostering of these views within the Party;
6 in the tendency not to implement the policy of ukrainization in the cities and among the proletariat and to limit it only to the villages;
7 in an over-tendentious exaggeration of individual distortions which have occurred in the implementation of ukrainization, and in the attempts to represent them as a complete policy of encroachment upon the rights of national minorities (Russians, Jews).[2]

In 1927 the Russian nationalist deviation was condemned. And in 1932 Stalin sharply reversed this and sent his trusty men (who had quite likely belonged to the same Russian nationalist deviation group) to Ukraine ostensibly to exterminate

'Ukrainian bourgeois nationalism', but in reality to eradicate all manifestations of Ukrainian nationality, and national life, and to liquidate national cultural, educational, scientific and Party cadres. Up to that time people had boasted of the successes in ukrainization, but then it became fashionable and a mark of valour to vaunt the annihilation of Ukrainian culture, to report the numbers of liquidated teachers, writers, etc. At the XII Congress of the CP(B)U (1934), reports such as this were heard:

> At the beginning of the November Plenum alone, 248 counterrevolutionaries, nationalists, spies and class enemies, among them 48 enemies with Party cards, were exposed and sacked from the scientific research establishments of the VUAN[3] and of the People's Commissariat of Education, but these figures are out of date [!]. Now much more of this element has been sacked from these establishments. Thus, quite recently, in December, we had to close down completely [!] the Bahaliy Research Institute of the History of Culture, because this institute, again like a number of other learned bodies, such as the Ukrainian Soviet Encyclopedia or the Shevchenko Institute, with Pylypenko as its boss, was revealed to be a refuge for counter-revolution.[4]

Almost the whole of Ukrainian culture was revealed to be 'counter-revolutionary' (as in certain later times, 'unrewarding'). This is why scholars and writers of world renown, hundreds of talented people in all spheres of culture, and thousands upon thousands of the rank-and-file intelligentsia were destroyed. 'At the same go' several million peasants were wiped out in the artificial famine of 1933. Let us bear in mind: this was long before notorious 1937.[5]

> Meanwhile Stalin kept sending telegrams to Ukraine: 'At last you are getting down to business in a Bolshevik fashion ... Rumours have reached us that the measures taken you consider to be sufficient. If this is so, such a policy could ruin the whole undertaking. In point of fact, the measures taken by you are only the first step ...'

It is hard to calculate and to imagine to what extent the strength of the Ukrainian nation was undermined and how catastrophically its cultural potential was lowered. And after this, how many pogroms followed ...

Today the policy, the constructive methods and the spirit of ukrainization are safely forgotten and deeply buried. And the Party documents from the period of ukrainization can be used to frighten and shock today's orthodox Party official.

As a psychological experiment we might offer to today's administrators of the nationalities policy a quotation from the resolutions of the XI Congress of the CP(B)U of 1930:

> The ukrainization of schools, establishments of higher education, secondary and higher technical schools guarantees the training of the new generation in the spirit of the Party's policy on the nationalities question and guarantees the preparation of Ukrainian cadres for industry and agriculture.

Further on, mention is made of the growing proportion of Ukrainian printing: in May 1930 the share of Ukrainian-language newspapers was 89 per cent, that of Ukrainian books 80 per cent. There was reported to be:

> ... a rapid growth of ukrainization among the proletariat and especially among its basic cadres. Moreover, there is an undoubted systematic

growth in the Ukrainian contingent among the proletariat, with the process of ukrainization by far outstripping the growth of new cadres. In the past three years there has been a great increase in the numbers of people speaking, reading and writing Ukrainian. Among the core of the proletariat, the metalworkers, the number of those who read Ukrainian has risen from 18 per cent to 42 per cent, and the number of those who can write has risen from 14 per cent to 35 per cent ... The working class of Ukraine is taking the development of Ukrainian Soviet culture directly into its own hands, is becoming its actual builder and creator. In connection with this enormous change in the working class with regard to the realization of the Leninist nationalities policy, special duties fall to the trade unions. The unions in the chief industrial districts are not only still failing to lead the working class in its aspiration to master the Ukrainian cultural process but are clearly falling behind in this movement. Notwithstanding the considerable upward trend of ukrainization in club work and all mass cultural work, all this undeniably lags behind the requests and demands of the working masses. The trade unions of Ukraine must assume control over the provision of cultural opportunities in the Ukrainian language for the masses, over the movement of the working masses toward culturalnational construction, they must speed up and develop this movement still further, and must themselves lead the masses.

These three elements – schools, the press and the ukrainization of the proletariat – are the firm basis which genuinely guarantees within the shortest term an unprecedented development of Ukrainian culture, national in form and proletarian in content.[6]

Where is all this today? Where is the 'ukrainization of establishments of higher education, secondary and higher technical schools'? Where are those percentages, unbelievable by today's standards, of Ukrainian book production? Where is the ukrainization of the proletariat and the engineering and technical cadres? The ukrainizing role of the trade unions is too ridiculous to speak of. Not to mention that if someone took an interest today in 'the numbers of people speaking ... Ukrainian' and in 'the number of those who can read and write' he would be branded as a zoological nationalist, spat upon or suspected of being a spy ... After all, even such elementary, sociologically indispensable statistics as those on the number and trends of Ukrainian and Russian schools and the pupils in them, books, press circulation, etc., are classified as a state secret which must remain unpublished. Not without good reason, of course ...

What can be added to all this? Perhaps that even without the 'firm basis' envisaged by the XI Congress of the CP(B)U we contrive to boast of the 'unprecedented development of Ukrainian culture'.

---

1 Lenin, CW, XXVII, p. 261.
2 Ibid., XX, p. 219.
3 Cf. V.N. Kokovtsov's speech of 28 October 1911 in Gosudarstvennaya duma. Stenograficheskiye otchoty. Tretiy sozyv. Sessiya 5, chast' I, St Petersburg, 1911, cols 701, 758.
4 Is this not the kind of recognition with which we often content ourselves?
5 Lenin, CW, XX.XI, p. 147.
6 Lenin, CW, XXXVI, p. 608.

10
Russification and its mechanics

Ukrainization was replaced by russification. To be more exact: the fly-wheel of russification, which had been braked somewhat, was again accelerated with renewed force.

Even in conditions of formal equality, actual inequality cannot fail to lead to russification and to become its powerful driving force. At the same time the mechanics of this inequality are the 'material' mechanics of russification.

The second, psychological and ideological, force of russification is Russian Great-Power chauvinism. It constitutes the 'psychological' mechanics of russification, its 'soul'.

This question has already been in part discussed earlier on. But some things have to be added and defined.

The term 'russification' is very unpopular today with the authorities; it is considered politically too dissonant to be used in public; and, of course, only a hardened 'nationalist' can speak today about the russification of the Ukrainian population.

In Lenin's time this sad privilege fell to outstanding communists. The Party qualified as russification, and so condemned, phenomena which today are described as successes of the policy of the friendship of nations (for instance, when Ukrainians abandon their nationality and language, when parents send their children to Russian, instead of to Ukrainian, schools and the like).

Extremely sharp pronouncements of Lenin against Great Russian chauvinism and various 'attempts at russification' have been quoted above. Here I will quote several speeches of other Party workers, in the spirit and under the direct influence of Lenin's declarations. Here is a fragment from a speech by delegate Yakovlev at the XII Congress of the RCP(B):

> I think that Comrade Rakovsky[1] is mistaken when he reduces the question to the unification or separation of Commissariats.[2] I should like to ask Comrade Rakovsky: In your independent Commissariats ... isn't there the same spirit of Great Russian chauvinism and nationalism, isn't there the same bureaucratic staff made up of Russians and Russified Jews, who are the most consistent champions of Great Russian national oppression? In reality they pursue the same line of national oppression. What language is used in the district administrations? In what language are documents drawn up in the villages, in what language do your Commissariats speak? The problem lies not only in the setting up of relations between the Commissariats of the independent Republics and the unified Commissariats, but in the work of the Commissariats themselves. I know what enormous resistance – unconscious on the part of the Party, which is overwhelmingly Great Russian, conscious on the part of the bureaucratic staff of the Commissariats – is offered to such a simple thing as the duty to change over to a given language in clerical work and correspondence, the duty to learn the given language of the Republic involved. But I think the Congress must affirm that it is better to force ten Great Russian chauvinists and nationalists to learn the language of the country in which

they live than to force one peasant to torture his native language in a government office.³

Later they began to do the opposite: force ten peasants 'to torture their native language' just not to disturb one 'Great Russian chauvinist and nationalist'.

State and economic machinery is one of the most important and effective levers of russification. Where 'the authorities' speak Russian, soon everybody will also be forced to start speaking Russian. The language of the 'commanding elements' gradually triumphs over the whole environment. History shows many analogous examples concerning other nations. And here the national question again develops into a social one: we see that in city life the Ukrainian language is in a certain sense opposed as the language of the 'lower' strata of the population (caretakers, maids, unskilled labourers, newly hired workers [from the village], rank and file workers, especially in the suburbs) to the Russian language as the language of the 'higher', 'more educated' strata of society ('captains of industry', clerks and the intelligentsia). And it is not possible to 'brush aside' this social rift. The language barrier aggravates and exacerbates social divisions.

And here is another rather weighty little fly-wheel in the mechanism of russification. I quote from the speech of M. Skrypnyk at the XII Congress of the RCP(B):

> To this day the Army has remained an instrument for russifying the Ukrainian and the whole non-Russian population. Admittedly, the PUR⁴ has begun latterly to subscribe to newspapers in the national languages. But the whole task still lies before us, and we must ... adopt measures to prevent our Army from being an instrument of russification ...⁵

This thought was developed by another speaker at the Congress:

> Comrade Skrypnyk has just touched upon this question. That is the question of the Army. But he did not dot the i's and cross the t's. For we should not forget that the Red Army is objectively not only an instrument for educating the peasantry in a proletarian spirit, it is an instrument of russification. We transfer tens of thousands of Ukrainian peasants to Tula and force them to grasp everything in Russian. Is this correct or not? Obviously not. Why should the proletariat need this, nobody can say. Here is the inertia of the Great Russian command structure; our top command is overwhelmingly Russian. For even these Ukrainian peasants, transferred to Tula and placed under Russian command, could still receive political and cultural education in the Ukrainian language. Then there is the second question, the question of creating army cadres who will speak the national language.[6]

To this we might perhaps add that this particular question was of special interest not only to one or two delegates, but invariably attracted the attention of the entire Party. As we all know, in those days decisions were made to create national military formations, while the VIII Congress of the RCP(B) had envisaged the prospect of territorial military formations. The X Congress of the CP(B)U in 1927 occupied itself especially with the question of ukrainizing the cultural-political work in the Red Army.

Naturally, all these genuinely internationalist Leninist measures shared the fate of other 'nationalist contrivances'. Now we cannot even speak of minimal safeguards for the most elementary national interests of Ukrainian youth (as well as for the youth of other Republics) in the Army. Millions of young Ukrainian men come home after several years' service nationally disorientated and linguistically demoralized and become in their turn a force exerting an influence for russification on other young people and on the population at large. Not to mention that a considerable number of them do not return to Ukraine at all. It is not hard to imagine how tremendously damaging all this is for national development. Let us consider if the government of any socialist country, Poland, Czechoslovakia, Hungary, Romania, etc., would have agreed to anything like it.

Our cities have been, and unfortunately remain, gigantic russifying mincing machines. Formerly this was true chiefly about large cities, today it is already also true about small towns. According to the words of a Russian writer, the cities were the abode of 'ten generations of Russifiers', the source and symbol of national oppression and of the colonial offensive of tsarism. We speak, of course, not about the city as such, as a focus of culture and of the revolutionary movement, but about the city of bureaucrats and of the petty bourgeoisie, the city of colonizers, of 'Tashkentians', as Shchedrin called them. Its poison of russification, its nationally oppressive action has been well demonstrated in Ukrainian classical literature, as well as in literature of other oppressed nations. Lenin's Party saw clearly that the russifying element of the city with its 'ten generations' of colonizers represented a great danger for socialist nation-building. That is why the Party planned a series of measures designed to de-russify the great cities and to restore their national character. Even Stalin, who as we know was not a great sympathizer with 'nationals', declared under the pressure of Lenin's ideas at the X Congress of the RCP(B):

> It is obvious that although Russian elements still predominate in the Ukrainian towns, in the course of time these towns will inevitably be

ukrainized. About forty years ago, Riga had the appearance of a German city; but since towns grow at the expense of the countryside, and since the countryside is the guardian of nationality, Riga is now a purely Latvian city. About fifty years ago all Hungarian towns had a German character; now they have become magyarized. The same can be said of those cities in Ukraine which have a Russian character and which will be ukrainized because cities grow at the expense of the villages. The countryside is the guardian of the Ukrainian language, which will enter all the Ukrainian cities as the dominant element.[7]

Since the time these words were uttered, forty-five years have passed, a sufficiently long period for the Latvian and Hungarian cities mentioned to have regained their own national character. Why then have Ukrainian cities become even more, incomparably more Russified in this time, in spite of the enormous and constant inflow of Ukrainian population from the villages?

Why have Ukrainian cities with their immense growth become immensely grandiose laboratories of russification? Why do millions of Ukrainian boys and girls, after coming to work in the city, 'forget' their language after a year or two and begin to speak some broken impoverished jargon?

The Party's plans for de-russifying the cities of Ukraine were not carried out, and development was channelled in the opposite direction. Thus, the spirit of Russian cultural and linguistic superiority and of contempt for Ukrainian culture and language has become even more firmly entrenched in the cities. Naturally, no decrees will change this situation. However, the situation itself results from a certain policy and can gradually be changed by changing this policy.

For some time past, russification has been creeping inexorably into the smaller towns and centres of rural districts, accompanied by proliferation of officials and bureaucrats in them who, naturally, speak or attempt to speak Russian and thus force their subordinates to do likewise, accompanied by the decay of folk customs, folk art and cultural entertainment, which are being replaced by the faceless hack-work of professional cultural 'landing parties', accompanied by the ascendancy of Russian newspapers, books, broadcasting and films ... As a result, there is developing a language which is neither Ukrainian nor Russian but a hideous mixture, popularly called *surzhyk*; there is developing not a culture but a vulgar ersatz, a shoddy mass product with pretensions to 'the city style'; there is developing the historically well-known type of the 'khokhol turncoat with a low cultural outlook' (from the declaration of the All-Ukrainian Federation of Proletarian Writers and Artists). A tragedy is unfolding in vaudeville style.

The main action is taking place in the areas of culture and language.

1   CULTURE

In keeping with firm instructions from Lenin, the XII Congress of the RCP(B) in 1923 determined clearly and precisely:

> Talks about the advantages of Russian culture
> and propositions about the inevitable victory
> of the higher Russian culture over the cultures
> of more backward peoples (Ukrainian, Azer-
> baijani, Uzbek, Kirghiz, etc.) are nothing
> but an attempt to confirm the domination
> of the Great Russian nationality.[8]

Today talks and notions of such a character are not only legalized and dominant in everyday civic and Party life, but diverse 'allegorical' variants of these 'talks' have also long become stereotyped in official theory and propaganda, even finding their way into textbooks for Ukrainian children as the alpha and omega of truth. What is more, today everything is apparently being done so that this 'superiority of Russian culture' should not only be the subject of talks and wishes but the *manifest reality* in Ukraine. At the same time a rare, pitiful helplessness, unheard of anywhere else in the world, is displayed every time it is necessary to support Ukrainian publishing, Ukrainian culture, the Ukrainian word ... (Not to mention the implementation of the Party's old and well-known resolutions about its responsibility for the development of Ukrainian national culture, about the necessity of leading it within the shortest possible term to the highest level on the world scale and of making it the culture of the proletariat: today one can only mention actions running counter to those resolutions.) Up to the present, Lunacharsky's expectations have not been fulfilled: 'We can expect the most gratifying results from the independent cultural development of the Ukrainian people, for there is no doubt that it is one of the most gifted branches of the Slavic tree.'[9]

Our literature is far from being on the level on which it should and could be. The Ukrainian theatre is in obvious decadence. The Ukrainian cinema is virtually non-existent in spite of the existence of studios in Kyiv, Odessa and Yalta: the films they make are either unbelievably bad or (with very few exceptions of late[10]) not Ukrainian at all.

Anything that is interesting and promising does not usually receive support but attacks, obstacles and suppression .

What is the matter? Could it be that the Ukrainian land has lost its energies and talents? Hardly, if you observe to what an extent it is bestowing these upon Russian culture and learning. Surely there are other serious causes, both subjective and objective.

The strength, abundance, health and future of any national culture depends directly upon its position in society, upon how much this society is interested in it and devoted to it, and upon how large a mass of this society is permeated by it and contributing to it, actively or passively, linking their conscious spiritual existence with it.

In discussing these matters, Lunacharsky in his time approvingly quoted a German Marxist:

> What does the strength and greatness of
> a nation depend upon? asks Braun, and answers:
> It depends upon whether its national body
> is healthy and whether its whole people are
> permeated by their culture. Capitalist exploita-
> tion destroys the strength of a nation, robbing
> the class which constitutes the majority of its
> health and blocking its access to national culture.
> None the less the nationalists are quite often
> defenders of capitalism. Hereby they prove
> at once that they do not fight for their nation
> but represent the interests of its ruling classes.
> Only socialism will permit the whole nation
> to be definitively permeated by its national
> culture. But the struggle for this culture against
> the bourgeoisie must and does proceed only
> in an international framework. The con-
> clusion is clear: the socialist international is
> the best champion of genuine nationalism.[11]

The Ukrainian communists of the 1920s understood the direct and constantly active interrelation between the strength of a national culture and its hold over society. This is why they placed such emphasis upon the task of drawing all strata of the working population of Ukraine (and especially its proletariat) as speedily and closely as possible into the process of assimilating and creating Ukrainian national culture. This, they felt, was essential for the development and spiritual health both of Ukrainian culture and of the Ukrainian proletariat (the relevant documents have been quoted earlier). Finally, they intended to raise Ukrainian culture from its secondary position in Ukraine and to overcome the inequality existing between Russian and Ukrainian culture, and the actual domination and preponderance of that Russian culture in Ukraine.

> In the short time that the Soviets have been in power in Ukraine ... much has already been done to aid the development of Ukrainian culture, schools and publishing,' read the resolution of the All-Ukrainian Central Executive Committee and the Council of People's Commissars. 'But this work could not eliminate the inequality of cultures that had been created by centuries of oppression.'
> This is why it must be the immediate task of the Government to eliminate this inequality in the sphere of national culture.[12]

However, the repression of ukrainization put an end to the measures that were to make national Ukrainian socialist culture the culture of the whole of Ukrainian society.

As a result, Ukrainian culture has not only failed to take its rightful leading place in Ukraine but has not even caught up with Russian culture, remaining a poor second and a makeweight. Furthermore, the overwhelming majority of the working class, of the scientific, technical, engineering and other intelligentsia and of the town population in general remains beyond the sphere of Ukrainian culture, which Russian culture has for them supplanted completely. This is borne out by the actual position of Ukrainian books, press, school, theatre, etc., as well as by the degree of interest shown by society in them and Ukrainian culture in general. We all know what a miserable percentage of those above-mentioned strata, which are culturally the most active, is interested in Ukrainian culture and links the satisfaction of its spiritual needs with it. And this cannot pass without leaving its mark. This keeps draining the life-blood from Ukrainian culture, undermining it materially and spiritually. Narrowing the circle of readers, listeners and users is not simply a mechanical but a complex psychological process, which on the one hand diminishes the spiritual current flowing out to the reader and on the other weakens the force of the spiritual feedback for the creators, not to mention the fact that this drains and silts up catastrophically the sources providing national culture with new creative forces, which are drawn more and more into the already incomparably more powerful stream of Russian culture.

But even this is not the end of the story. Most poignant of all, the forces that even in these arduous conditions selflessly remain faithful to their national culture are not helped as they should be, but on the contrary are very often hindered, in fact in a systematic and purposeful way, by all sorts of obstacles and bedevilments.

Brilliant talents and innovatory experiments are not so much discouraged but they simply run against an impenetrable line of bayonets in the official press. Let us only remember the witches' sabbath which not so long ago broke loose around the work of certain young poets who were falsely accused of formalism. Let us remember that a good many poets, from Lina Kostenko to V. Stus, from Hryhoriy Kyrychenko to Mykola Kholodny, from Ihor Kalynets' to Borys Mamaysur, have for years been unable to publish their collections. Let us remember that the Czechs in their anthology of young Ukrainian poets print those who for years have been denied recognition in our country, and that even older, honoured writers get into trouble as soon as they say more than one is accustomed to hear from them (thus Yu. Smolych could not publish his memoirs about the literary life of the 1920s).

The situation is no better in the Artists' Union, where the work of a number of original young artists is being suppressed and discredited in various ways.

The situation in the Ukrainian theatre is almost catastrophic. The Kyiv Franko Academic Dramatic Theatre is in a state of permanent helplessness and drabness, while at the same time the talented young producer Les' Tanyuk was refused work until in the end he was forced to leave Ukraine. Now he works in Moscow, he is gladly invited to the best Moscow theatres, where the shows he directs enjoy tremendous popularity.[13]

However, much effort was expended by young theatrical enthusiasts trying to set up, at least on a voluntary basis, an experimental theatre, say, in Darnitsa, a huge workers' suburb of Kyiv, which has not a single theatre for a population of tens, if not hundreds, of thousands (apropos, Kyiv has only five professional theatres, while Warsaw and Prague, equalling it in size, have several dozen each). However much effort was expended by theatrical youth to achieve this, they were permitted nothing.

The young Ukrainian composer Leonid Hrabovs'ky, whom Shostakovich places among the most original young talents, has for years been unable to get his innovatory works performed in Ukraine. Meanwhile they are gladly being performed by the leading ensembles of Moscow and Leningrad. Even his wonderful 'Four Ukrainian Songs', which won an award at an all-Union competition and were recorded in Leningrad, have not been performed in Ukraine to this day.[14] The young Ukrainian composers Syl'vestrov, V. Huba and others are in a similar position. And how many difficulties are being placed in the way of the talented choirmaster and producer Ihor Polyukh's organizing of a national instrumental-vocal variety ensemble, how much it is being forced into the rustic mould!

Sergey Paradzhanov's film *Shadows of Forgotten Ancestors* marked a turning point for the Kyiv Dovzhenko Film Studio, which in latter years had enjoyed the worst possible reputation, and regained for it international recognition. And here Paradzhanov is being hindered in the production of his second film and is virtually being turned out of the studio. Yuriy Il'chenko's and Ivan Drach's film, *The Well for the Thirsty*, has in fact been banned, a film '...which according to the judgement of most professionals is an outstanding achievement of national cinematographic art and could, together with *Shadows of Forgotten Ancestors*, take the Ukrainian cinema to the international level'. A threat also hangs over other brilliant films being prepared in the studio, and one hears that it is necessary to 'tighten up' somewhat ... All kinds of obstacles are placed in the way of the young Ukrainian film directors Leonid Osyka and Rollan Serhiyenko who are expected to produce official drabness and 'happy endings'. Similar examples are countless.

One's impression is that whenever new forces appear in some sphere of Ukrainian culture and some sort of revitalization begins, the bureaucrats pass sleepless nights and lose all tranquillity until this revitalization is repressed and everything returns to the 'normal' primitive level. A few years ago, the young editorial staff of the Kharkiv magazine *Prapor* [The Banner] began to produce a fresh, interesting journal. A brutal 'dressing-down' was not long in coming, and now *Prapor* has become a commonplace, boring little provincial magazine. Two years ago, an energetic man of good taste, R. Bratun', became the editor of the L'viv magazine, *Zhovten'* [October]. The formerly languid magazine soon became one of the best in Ukraine, gained great popularity, and showed a steep increase of its circulation figures. And before long the L'viv Provincial Committee of the Party decided to remove Bratun' from his post as chief editor and condemned his activity. Admittedly, for the time being the Writers' Union has succeeded in vindicating R. Bratun', but in such a situation it is difficult to expect from an editor great daring and initiative. In any case, everything is done to eliminate these qualities. And how often the editors of *Ranok* [Morning] and *Dnipro* [Dnieper] 'catch it', just because these journals are somewhat fresher than others. It is precisely for the best material that the appropriate departments 'give them the treatment'.

Thus our culture is being deliberately held back and impoverished by various measures, by administrative brutality, by a caveman cultural level, by a 'deeply echeloned' bureaucratic 'vigilance', and by an automatically repressive reflex. Our culture is being compromised in the eyes of a mass public which has no opportunity of seeing this concealed 'restricting and suppressing' mechanism in action and therefore attributes all the backwardness of our culture to its own allegedly innate traits.

A second factor limiting the appeal of Ukrainian culture for millions of readers is the artificial impoverishment of its past attainments and traditions, a pillaging in fact of Ukrainian cultural history.

What other nation in the world can boast a situation in which its greatest scholars in the field of the social sciences, M. Hrushevs'ky and M. Drahomanov – men of worldwide reputation – are unknown in their own country? The name of the former is still banned, while an undeclared ban has only recently been lifted from the latter. However, the works of both remain equally unpublished and inaccessible.

A paradoxical fact: prior to the revolution, in the conditions of the openly anti-Ukrainian policy of tsardom, epoch-making records of Ukrainian historic and social thought were published, such as *Istoriya rusov* and the Cossack chronicles of S. Velychko, H. Hrabyanka, and Samovydets'. They have not been republished now for several decades, although they have long since become bibliographical rarities, which even scholars cannot lay their hands on.

The same holds true of the monumental collections of Ukrainian folklore by P. Chubyns'ky, M. Drahomanov, V. Antonovych, Ya. Holovats'ky and others, published in the nineteenth century.

As for the works of Ukrainian historians – V. Antonovych, M. Maksymovych, O. Bodyans'ky, M. Kostomarov, O. Lazarevs'ky, or those of P. Kulish, a more than remarkable figure – where are they? (Meanwhile in Russia S.M. Solov'yov and V.O. Klyuchevsky have been republished in full.)

And where are the works of Ukrainian social scientists, sociologists and economists – M. Pavlyk, S. Podolyns'ky, F. Vovk, O. Terlets'ky, N. Ziber (whom Marx esteemed so highly) and many others? of F. Vovk, M. Tugan-Baranovs'ky, V. Levyts'ky, L. Yurkevych and others, whose activity and works need historical and objective treatment, and should certainly not be concealed.

But why talk of this, if the private Shevchenko Scientific Society in Galicia [Western Ukraine], not supported at all financially but in every way hampered by the Austrian, and later the Polish, authorities, managed in the few decades of its existence to publish such a quantity of literature on Ukrainian studies, particularly history, folklore, statistics and the study of documents, as, in the conditions at present obtaining in the Ukrainian SSR, all its State Publishing Houses would probably require for this kind of work several centuries to produce, not to speak of the scholarly level of execution and selection of material involved.

As for the works of dozens of great Ukrainian scientists in various branches of the natural sciences, if they are published, then it is in most cases only in Russian, and not in Ukrainian.

Should we be surprised then that the documents and personalities of the national political struggle at the end of the nineteenth and the beginning of the twentieth century are consigned to oblivion? As a slavish tribute to anti-scientific, chauvinist conceptions all this has been assigned to 'zoological nationalism'. This runs counter to Lenin's direct indication of the necessity for distinguishing on principle between the aggressive nationalism of a ruling nation and the defensive nationalism of an oppressed nation, the nationalism of any oppressed nation having a general democratic content.¹⁵ It also runs counter to the clear definition of the role even of the 'nationalist petty bourgeoisie' given by the Central Committee of the CP(B)U in 1927: 'Before the October Revolution its movement had an undoubted revolutionary importance and played its role in the overthrow of first, tsarist, and then, bourgeois imperialist, power.' Only after the October Revolution did this movement become anti-Soviet.¹⁶ In our case it is not even a question of the 'nationalist petty bourgeoisie' but of national liberation radicalism of the intelligentsia or 'revolutionary democratic nationalism', as Lunacharsky defined Shevchenko's ideology, basing himself on Lenin's thesis about two nationalisms.¹⁷

Even a number of works by I. Franko – *Ukraina irredenta, Shcho take postup?* [What is Progress?] – are being concealed and withheld from publication. The journalistic works of B. Hrinchenko (*Lysty z Ukrainy Naddnipryans'koyi* [Letters from the Dnipro river banks in Ukraine]), I. Nechuy-Levyts'ky and others are printed with great excisions, as they sharply formulate the question of the colonial oppression of Ukraine and the necessity of struggling for its liberation and national state independence.

Likewise concealed are the literary-political writings of the 1920s and works on the nationalities question by M. Skrypnyk and others. The resolutions on the Ukrainian question passed by the Comintern, the RCP(B), and the CP(B)U in Leninist and early post-Leninist times and in particular their ideas about national cultural construction in Ukraine are also not made available to the general reader.

Huge breaches have been made, and still gape wide, in the Ukrainian literature and art both of pre-Soviet and Soviet times. Whilst in Soviet Russia Bunin has long been recognized and published, in Soviet Ukraine there can be no question of it as regards V. Vynnychenko, who had been incomparably more 'left' in prerevolutionary days. In the 1920s, however, his collected works were published successfully without the Soviet system being rocked to its foundations. After all, how can the history of Ukrainian literature be written without the inclusion of Vynnychenko?

While in Soviet Russia the works of Averchenko, Mandel'shtam and Maksimilian Voloshin are being prepared for publication, and you even hear some mention of Gumilyov who had been executed as a White Guard, in Soviet Ukraine there can be no question of it not only for Hryhoriy Chuprynka (who, by the way, had also been published in the 1920s) or M. Yevshan, but even for V. Pidmohyl'ny, M. Khvyl'ovy, O. Slisarenko, M. Ivchenko, M. Yohansen and many others. Mykhaylo Semenko, Geo Shkurupiy and many others of the *avant-garde* are only mentioned for the sake of their denigration and are represented in anthologies by only a few carefully selected little poems. P. Fylypovych and M. Dray-Khmara are virtually nonexistent for our literature. The same can be said about the encyclopedic M. Zerov, since his few 'vindicated' poems represent merely a drop in the ocean of his literary and scholarly work. Even in the case of Bazhan, Tychyna, Sosyura and others, far from everything is being reprinted that was published in their books of verse and in the periodicals of the 1920s.

And what about the literary criticism and scholarship of the Soviet period? Not a trace of Academician S. Yefremov, nor of the brilliant student of Western literatures A. Nikovs'ky, nor of M. Kalynovych, nor of the communist V. Koryak, nor of many, many others ...

And what about translation? What about bringing the Ukrainian reader the wealth of world culture in his own language? This is one of the great concerns to which every civilised nation has always devoted the maximum attention and effort. In the 1920s Ukrainian publishing houses were successfully carrying out a far-reaching plan for complete multi-volume editions of the world's literary classics and of the most outstanding works of philosophical, political, sociological, historiographical thought and art criticism, in good translations, with *apparatus criticus* and with the participation of eminent specialists. Now these translations have become such bibliographical rarities that it is virtually impossible to get hold of them. New translations are being produced on a fairly miserable scale, so that we have only individual books from the world's classics. Some of our most brilliant translations, such as Goethe's *Faust* (translated by M. Lukash), Dante's *Commedia* (translated by P. Karmans'ky and M. Ryl's'ky) and others, are being published in such miserably small editions that it is impossible to acquire them no matter how much one may want to. The publication of the world's philosophical and sociological literature in Ukrainian translation is out of the question. But these are the things that must make up the tangible cultural life of a modern nation, if it is not to fall into a state of spiritual inferiority. If we failed to provide these for the Ukrainian nation and if we suggested that it could reach the world's intellectual life through the medium of Russian culture rather than directly, we would actually refuse it one of its most basic rights, and transform into parasitism and dependence what should and could be friendly reciprocal help. Also, we would actually increase the backwardness of Ukrainian culture and push the Ukrainian language yet further into the background, since translations are not liabilities but rank among the greatest assets of every culture.

The Ukrainian reader wants and must have in his own language the achievements of universal culture, particularly the literary classics of the world.

> In our country there is a great demand for world classics in translation.
> Experience has shown that the editions of good translations from world literature into Ukrainian, such as Homer's *Odyssey* (translated by Borys Ten), Dante's *Commedia* (translated by M. Ryl's'ky and P. Karmans'ky), Goethe's *Faust* (translated

> by M. Lukash), or Aesop's *Fables* (translated by Yu. Mushak), were sold out very quickly.
>
> It is time to bring greater method, scope, initiative and persistence to this matter which is so important for the development of the culture of the people.
>
> In our opinion it would be worthwhile creating a special publishing house that would bring out works from foreign literatures and from the literatures of the peoples of the USSR in Ukrainian translation. Such a publishing house could rally to itself highly qualified translators and could meet the demands of Ukrainian readers more fully.[18]

However, to this day there have unfortunately been more words than action in this matter. In the sphere of translation, we have only a miserable part of what we actually had in the 1920s.

We also do not treat the achievements of the Ukrainian people well in other spheres of culture and art.

In music we have almost forgotten the great Ukrainian composers Maksym Berezovs'ky and D. Bortnyans'ky as well as the Galician composers of the nineteenth and twentieth centuries. Until recently no mention was made of the great and celebrated singers Solomiya Krushel'nyts'ka, Oleksandr Myshuha and Modest Mentsyns'ky, and even now we do not have their recordings, although such recordings exist in the West, where they enjoy great popularity. We make hardly any mention of the Koshyts' choir or of a number of other famous performer groups and do not have their recordings.

In our entire Republic there is not a single record factory.

In painting and sculpture, we do not know such a giant as Archipenko, whom the artistic world places alongside Picasso. We do not know M. Butovych, M. Parashchuk and P. Kholodny, we almost do not know P. Obal',

O. Novakivs'ky and O. Bohomazov. To this day silence covers a whole constellation of talented artists, the 'Boychukists', who created an original school in Ukrainian art in the 1920s. Only now do we begin to mention A. Petryts'ky ...

Insufficient attention is paid to Ukrainian folk art which has long been recognized throughout the world as one of the finest jewels of beauty and human culture. As a result, the renowned centres of folk art in Upishnya, Petrykivka, Kosiv and other villages are, to put it mildly, not in the best of states ...

Is it not a fact that Pavlyna Tsvilyk, whose products are so highly valued in the artistic world, lacked the elementary facilities for work? The same was until quite recently true of Prymachenko and a number of other folk artists.

In our museum galleries, too much space is given to imposing hackwork and the dreary output of honoured time-servers, whilst the latest artistic strivings of less 'comfortable' contemporary talents are not represented. Many brilliant works from earlier periods, especially the 1920s, are languishing in store. In L'viv hundreds of first-rate examples of Ukrainian icon art of the fifteenth to seventeenth centuries lie virtually buried in the Armenian Cathedral. These icons could adorn many a museum (or why should not a special museum of ancient Ukrainian art be created?); they could provide material for a wonderful art album, which would sell all over the world (and how many themes for such albums Ukrainian art could provide!) ... We could quote so many more similar examples of how the artistic attainments of the Ukrainian nation are belittled and its spiritual history is diminished.

But even these things which have not come under any official or unofficial taboo, things that seem to have been given a place among the assets of Ukrainian culture, are being very insufficiently disseminated amongst the mass of the public. As a result, large sections of the population know very little about the enormous riches of Ukrainian culture, show no interest in it and consider it beneath their notice. Let us recall how seriously the CP(B)U in the 1920s concerned itself with the absorption of Ukrainian culture by the broad working masses, and how it considered national culture and language a powerful instrument of communist cultural construction and education. Now we are faced with the total antithesis of this: Ukrainian culture, and in particular the printed word, is being steadfastly ignored and replaced in its entirety by Russian culture and Russian books. This is what is happening, if not everywhere, at least among considerable sections of the city populations, and especially in the 'upper strata' of society. The case is the same with the public authorities, which do nothing to disseminate Ukrainian culture among the population, especially not amongst its younger members. This deliberate neglect takes on such egregious forms that it cannot fail to shock anyone who feels the least concern for Ukrainian culture. Worried voices percolate even into our press, which, mildly speaking, tends to be rather cautious on such matters. Let us look through *Literaturna Ukraina* [Literary Ukraine], *Kul'tura i zhyttya* [Culture and Life] (formerly *Radyans'ka kul'tura* [Soviet Culture]), *Robitnycha hazeta* [The Workers' Gazette] and others, and we will find a good many voices raised in concern and protest against the manifestations of an openly neglectful and scornful attitude towards the popularization of Ukrainian books and culture, voices which complain of the complete absence of any organized dissemination of them.

In the Ukrainian Soviet State, the responsible authorities, first and foremost the Government itself, in no way endeavour to make Ukrainian Soviet culture truly accessible to the whole nation.

2   THE LANGUAGE BLOCKADE

More than fifty years ago, in tsarist Russia, the Imperial Academy of Sciences was forced to declare in its memoir

'Ob otmene stesneniy malorusskogo pechatnogo slova' [Concerning the Abolition of Restrictions against the Little Russian Printed Word]:

> We cannot but admit that a scornful attitude towards one's native language also leads to a negative attitude towards one's family and native environment, and this cannot fail to have a most grievous effect on the moral constitution of the ... Little Russian population.[19]

This admission was forced and belated but nevertheless just. It was made under the pressure of circumstances, under the influence of many authoritative scholars of the first rank. In scientific and pedagogic thought it has long been an accepted view – developed by philosophers, pedagogues, linguists and writers – that all culture begins with a knowledge of one's native language and native culture; that contempt of one's language is a form of depersonalization and selfrenunciation and is evidence of a certain demoralization; that a man's attitude towards his native language reflects his moral and intellectual level; that language is the living symbol of a people's collective individuality; that the decadence of a national language directly attests the decadence of that nation and thus represents an enormous loss for the spiritual treasure-house of humanity; that for every spiritually integrated person any encroachment upon his language is an offence against his individuality and his people, which he will inevitably resist.

For any thoughtful communist these sociological truths are incontrovertible. Hence the tremendous importance of the language factor in the general task of communist national construction.

Therefore the Politbureau of the Central Committee of the RCP(B) resolved as early as November 1919:

> RCP members on Ukrainian territory must put into practice the right of the working people to study in the Ukrainian language and to speak their native language in all Soviet institutions; they must in every way counteract attempts at russification that push the Ukrainian language into the background and must convert that language into an instrument for the communist education of the working people. Steps must be taken immediately to ensure that in all Soviet institutions there are sufficient Ukrainian-speaking employees and that in future all employees are able to speak Ukrainian.[20]

As we know, this resolution was written in Lenin's own hand. Foreseeing (and seeing already) resistance to its implementation, three years later in his last instructions he declared categorically:

> ... The strictest rules must be introduced on the use of the national language in the non-Russian republics of our union, and these rules must be checked with special care. There is no doubt that, our apparatus being what it is, there is bound to be, on the pretext of unity in the railway service, unity in the fiscal service and so on, a mass of truly Russian abuses. Special ingenuity is necessary for the struggle against these abuses, not to mention special sincerity on the part of those who undertake this struggle. A detailed code will be required, and only the nationals living in the republic in question can draw it up at all successfully.[21]

According to this instruction from Lenin, the XII Congress of the RCP(B) resolved in particular: that it is necessary 'to promulgate special laws guaranteeing the use of the native language in all State bodies and institutions ... laws prosecuting and punishing all transgressors of national rights with full revolutionary harshness'.[22]

Over forty years have passed since then, more than enough time to have implemented these direct instructions and achieve the end clearly expounded by Lenin. What do we have instead? Everything contrary has been done. Today it is ridiculous even to speak about the use of the Ukrainian language in official institutions. Any such things as 'rules' or 'a code' regarding the use of national languages have passed into total oblivion. In any case, they would look foolish nowadays. The spirit of 'unity' (not 'railway' or 'fiscal', but total, absolute and ruthless) has had its complete triumph long ago. As for 'pushing the Ukrainian language into the background', this has already been done, as a corollary of the above, in all possible respects, and very firmly, truly, 'uncompromisingly' at that. To anyone who is capable of honestly admitting facts all this is so plain and obvious that it needs no further discussion.

It only remains for us now to point out that the actual secondary position of the Ukrainian language (in the actual literal sense of the word, since formally and legally it naturally enjoys full rights) has produced a luxuriant flowering of contempt and even of hatred for it, not only on the part of the petty bourgeoisie, but also on the part of those 'communists' about whom Lenin said: 'Scratch some communists and you will find Great Russian chauvinists,'[23] and finally even on the part of Ukrainians themselves, those Russianized nonRussians about whom Lenin said that they especially 'overdo [the truly] Russian frame of mind'.[24] What greater moral collapse can there be than contempt for your own language and culture? And what can society expect from such mother-haters?!

Ukrainophobia, which we have discussed earlier, is for many Ukrainians the logical result of the renunciation of their native language. This happens in accordance with a general psychological law which holds true for members of any nation:

> As many outstanding psychologists and pedagogues (for instance, Fichte, Diesterweg and others) long ago observed, such a renunciation[25] results in a certain distortion of man's spiritual nature, on the one hand often expressed in such people by a certain enfeebling of their thoughts, feelings and will, which sometimes even results in a decline in their personal character and disposition, and on the other by an inevitable dwindling of their natural affection for their native environment, for their people, and their country, frequently leading to complete indifference to everything social, or to a generally reactionary mood accompanied by misanthropy and antipathy directed primarily towards everything native.[26]

Many people who think superficially do not attach any great importance to the facts of denationalization and the loss of the native language and consider this 'tolerance' or indifference of theirs to be a manifestation of nobility and breadth of outlook. But they are mistaken. Language is so intrinsically linked with the deepest sources and most subtle manifestations of individual and social spiritual life that its renunciation, either by linguistic assimilation or a mass transition to another language, cannot occur without leaving some mark on the individual and on society as a whole. It cannot fail to produce certain dislocations, certain disturbances in the 'alveolar' system of the spiritual 'microstructure', disturbances that may be imperceptible, but can in time produce indirect but nonetheless grave consequences and complications. First of all this causes an inevitable impoverishment, a certain drying up and silting up of the springs of the spirit, which may not be noticed immediately, just as rivers do not run dry immediately after the drying up of forest springs; for with the loss of your native language you lose an unfathomable world of the subconscious, you lose the whole national psychological spiritual subsoil, all the underground springs and secrets of the great collective soul, of the collective experience of the people. The acquisition of a new language without doubt only enriches a man when his native language retains its original place, but when there is an exchange the acquisition only partially compensates him for his losses. Even with the best knowledge, a foreign language is up to a certain point assimilated in a schematic, somewhat depleted way, without the vast depths of the subconscious, without the unique patterns of association, with perhaps imperceptible but innumerable ruptures of the 'alveolar radicles'. This is the undoubted source of spiritual, aesthetic and ethical losses. This is why the great Potebnya warned against the inevitable 'abomination of emptiness' linked with denationalization, with linguistic assimilation. This is why all great experts on the human psyche – writers, psychologists and pedagogues – were so emphatic in defending the native language. Let us recall the words of F. Adolf Diesterweg:

> What individuality means for the person, nationality means for peoples ... To kill a person is a single, complete act. But to rob people of their nationality is continuous, prolonged murder. How frightening! ...
> Language is sacred to man. To encroach upon it, to rob man of it, to impose a foreign language upon him is equivalent to striking at the roots of his life. Any people in the world would consider such an action a crime against its selfhood and not let it pass unpunished. A people lives through its language; its spirit is embodied in it.

> A cultivated language is a great thing, the mark and expression of a people's innermost being.

Another great pedagogue, K. D. Ushinsky, reached similar conclusions:

> The language of a people is the best, unfading and eternally renewed flower of its whole spiritual life, which begins far back in prehistory. It is the spiritual expression of a whole people and of their whole country. Through the creative force of the people's spirit, a language transmutes into thought, image and sound the sky of the native country, its air, its physical phenomena, its climate, its fields, mountains and valleys, its forests and rivers, its tempests and thunderstorms – the whole profound, meaningful and emotive voice of native nature which speaks so eloquently through man's love for his sometimes austere native land, expressed so clearly in native songs, in native melodies, in the voices of the people's poets. However, the bright, transparent depths of a people's language reflect not only the nature of their native country but all the history of the people's spiritual life. Generations come and go, but the results of each generation's life remain in the language as a legacy to posterity. One generation after the other accumulates in the treasure-house of the mother-tongue what it has culled from deep movements of the heart, from historical events, beliefs, opinions, and marks of sorrow and of joy, in short, the people carefully preserve all the traces of its spiritual life in its language. Language is the most vital, the richest, and the finest bond of uniting past, present and future generations of the people into

a single great, historic living whole. It not only expresses the vitality of a people, but is its very life. When a people's language disappears, the people ceases to exist! This is why, for instance, our western brethren, having suffered all kinds of violence at the hands of strangers, understood when this violence finally touched their language that it was a question of the life or death of the people itself. As long as a language lives in the mouths of a people, that people is alive. There is no violence more intolerable than that which attempts to rob a people of its heritage created by countless generations of its ancestors. Take everything from a people, and it will be able to recover all; take away its language, and it will never recreate it; a people can create even a new homeland but never a language; when a language has died on the lips of a people, the people is also dead. But if the human heart shudders before the killing of a single transitory human being, what then should it feel, making an attempt upon the life of the age-old historic personality of a people, this greatest of all God's creations on earth?[27]

If to rob a people of its language is to kill it, and if this crime is immeasurably greater than any other, what then can we say when such a murderous policy hides behind noble words; when its perpetrators, assuming the role of both judge and jury, declare any instinctive self-defence a crime – including a people's defence of its own language – and are not honest enough to show their faces, but assure us that it is not they who are robbing a people of its mother tongue, but that it is the people itself which is renouncing its language of its own accord?

If a people were to renounce its language, this would mean that it was renouncing itself. Obviously, such a thing cannot be. To this day history has shown us no example of such *voluntary* self-abnegation, such *voluntary* suicide by a people. There never has been nor could there ever be such a thing, just as surely as humanity cannot seek its own destruction.

Neither does the Ukrainian people, nor any part of it, *voluntarily* renounce its identity and language today. What appears *voluntary* at first glance is not really so. Instead, we find the *pressure of circumstances* and the *effects of deep-seated causes*, forcing some Ukrainians to renounce their language, with all the accompanying abnormal consequences for their society.

'Who stops you from speaking Ukrainian?' is the favourite damning question of ukrainophobes poorly masked as internationalists, or of russifying 'members of mankind', too immature for true human culture.

'Who prevents you from speaking Ukrainian?' is the surprised query of well-meaning but politically naive people, indifferent to the 'artificial' nationalities problem.

'Who forbids you to speak Ukrainian?!' the high officials thunder, demonstrating by their wrathful mien that any compulsion is totally impossible.

Who forbids? ... Can there be a more false or empty question? And who, in tsarist Russia, forbade people to speak Ukrainian, Polish, Georgian, etc.? Even writing and printing was not prohibited all the time. And yet why, in spite of the absence of a legal prohibition to use it in daily speech, did our 'dear fellow-countrymen', to use Shevchenko's words, 'patter Muscovite'?[28] Who forbade the Africans to speak their languages, and yet why did the French or English language take over in a considerable part of Africa, so that the young African states are now confronted with the important task of emancipating the native languages? Why has the English language gained such a strong hold over certain sectors of Indian society so that now, as we know, the government's de-Anglicizing measures are meeting with desperate resistance from these circles? And who, in general, forbids all the peoples of the earth to be cultivated, educated, good, friendly, intelligent, happy? And who forbids you, honourable russifiers and ukrainophobe 'internationalists', to rid yourselves of your russification and of your ukrainophobia, to understand the national needs of the Ukrainian people, to see its actual national situation, and to see the russifying mechanism which you yourselves have set up?

You forbid (stop, prevent), if you still insist on your rather dishonest question and want an answer to it – you, yourselves, that is to say, the *circumstances* of life that you have created. 'The inequality which obtains in actual practice',[29] the actual secondary position of the Ukrainian language (and culture) – with implacable force, past comparing with that of any whip, any rod, any command or legal enactment – with all-crushing might *compels* and *forces* the individual Ukrainian and the Ukrainian masses in general to speak Russian and to renounce their mother-tongue. Some people simply stop feeling the need for the Ukrainian language, since everywhere life imperiously demands Russian (as an unpublished letter to *Literaturna Ukraina* justly observed: with the Russian language you can travel all over Ukraine and manage without Ukrainian, but you cannot manage in Ukraine with Ukrainian and without Russian); others again would like to speak Ukrainian, but they are ashamed to: at best, people look upon someone speaking Ukrainian in a town as a crank. This actual inequality of languages and cultures, as we have said, was produced prior to the revolution as a result of the colonial position of Ukraine. It was honestly recognized in the 1920s and the task of gradually overcoming it was set. Thus, for instance, on 1 August 1923 the All-Ukrainian Central Executive Committee and the Council of People's Commissars of the Ukrainian SSR decided

> to concentrate the attention of the State on spreading knowledge of the Ukrainian language

... As a result of the relatively poor development of Ukrainian schools and Ukrainian culture in general, as a result of the lack of the necessary school textbooks and sufficiently well-trained personnel, reality, as we see from experience, produces an actual preponderance of the Russian language.[30]

This *actual* preponderance of the Russian language in reality, a preponderance which has not only been preserved since then but which has grown (since the policy of ukrainization has been replaced by a policy of russification) is the crux of the matter.

We have already seen how it manifests itself in various spheres of social and everyday life and how the powerful and well-tuned machinery of russification functions. Finally, I would like briefly to enumerate some of its cogwheels, some of its main outlines.

1 *Official life and official relations* are, with rare exceptions, conducted in Russian, contrary to the decision of the All-Ukrainian Central Executive Committee and the Council of People's Commissars of the Ukrainian SSR of 1 August 1923: 'to select Ukrainian as the predominant language for official relations'.[31] Individual exceptions may occur in Kyiv as the capital of the Ukrainian SSR on some public occasions (a Shevchenko jubilee, a government reception, a rally, etc.) and they have a forced or sometimes even farcical character. In all the other sectors of official life and official relations the Russian language reigns supreme in the entire Republic, from top to bottom (at least as far down as the district centres).
2 *Party, Communist Youth League,* trade union and other social and civic activities are also conducted almost exclusively in Russian.

3 *Economic life and economic relations* in all their endless ramifications are conducted in Russian. A whole series of direct decisions taken to safeguard the functioning of economic agencies in the language of their given republic, including the resolution of the x Congress of the RCP(B),[32] have remained on paper.
4 *Business administration*, likewise.
5 *The Army* since the 1920s has been beyond comment in this respect, and has become an even more powerful instrument of russification.
6 *Higher, secondary technical and professional education* has been and is everywhere conducted in Russian (although in some establishments of higher education a gradual introduction of the Ukrainian language seems to be planned, starting from this year [1965–6]; however, it seems to have been already decided 'not to hurry' with this).
7 *Factory, trades and similar schools* recruit predominantly rural youth and for several years mercilessly mutilate their language.
8 *Secondary education, secondary schools.* In the cities of Ukraine in 1958 only 21 per cent of the children attended Ukrainian schools (in 1927, 75.9 per cent did so). Also, in 1958 even in the capital of Ukraine, Kyiv, there were only 22,000 pupils in Ukrainian schools, but 61,000 in Russian schools. It is well known that in a number of large cities (Kharkiv, Donetsk, Odessa and others) Ukrainian schools are the exception. In this respect the state of school education in the cities of Ukraine is so scandalous that the relevant statistics have not been published for a long time, and the data about the numbers of Ukrainian and non-Ukrainian schools and of the pupils in them seem to be classed with the greatest state secrets.

But even schools that are called Ukrainian are not really so. It is enough to visit any 'Ukrainian' school in Kyiv, for instance, to convince oneself that apart from the instruction itself the whole internal life is Russian and even the teachers themselves are 'ashamed' to speak Ukrainian to each other, not to mention the pupils. All this amounts mostly to make-believe and a superfluous show for the sake of statistics and 'for foreigners'.

But worst of all, the 'Ukrainian' schools – and this applies now both to those in cities and in villages – do nothing to instil a sense of national dignity and national feeling, nothing to give an elementary consciousness of nationality and of the duties connected with it. They do not even assure for the pupils a minimal knowledge of Ukrainian history and culture. For in most of them there is the same all-pervading atmosphere of the superiority and 'preferability' of Russian culture and of the inferiority of Ukrainian culture regarded as a make-weight. Thus, it is not surprising that the school-leavers from Ukrainian schools are for the most part totally ignorant of Ukrainian culture.

> An essay was set on 'The Role of Literature and Art in the Life of Soviet Man'. The teachers were disturbed. Not one of the 230 essays so much as mentioned the names of Lysenko, Lyatoshyns'ky, Stepovy, Leontovych, Nishchyns'ky, Mayboroda, Filipenko, Kos-Anatol's'ky, Lyudkevych, Pymonenko, Vasyl'kivs'ky, Trush, Yizhakevych, Manastyrs'ky, Zan'kovets'ka, Sadovs'ky, Krushel'nyts'ka, Myshuha, Kurbas, Petryts'ky, Dovzhenko ... It transpired that some of the secondary school leavers had never heard of these artists who have made a considerable contribution to our cultural riches ...
> ... Can we lay all the blame at the door of the teachers? Obviously, it is not solely their fault.

Indeed, not even the most conscientious village teacher will find even postcard reproductions of the works of Ukrainian painters. There are none either in bookshops or in art shops. And they ought to be sold at every bookstall, like the reproductions of Shishkin or Perov.

It is a very good thing that our schoolchildren know the names of Tchaikovsky and Repin. They may well have heard about them from their first to their very last form. In many schools such talks are repeated from year to year: 'Repin, the Great Painter', 'Tchaikovsky, the Great Composer'. This, we repeat, is good, but clearly insufficient. Thus, we should not be surprised at what happened last year in one of the schools in Lutsk. A teacher once gave a talk to the fifth form in the presence of a number of form-teachers about the painter Yizhakevych. During the exchange of opinions one of the teachers declared that 'the subject is clearly unfortunate, why not take some known painter, for example Repin or Shiskin, because not even all the teachers have heard of Yizhakevych'.[33]

Comment, as the saying goes, is superfluous.

9 *Kindergartens and day nurseries* present one of the most terrible and criminal aspects of russification. Here an irreversible 'grafting' on to the defenceless minds of children is taking place. Kindergartens and day nurseries in the cities are, but for a few exceptions, completely Russian. How then can there be Ukrainian children in the cities, where and how can they be brought up?

I will permit myself to quote an interesting document, one of many letters concerned with the language question received by various official bodies in the Ukrainian SSR:

To the Ministry of Education of
the Ukrainian SSR, Kyiv.
From mothers of pre-school children.

Complaint

We, the Ukrainian mothers of pre-school children, address this complaint to you on the question of putting a stop to the reactionary language policy of the Ministry of Health as it is practised in the day nurseries and kindergartens of our locality and likewise of the whole of the Ukrainian SSR.

We protest and demand that in kindergartens and similar institutions the mother-tongue (in our case Ukrainian) should be introduced into the pre-school education of our little ones.

When they enter the kindergarten, our children understand no other language except their mother-tongue, and there can be no educational method when the teachers [!] speak Russian to them. No doubt this also creates difficulties for the teachers of primary schools in teaching the Ukrainian language to children who have been educated in this kind of institution.

We are against the spoiling and mutilation of the Ukrainian language, against the reactionary language policy of the Ministry of Health of the Ukrainian SSR. However, we are not against our children learning other, foreign languages, especially Russian, but only if they first learn their mother-tongue well.

The language policy of the Ministry of Health in the Ukrainian lands is anti-constitutional, anti-Leninist, anti-Party and anti-Soviet. It can suit only all sorts of anti-Soviet elements.

It feeds the flames of anti-Soviet propaganda abroad. It differs in no respect from the policy of powers which formerly occupied Ukraine.

As a result, such a Great Russian chauvinist and reactionary method of education as adopted by the Ministry of Health of Ukraine will not lead to the victory of communism.

According to the teachings of Marx and Lenin, all peoples of the world, even if they are stateless, have a sacred right to the development of their own native culture, and in this way each people contributes its part to the creation of a beautiful stained-glass window. It (this reactionary policy) will bring the Ministry of Health neither honour nor the hoped-for success. On the contrary, it will remain as a blot of Black-Hundred reaction and will sap both Ukrainian and Russian culture, increasing the cadres of uneducated language paralytics. It will cause general indignation and censure against the policy of the Soviet Union from the progressive public of the world.

There are seventeen signatures on the letter. At the top, the incoming and outgoing references and the decision taken. What do you think it was? Perhaps, to punish severely those responsible for the violation of both the Leninist nationalities policy and the national rights of the Ukrainian population (as the Congresses formerly decided) 'to punish those who violate national rights with the full harshness of the revolutionary laws'?[34] Perhaps to enter into communication with the Ministry of Health with a view to reversing the abnormal situation in its educational institutions? Not at all. Quite the contrary. Decision No. 6–493 says this, word for word: 'Please send [this] letter to the Regional [*Oblast'*] Education Office, have them discover [!] the authors of this letter and explain to them the Leninist nationalities policy of our State.' Very simple and efficient: received on 4 November 1965, already answered on 6 November. Nowadays such matters are dealt with very efficiently: one has a practised hand. Any letters on similar topics are brushed aside in the same manner, the tragedy of a whole nation is brushed aside. And lest this should seem bureaucratic or undemocratic, they 'explain'. Would it not be better for the Leninist nationalities policy and for us all if instead of the bureaucrats (of any rank) 'explaining' it to the people, the people were to explain it to the bureaucrats? Let us be honest: the letter of the not very literate mothers shows much more understanding of the Leninist nationalities policy and internationalism in general, and much more elementary human decency besides, than do all such decisions taken together, and more than many 'theoreticians' and publicists who take up these subjects possess ...

10. *Cultural-educational centres, libraries, etc.* Artistic amateur activities, circles, etc., have gained a tremendous impetus in our country. But their cultural level is far from being always satisfactory, if we do not consider outstanding individual groups but take them as a whole. I do not know who is responsible for the repertories and performances of these innumerable ensembles and circles, but it must be admitted that in the overwhelming majority of cases they are by no means propagators of Ukrainian art and do not base their productions on Ukrainian national culture. Quite the contrary, their work, their programmes (at least in the cities) have either no Ukrainian content whatsoever, or one or two numbers as 'padding', for exoticism (or for the activities report). To convince oneself of this it is worth paying a random visit to any of the countless

amateur concerts (I am speaking, of course, about the spontaneous ones, not about the 'special orders', such as the republican amateur competition, some festival or the like). And it is in these lower reaches of mass cultural-educational work, in these mass leisure activities, that the tastes, sympathies and inclinations of the widest public are cultivated (and sometimes debased). Here the cultural interests and energies of youth, especially working-class youth, are directed in one way or the other. All this could exert a tremendous pull on the widest masses to attract them to Ukrainian culture. It is difficult to overestimate the importance of a well-organized programme of this kind for the education of the working people and for raising the 'coefficient' of the active participation in Ukrainian culture, with all its tremendous past, and considerable present, attainments, in creating a spiritual atmosphere of communist society. But nobody is giving a really purposeful lead in this matter.

But then, why should we speak about amateur activities when even the Kyiv Republican Philharmonic (not to mention most provincial ones) hardly practises any artistic reading in the Ukrainian language at all. Those few readers, masters of the Ukrainian word, who out of decency are still being kept, live virtually on 'hunger rations' and have to endure endless annoyances. Or another aspect. You might think that the one thing that is certainly being popularized in our country is Ukrainian song. But on closer examination even here a quite different, and not very happy, picture appears. Yes, day and night, year after year, you can hear a few songs, but always the same ones (and often in hackneyed renderings), which end up by boring people, and in point of fact contribute nothing much to cultural life. To the public mind they represent the wealth of Ukrainian song, and how is anyone to guess that over 200,000 Ukrainian songs have been collected (specialists claim that these are still not all, and that no other nation in the world can boast of such a wealth of song). Who popularizes these songs, who concerns himself with them, except for those who make use of them in the archives of the Institute of Folklore for higher degrees? Enormous cultural riches are being wasted and forgotten.

And where is the Ukrainian music-hall (Ukrainian not by territory but by the nature of its repertory), where the popular, jazz and other youth ensembles are? And yet, experience shows that where they are created, as in L'viv, they soon gain great popularity among young people.

Vast numbers of students and young workers live in hostels. Not only does the educational, cultural and day-to-day atmosphere lack any Ukrainian character, one can hardly find a Ukrainian newspaper, magazine or book in their 'red corners' or libraries. The situation is most deplorable in workers' hostels, although they are inhabited predominantly by Ukrainian youth.

> How is Ukrainian culture disseminated in our hostels? Very unsatisfactorily. It will suffice to point out one single fact: in the hostels of Krivyy Rih, in each of which over a dozen newspapers and magazines are subscribed to – at state expense,[35] by the way – it is difficult to find Ukrainian periodicals.[36]

The same situation exists in thousands of youth and workers' hostels. And what about trade union and department libraries, which again are maintained at the expense of the Ukrainian working people? Year after year most of them do not subscribe to any

Ukrainian newspapers or magazines (except for the compulsory general political ones), and the percentage of their Ukrainian book holdings is miserable.

But then, why speak of trade union libraries, if even in the libraries of schools and establishments of higher education we can see, for example, the following picture:

> We enter School No. 118. It is considered to be the best in the Podil district of the capital. Seven hundred pupils receive instruction here in 17 classes. There are 6,136 books in the school library.
>
> Ukrainian classical and contemporary literature is represented by only 400 books. The editions are old. They are intended for the higher classes. For the children of the lower and intermediate classes (it is a school with eight years) there is not a single Ukrainian book!
>
> In School No. 20 with 600 pupils the library holds 16,000 volumes, of which only 480 represent both classical and Soviet Ukrainian literature.[37]

The Central Committee of the CP(B)U used to adopt special resolutions dealing with such shocking facts ... For instance:

> While even in the industrial unions Ukrainian workers constitute the majority, we observe an intolerable phenomenon in workers' libraries: Ukrainian books, which should provide for the cultural needs of Ukrainian workers, constitute a miserable percentage (in fifty miners' libraries in the Stalino region Ukrainian books comprise only 7.7 per cent, in the builders' libraries of the same region, only 9 per cent).[38]

And decisive measures were planned to improve the situation ...

But now such a situation is accepted as normal and the matter is raised only in comments from individuals in the newspapers, particularly in the newspaper which those criticized do not themselves take, and year in, year out such comments produce no result.

11 *The press, books, publishing, the readers' market in general.* We have already said enough about the fact that Ukrainian publishing lags catastrophically behind Russian publishing, that its Ukrainian-language production is unfairly small in relation to the percentage of the Ukrainian population, and that Russian-language production is overwhelmingly predominant on the readers' market in Ukraine. At the same time Ukrainian-language production not only fails to be properly publicized, but even the basic spontaneous demand for it frequently remains unsatisfied. Everywhere you hear complaints about the shortage of some Ukrainian book or other, and in the newspapers you can often read something like the following:

> *Veselka* (Rainbow) and *Molod* (Youth) should not publish books in such miserably small numbers of copies as we receive now. Can anyone hold with the fact that with thirty thousand schools and seven million pupils in the Republic children's books are printed in thirty thousand copies?[39]

Talk about this has been going on for years, and for years the numbers of copies printed have remained the same. There is either a shortage of paper or of something else. Meanwhile the central, Moscow publishing houses manage somehow. (Once upon a time, Party resolutions used to qualify such contempt for the needs of the Republics as one of the manifestations of Russian Great-Power chauvinism.)

I would like to draw attention to one more fact. Russian-language publishing has the superiority not only in numbers but also in quality. Many factors contribute to this. All serious scientific and scholarly works appear in Russian, while in Ukrainian we get mainly *belles-lettres*, social-political, popular and similar literature. The central publishing houses have incomparably greater financial resources, they offer higher salaries and royalties and attract the best cadres and the best authors. (Although the situation here is more complex than that, let us say, in sport or in opera, when they simply whisk off the best performers to Moscow without further ado, something similar certainly does take place in the field of publishing.) There are also a number of other factors whose adverse (in relation to the national needs of the Republics) influence is not combated (not to mention the guarantees and 'concessions' which Lenin tried to elaborate).

And so it turns out that the Russian-language production of the central publishing houses has a greater appeal for the mass reader than the Ukrainian production, which he often disdains (sometimes justly, sometimes unjustly).

The mechanics of this 'qualitative inequality' could also be detailed, but for reasons of space I shall give only one example. The central Moscow newspapers keep their readers informed about current events from 'primary sources' and arrive in most Ukrainian cities on the day of issue. The republican newspapers not only print translated, and thus often belated and incomplete, information, but also do not arrive in most Ukrainian cities until the second or third day. Let us consider whether in these conditions many people will feel a particular interest in these republican newspapers. And yet in the 1920s Ukrainian newspapers had their foreign correspondents, RATAU (Radio-Telegraphic Agency of Ukraine) maintained direct contact with many world capitals, we received our information ourselves, often faster than from Moscow, and thus the republican press and radio offered an independent source of interest. Why should we not think about this now too? Why should we not think about having the runs (or part of the runs) of *Pravda, Izvestia* and other papers, which are intended for Ukraine, printed in Ukrainian for the Ukrainian reader? This would be just. This is done even in some bourgeois countries: a popular newspaper is printed at one and the same time in the different languages spoken in the country. There is all the more reason to do this in a socialist country. Unnecessary expense? Not very considerable, and besides one should be ashamed to speak of expense when it is a question of justice. In Lenin's time expense was a much more weighty consideration, and yet in elaborating the guarantees for national minorities he did not count their cost in roubles. He knew that a rouble saved in this way would result in a loss in more valuable things.

It would be possible to describe many more channels of russification. But what has been said is quite enough. I only want to stress that in my opinion the most alarming factor in this complex situation is still the spiritual-psychological one: the overwhelming pressure of Russian Great-Power chauvinist sentiment, coupled with a total lack of communist national education or a communist understanding of the nation and man. Hence the thoughtlessness, indifference, cynicism, acquiescence, servility and 'couldn't-care-less' attitude towards the national cause. Hence the national self-destruction.

All this creates a favourable climate for the successful workings of the mechanism of russification, all this is a powerful catalyst for the denationalizing and russifying processes which never have brought nor will ever bring any good either to the Ukrainian or to the Russian, people and even less to communism, the future society.

1   At that time the Chairman of the Council of People's Commissars of Ukraine.
2   With, or from, the all-Union ones.
3   XII s'yezd RKP(B), p. 596.
4   The Political Administration of the Workers' and Peasants' Red Army.
5   XII s'yezd RKP(B), p. 571.
6   Ibid., p. 597.
7   X s'yezd RKP(B), p. 213; an incomplete English translation in J.V. Stalin, *Works*, V, Moscow, 1953, p. 49.
8   KPSS v rezolyutsiyakh, I, p. 713.
9   Cf. note 79 above.
10 Yuriy Il'chenko's and Ivan Drach's film, *The Well for the Thirsty*, has in fact been banned, a film which according to the judgement of most professionals is an outstanding achievement of national cinematographic art and could, together with *Shadows of Forgotten Ancestors*, take the Ukrainian cinema to the international level.
11 Lunacharsky, 'O natsionalizme ...', *Ukrainskaya zhizn'*, No. 10, 1912, p.14.
12 *Kul'turne budivnytstvo v Ukrains'kiy RSR: vazhlyvishi rishennya Komunistychnoyi partiyi i Radyans'koho uryadu, 1917–1959. Zbirnyk dokumentiv*, I, Kyiv, 1959, p. 243.
13 However much effort young theatrical enthusiasts expended trying to set up, at least on a voluntary basis, an experimental theatre, say, in Darnitsa, a huge workers' suburb of Kyiv, which has not a single theatre for a population of tens, if not hundreds, of thousands (apropos, Kyiv has only five professional theatres, while Warsaw and Prague, equaling it in size, have several dozen each) – however much effort theatrical youth expended to achieve this, they were permitted nothing.
14 The young Ukrainian composers Syl'vestrov, V. Huba and others are in a similar position.
15 Lenin, *CW*, XXXVI, p. 607, and XX, p. 412. (Lenin's italics.)
16 I V. Koryak (ed.), *Shlyakhy rozvytku ukrains'koyi proletars'koyi literatury*, Kharkiv, 1928, p. 343.
17 A.V. Lunacharsky, *Stat'i o literature*, Moscow, 1957, p. 429.
18 M. Humenyuk, 'Vid rozmov – do dila!', *Literaturna Ukraina*, 24 September 1965, p. 3.
19 As quoted by Lunacharsky, 'O natsionalizme voobshche i ukrainskom dvizhenii v chastnosti', *Ukrainskaya zhizn'*, No, 10, 1912, p. 18.
20 Lenin, *CW*, XXX, pp. 163–4. (Italics by the author.).
21 Lenin, *CW*, XXXVI, p. 610. (Italics by the author.)

22 KPSS v rezolyutsiyakh, I, pp. 716–17.
23 Lenin, CW, XXIX, p. 194.
24 Lenin, CW, XXXVI, p. 606.
25 Of the native language.
26 K. Mikhal'chuk, 'Chto takoye malorusskaya (yuzhnorusskaya) rech'?', *Kievskaya starina*, LXVI, August 1899, p. 185.
27 K.D. Ushinsky, 'Rodnoye slovo', in his *Sobraniye sochineniy*, II, Moscow Leningrad, 1948, pp. 557–8.
28 T. Shevchenko, 'Son (komediya)', in his *Povne zibrannya tvoriv u shesty tomakh*, I, Kyiv, 1963, p. 250; an English translation in his *Selected Works*, Moscow, 1964, pp. 133–4.
29 Lenin, CW, XXXVI, p. 608.
30 *Kul'turne budivnytstvo v Ukrains'kiy RSR ...*, I, Kyiv, 1959, p. 243.
31 Ibid., p. 244.
32 x s'yezd RKP(B), p. 603.
33 S. Zabuzhko, 'I vse shche prohalyny ... Notatky z vstupnykh ekzameniv', *Literaturna Ukraina*, 3 September 1965, p. 2.
34 Cf. note 259.
35 That is to say, at the expense of the Ukrainian people.
36 K. Hryb, 'Dim chy prytulok?', *Literaturna Ukraina*, 28 September 1965, p. 4.
37 K. Hryb, 'Shcho chytaty dityam?', *Literaturna Ukraina*, 23 October 1964, p. 1
38 *Kul'turne budivnytstvo v Ukrains'kiy RSR ...*, I, Kyiv, 1959, p. 424.
39 K. Hryb, loc. cit.

11
The Russification of other peoples and denationalization run counter to the interests of the Russian people itself

'Has it really never occurred to you when reading Pushkin, Lermontov or Gogol, that there is another Russia besides the official, governmental one?' Herzen once asked.[1] Today we must address this question to those who elevate to the sacrosanct level of official theory the ill-omened thesis about the USSR being the heir of the Russian Empire; who want all its victims and prisoners – the occupied and deceived peoples – to consider this empire, this prison of the nations, as their common historic 'Fatherland'; who glorify all sorts of 'reunions', 'annexations' and 'territorial acquisitions', things done by 'official, governmental Russia', and forget that the 'other' Russia had nothing to do with any of this, that it opposed all this and demanded its renunciation.

A strange fact emerges: our historians and theoreticians consider themselves the ideological heirs of Chernyshevsky and Herzen, and by no means those of S. Solov'yov or M. Katkov, and yet in their judgements on the 'gathering together' of the Empire and in their concepts of the historic 'Fatherland' they make common cause with the latter and not with the former. Do they think that to call themselves the heirs of Chernyshevsky and Herzen, it is enough to celebrate their jubilees from time to time and to enshrine them in anthologies?! Does it suffice to honour the *names* of the representatives of unofficial Russia in order to assimilate their ideas? Hardly. Just as allowing the *names* of the champions of official despotic Russia to pass into oblivion does not necessarily imply forgetfulness of their ideas.

Who today would dare to tell the truth about the colonization of the Caucasus, as Lermontov told it, that story of blood, crimes, tears and vengeance?

Who today would dare to tell the truth about Mazeppa and Voynarovs'ky as recounted by Ryleyev? Or at least what Pushkin said in 'Poltava'? Today we are expected to drone out what the Church chanted for two hundred years at the behest of Peter I: 'Curses and anathema not only twofold and threefold, but also manifold.'

Who would treat the history of Ukraine in the way I.G. Pryzhov or Herzen treated it?

Who would tell what Aksakov the Elder told about the colonization of Bashkiria?

Who would repeat today what Herzen and Bakunin said about Russia's policy towards Ukraine, or at least what Lunacharsky said about Taras Shevchenko?

Who today would repeat Turgenev's words for all the country to hear: 'If I were a Ukrainian, I should consider personal indifference towards my nationality a crime; I would not want to be a Russian'?

Who today would be capable of writing what N.N. Zlatovratsky wrote about Shevchenko's grave?

This series of rhetorical questions could be continued ad infinitum. This alone shows what ideological and moral losses and devastation *present-day* Russian intelligentsia and youth suffer, from the necessity for their understanding of the past to be adjusted so as to conform with the falsely interpreted current needs.

Is it possible that you really do not feel the tragic loss of those values and concepts, of those high standards of conscience, of regard for the truth, of the sense of responsibility, and of that ethical potential, which were attained by generations of the revolutionary Russian intelligentsia amidst the stupefying murk of official hypocrisy? Is it not frightening that the words of the man who according to Lenin saved the honour of Russian democracy, the words of the man who was the conscience of Russia – Herzen – have no meaning or binding force for today?!

> We do not believe in the prosperity or the permanence of monstrous empires, we do not need so much land in order to love our native country. The desire for territorial expansion marks the growing stage of a people, and if this desire outlives the childhood stage, this in itself only demonstrates that such a nation is incapable of maturity. Everything undeveloped – organic sculpture, primitive art – plunges into the quantitative, everything unwise depends on the strength of the fist ...
>
> The unity of the agglomeration, the preservation of its excrescences, the defence of undigested pieces swallowed with difficulty – all this is extraneous and inimical to the fortunes of the people. In the name of a strong, invincible Empire the people were crushed and fleeced; in its name serfdom, bureaucracy and compulsory conscription were maintained. And this is not all. While robbing the ordinary man of all his civil rights, they maintained in him, a total slave, the conceited notion of the invincibility of the Russian Empire, which developed in him an arrogance towards foreigners coupled with a cringing servility before his invincible authorities.[2]

What is left today in our country of such an understanding of the Russian Empire, of such an understanding of the past?

And without nobility of mind in our judgement of the past, can there be nobility of mind in our assessment of the present?

And so we rejoice at the denationalization of dozens of peoples, at the 'successes' of russification, at the fact that according to the last census over ten million non-Russians in the Union gave Russian as their 'native' tongue and renounced their own language. And we put this down to the credit of the 'great and powerful Russian tongue', forgetting that Turgenev's hymn to the mother-tongue sprang from exactly opposite sentiments,[3] that Turgenev did not want to russify anyone, and that all great Russians by no manner of means perceived in the grandeur and beauty of their language an alleged capacity for dislodging and supplanting other languages; they glorified it only inasmuch as it was a question of defending it for themselves and not extending it to others. When it was a question of the latter, of russification, their true love for their own great language made them write bitter words about this:

> Let us admit once and for all ... that it is not necessary to russify or *polonize anybody* ...
>
> Why should a Ukrainian, for instance, exchange his openhearted language – the one that he used in his free councils, the one that has a record of all his history in song – for the language of a treacherous government which has constantly deceived Little Russia, for the language of that criminal woman who with one hand armed the *haydamaks*, while with the other she signed ukazes committing the Cossacks into bondage to her paramours? Is the Great Russian language in Western Russia[4] not the language of Tsar Nicholas, the language whose Cyril and Methodius are Bibikov and Semashko? Let our language first wash off all traces of servility, slavery, vulgar turns of phrase,

and the insolence of both sergeant and lord, and only then begin to teach our fellow men.[5]

These are the words of a man who loved his native Russian language and valued its greatness. But those who were implanting it among non-Russians and assuring them that it alone could bring them civilization were not knights of the Russian language but 'robber barons' of Nicholas's tongue. Likewise, those who today rejoice at the ten million Russified (in reality, more), at the mass switch in the national schools from their own language to Russian as the language of instruction, at the disappearance of entire nationalities (see below), are not knights of the Russian language and Russian culture but its hangers-on and enemies, the vanguard of tongue-tied and vulgar bureaucracy.

On the contrary, genuine workers in the field of Russian language and culture are becoming progressively more disturbed that the linguistic-national demoralization of other peoples is having a sad effect (and in fact cannot fail to have it) upon the Russian people. A profound concern about the gradual 'denationalization' and bureaucratization of the Russian language can be sensed in a number of articles on this fundamental issue by L. Leonov, K. Paustovsky, K. Chukovsky and others. A considerable response was evoked by V. Souloukhin's noble articles against the russifying zeal of certain 'people of other nationalities who have become Russified' and who 'overdo [the truly] Russian frame of mind'[6] and against the decline of folk customs and of everyday folk culture in *Russia Today* – not all Russians, especially educated Russians, as yet understand their concern, but more and more voices keep joining with them. More and more Russians will see what a threat hangs over their national language and culture as it is diluted by heterogeneous and chaotic admixtures.

Potebnya, too, rightly said that a nation which assimilated dozens of other nations ceased to be itself and would also bring 'the abomination of emptiness' upon itself. The first signs of this can already be observed today in such things as the Union-wide national vulgarity with its Philistine-bureaucratic cynicism and Volapuk which invades present-day variety shows, television and amateur art in all the Republics and is advancing ever more massively towards all spheres of culture.

But this is not the only evil. There is another, no smaller than the first. If dozens of nations in the USSR are to lose their languages and nationalities 'voluntarily', a very great deal of falsehood and injustice will be necessary. (For, indeed, in an atmosphere of truth and justice the very formulation of such a question and such an aim is senseless and absurd: that entire peoples should purposely renounce their language and their nationality ... Whatever for? and why? and for whose and for what benefit?) A very great deal of falsehood and injustice will be necessary regarding the past history of these peoples, regarding Marxism-Leninism, regarding the nature of communism, regarding the character of these processes which are taking place before our very eyes, regarding the values of human culture, regarding our needs for the future ... Will the burden of this untruth and injustice not press too heavily upon the shoulders of future generations? Will it be possible then to create that highly humane and moral atmosphere which we inevitably associate with communism? Can we arrive at truth through wrongdoing? These are questions which affect the future of all the nations of the USSR to an equal degree.

---

1 A.I.Herzen, 'Rossiya i Pol'sha', in *Kolokol. Izbrannyye stat'i A.I.Gertsena*, Geneva, 1887, p. 91.

2 I-r [Herzen], *Kolokol i Den'*. (Pis'mo k g. Kas'yanovu)', *Kolokol*, No. 167, 10 July 1863, p. 1375.

3 The Turgenev reference is to his poem in prose 'Russkiy yazyk' (1882).

4 That is, the colonized Polish and Ukrainian territories. 'Western Russia' included also the Byelorussian lands.

5 I-r [Herzen], 'Po povodu pis'ma iz Volyni', *Kolokol*, No. 116, 15 December 1861, p. 966.

6 Lenin, CW, XXXVI, p. 606.

12
The gap between theory and practice: covering up the tracks by deliberately false phraseology

'... We know perfectly well from our own experience that there is a difference between solving a problem theoretically and putting the solution into practice,' said Lenin at the VIII Congress of the RCP(B).[1]

He gave a special warning against the gap between theory and practice in the nationalities question, when the importance of this matter and the necessity of safeguarding the rights and the development of national minorities would receive merely formal recognition from people in practice governed by the reflexes of Russian GreatPower mania. Under Lenin's influence this was particularly stressed by delegates to the X and XII Party Congresses. Thus, Anastas Mikoyan said at the X Congress:

> ... At present the nationalities question ... is to be considered solely from the aspect of the practical implementation of the rights proclaimed by the Soviet Government ... At present it is not such a pressing matter in the borderlands whether there should be any Republics or not. There is not even any question of whether there is such a right or not, whether there is a right to the language, etc.

> These questions are not in dispute, only [the existing rights] are not being put into practice ...²

And here are analogous declarations by delegates to the XII Congress:

> On the theoretical plane the nationalities question does not give cause for any objections here. What our programme says, what the resolutions of the X Congress say, remains unshakable for all our comrades. But the theory, the programme, Comrades, is one thing, and the implementation of this programme and these resolutions is quite another.³

> The whole bourgeois and socialist world, and even more so the communist world, knows that our country represents Il'ich's school in the nationalities question, a school which has solved the nationalities question once and for all. We have been proud of this, we have looked at everyone with our heads held high and pointed out: look and learn how we can solve the nationalities question in our programme.
> We should have shown this in practice too. In this respect we have missed the mark. I contend that only because we have not succeeded in realizing our nationalities programme have the socalled deviations appeared ... I contend, Comrades, that many of our comrades have not rejected the nationalities programme in its present shape, they have not forgotten it but have simply put it aside. I happened to be present at one of the important sessions at which a Central Committee member declared the nationalities question to be a question of tactics for us.

That Central Committee member forgot that this is not a tactical but a programmatic question.[4]

We have earlier quoted speeches by M. Skrypnyk, D. Zatons'ky, H. Hryn'ko and others, who expressed profound concern as to whether it would be possible to carry out in practice the programme of national construction as planned, and to give real life to Lenin's nationalities policy, or whether this would be obstructed by GreatPower chauvinist sentiments, indifference to national matters, and practical national-liquidationism, accompanied by lip-service to the Leninist principles. As we now know, this concern was a kind of foreboding of that reversal of the nationalities policy, when seemingly 'Leninist' phraseology was still being partly used, while under cover of it a completely contrary policy of destroying national cadres and limiting national state construction was being pursued.

It must be said that in Khrushchev's time this traditional gulf between theory and practice was supplemented by a peculiar theoretical confusion which consisted in: using exceedingly oblique terms, a kind of 'camouflaging' jargon which never gave things their proper names but described them in such a puzzling way that one did not know what was really meant; characterizing a phenomenon not in coequal terms, but in terms that were the most 'convenient' at the particular juncture; subordinating objective data and perspectives to subjectivist pre-judgements; deliberately giving misleading 'labels' to phenomena and developments; in brief, in using public phraseology to conceal the real non-public policies.

We have already said that in our country nationalities problems are not analysed in depth – sociologically, statistically, etc.; instead everything stays circling in the realm of mere scholastic generalities. In this way we 'cover up' a whole series of very grave problems. Thus, in particular, contrary to Lenin, commonplaces about equality conceal the fact that many nations, particularly the Ukrainian nation, are falling behind in a number of important spheres of social activity, as we have already said before. Various formulas about the special, leading role of the Russian people, culture and language frequently conceal low-grade Russian nationalism pure and simple. We have already said enough about these and similar things.

But here I wish to draw attention to a few more examples of the shocking gap between theory and practice of intentional theoretical falsification.

We have mentioned earlier that although the Constitution of the USSR prohibits the preaching of national exclusiveness,[5] such preaching nevertheless takes place everywhere. From childhood, through school and throughout his life, the citizen of the USSR is pursued by assertions (in textbooks, lectures, newspapers, books and on the radio) about the special, exclusive role of the great Russian people in the historical, present and future destiny of all other peoples of the USSR and the former Russian Empire. All this cannot fail to reinforce the sometimes even unconscious national exclusiveness and superiority complex of many Russians – already evolved in tsarist times – and the national inferiority complex of other peoples. And myriad examples indicate that such complexes really do exist.

Apropos of this, in our country anything Russian is consistently rated above anything national: 'the Russian and national languages', *The Russian Language in the National School* is the name of a journal. In such cases Lenin used the expression *inonatsional'nyy* ('of another nation' or 'of other nations') to stress that the Russian language is also a national language, whilst Georgian, let us say, belongs to 'another nation' as compared with Russian. Children's textbooks of Russian language and literature are called: *Rodnaya rech'* [Our Native Language], *Rodnaya literatura* [Our Native Literature], while Ukrainian ones are simply called *Chytanka* [Reader]. For how many years have our pedagogues been fighting to get them called *Ridna mova* [Our Native Language] – all in vain! This smells of nationalism, they say ...

We have not only made Russian the ruling language in practice, since in most Republics virtually the whole of public and economic life, science and specialized education are conducted in it, but we have theoretically and officially proclaimed it to be the 'second native language of all the peoples of the USSR', 'the language of international communication', etc. Is this not an open violation of the Leninist principles: 'to ... annul all privileges for any one language'?[6]

Such is the official position of the Russian language; unofficially we have gone much farther. Unofficially the Russian language is for the majority of the public a mark of 'culture' and a means of getting on in the world; national languages, on the other hand, are a mark of being 'odd', backward and without prospects.

In literature, the press and social life, during every day and every hour, at every step, in unbelievable dosages, noticed and unnoticed, the notion is infused that the Russian language holds a very special position.

Here is a fragment from a typical report in *Pravda*:

> Many years ago the old Mirgasan brought his dearest son Farrukh to the prominent revolutionary Nariman Narimanov and said: 'Dear friend, make a man of the lad. May he learn the great language, Russian, and become a teacher.'
> For half a century Farrukh Akhundov has worked in the village school, energetically and selflessly instilling in the pupils and in his children a thirst for knowledge and an ardent love for the language of the Revolution.[7]

To the author and editors of *Pravda* and to many readers all this seems perfectly normal and natural, because it reflects the real state of affairs today. And this is the most frightening thing. Let us ponder these words (similar ones are written and said every day and every hour). First of all, the formula 'the great Russian language is the language of the Revolution', this formula, which our propaganda loves so much, is essentially an anti-communist formula. For one thing, it is copied from P.B. Struve's formula 'Capitalism speaks Russian'. In addition, it reflects the notion of the socialist revolution as being imported from Russia, being brought on the tips of Russian bayonets. Genuine communists strove for Revolution to be multilingual and to speak the language of every land and not an imported one. This is why the International was created, and this is why the International is called international. Secondly, the desire to 'become a man' with the help of 'the great language, Russian' does not attest to the greatness of the Russian language (there are other proofs of that) nor yet to internationalism, but to the national servility and degradation instilled by the colonial policy of Russian tsarism. Soviet power considered it to be its main duty to struggle against the consequences of this national corruption, to develop a feeling of dignity and importance in the national minorities, and it actually encouraged them first and foremost to learn their neglected native languages and to conduct educational work in their native tongues. The authors and editors of *Pravda* ought to know that.

The practice of building up, elevating and favouring the Russian language at the expense of the native languages of the peoples of the USSR has gone so far that declarations of a kind which even the official Russifiers of pre-revolutionary times did not often permit themselves have now become quite common and 'natural'.

This, for instance, is how the Secretary of the Daghestan Regional Committee of the Party, Doctor of Historical Sciences A. Abilov, 'argues' his proposed mass change-over in the schools to Russian as the language of instruction and how he justifies russification in general:

> A soldier, when he goes into battle, chooses from all the types of weapon the most accurate and the one with the greatest range. The Russian language is one of[!] the sharpest types of ideological weapon, and the better the non-Russian peoples know it, the more successfully will they be able to develop their economy and culture, their exchange of spiritual values.[8]

It would befit a Doctor of Historical Sciences to know the history of this question, to know what category of political figures in Russia used to advance analogous 'arguments', and to know that this has nothing to do with Marxism-Leninism. Marxism-Leninism never reduced the language problem to the level of a soldier's choice of ammunition. Marxism-Leninism saw mad chauvinism and racialism in unscientific 'theories' which made the prospect of any nation's successful economic and cultural development depend upon this nation's acquisition of another culture and language, or what is more, upon this nation's change-over to another culture and language. (As we shall see, it is precisely the latter that the Doctor of Historical Sciences and Secretary of the Regional Committee of the Party has in mind.) What sounds most hypocritical are Abilov's assurances that in the case of a complete realization of his programme 'the non-Russian peoples ... the more successfully will ... be able' not only 'to develop their ... culture', but even to carry out an 'exchange of spiritual values'. May I ask what 'spiritual values' they will 'exchange'? What spiritual values of their own will they be able to offer in exchange, if they have lost their language and culture and have changed over to Russian ones? They will simply disappear as peoples, as nations. And this Abilov himself demonstrates to us excellently as soon as he leaves the sphere of propagandistic falsifications, and passes to a description of certain real developments. Boasting of the successes of 'international education' in his field, he stresses that while according to the 1896 census there were 80 national groups in Daghestan, according to the 1959 census there were 'already only eleven'.

Abilov's internationalism is further developed along this line:

> After the adoption of the school law giving the parents the right to decide for themselves in what language the children shall receive instruction, in Daghestan one can feel a growing urge on their part to have their children study in Russian from the very first class. The Government of the Republic and the education authorities have met these desires and started primary classes with instruction conducted in the Russian language in all the rural districts. The number of such classes is growing. Now more than half of the primary pupils have changed over to the Russian language at the wish of the parents themselves. Instruction has been completely changed over to Russian for the children of the Rutul, Tsakhur and Agul national groups.[9]

As you see, at this rate Abilov will soon over-fulfil the plan 're internationalism', will put the 'national groups' entrusted to him into uniform, and instead of multilingual trouble will introduce yearned-for uniformity ... Just wait for the next census!

But can Abilov and others of his ilk claim the palm for being first in the field with such exploits of 'internationalism' and 'voluntariness'? We cannot but admit that he has strong rivals from the past. Long ago, admittedly – as far back as the nineteenth century. That was the time when the campaign 'for introducing Russian organic laws into all regions of the Russian state' was fashionable, with its touching 'internationalism':

> The local inhabitants composing Russia [!] for 130 years should know the Russian language;

> if they do not, with such measures[10] they soon
> will: necessity is the best teacher. *Nothing
> so unites the vanquished with the victors as
> unity of language*; from this unity springs
> the unity of our feelings and desires.[11]

That was the time when civilization advanced triumphant in Russia: 'Russia, our fatherland, the fatherland of twenty different tribes, whose blood' has mingled to form a single people, happily united under a *single* sceptre, is making great strides towards enlightenment: the common goal of mankind.[12] In that same blessed time a special tsarist commission 'on peasant affairs in the Polish Kingdom', where the national insurrection (1863–4) had just been put down, reported to Alexander II:

> A most important fact concerning peasant affairs
> in the Polish Kingdom consists in the successes
> of the Russian language in that land. In the
> section of the *Kielce* Commission on Peasant
> Affairs (about one thirteenth of the Kingdom)
> teaching of the Russian language has been intro-
> duced in 159 boys' and 3 girls' village schools.
> The peasants learn Russian with obvious will-
> ingness where the relations of the government
> representatives and institutions with district
> authorities take place in Russian. No national
> prejudice against the Russian language can be
> noticed among the peasants, on the contrary,
> bewilderment is caused when documents in
> the Polish language are received by the district
> offices from various administrative authorities ...

Further on we learn that in other localities the change-over of primary schools to the Russian language 'proceeds with positive success'.

Discussing this document, the well-known Slavophile and PanRussianist, I.S. Aksakov, whom we have already met, honestly describes these successes of russification as 'a living political fact of Russian rule'.[13]

It is very strange when present-day public figures propose the same methods and think in the same terms, only changing their phraseology and values slightly, and are not embarrassed by such uncanny historical parallels. They are not even embarrassed by the fact that these risky historical echoes cast doubts on the authenticity of their phraseology and their theoretical formulas and objectively unmask the real meaning of the latter. However, this is done even more effectively by reality itself.

Let us take as a further example the so-called 'theory of bilingualism', one of the current camouflages of russification.

The journal *The Russian Language in the National School*, which is one of the most assiduous official propagators of this theory (is it not shameful that certain present-day pedagogical 'theoreticians' are in the vanguard of those agitating for a crime against pedagogy, the crime of depriving children of instruction in their native language, and one actually denounced in its fundamentals by K.D. Ushinsky), writes in an editorial:

> One may assert that the Soviet people as a clearly defined historical community is characterized in respect of language by the development of a stable, durable and purely voluntary bilingualism ...
> A constantly growing number of parents send their children to Russian schools or raise the question of the change-over, in a greater or lesser degree, of national schools to the Russian language of instruction ...
> The use of the Russian language as the medium of instruction is at the present time

a growing tendency in the development of the national schools of our country. In the Russian SFSR the process of the voluntary change-over of national schools to the Russian language of instruction from a certain class upwards in accordance with the desire of the parents is even now proceeding very actively in most Autonomous Republics, Autonomous Regions and National Areas. At present in the schools of thirty-six nationalities of the Russian SFSR instruction is conducted in Russian from the V, IV, III, II or I classes upwards.[14]

Here everything is intentionally or unintentionally confused and falsified. First of all, it is not true that the Soviet people is characterized by bilingualism. Even if we were to accept the theory of bilingualism, we would have to define it more precisely: its authors are far from conferring the privilege of bilingualism on the whole Soviet people, but do so only on the non-Russian nations, while the Russian nation is condemned to monolingualism. How do these theoreticians expect to wriggle out of this 'unfair discrimination' against Russians? Perhaps they will also gladden the hearts of the Russian people with a second mother-tongue: Ukrainian, or Tartar, or even Buryat? After all, one has to justify the formula that bilingualism is the characteristic trait of the Soviet people!

Secondly, by what stretch of the imagination can *Russian*-language instruction be considered a mark of the development of a given *national* (for instance, Kazakh) school? This seems to be not only a new discovery in the theory of the nationalities question but also in elementary logic. Is it not obvious that by changing over to *Russian* as the medium of instruction, a school loses its *specific nationality* (Ukrainian, Tartar, Kazakh) and becomes Russian? It will be interesting to see what the journal *The Russian Language in the National School* (which, incidentally, in an ungentlemanly way goes beyond its competence when it advocates not the Russian language in national schools, as it is supposed to do, but the russification of these national schools) will be called when all the national schools have changed to Russian-language instruction.

And this time is probably not far off, judging by the facts relished by the journal (see above). These facts, as well as those cited in Abilov's article, totally expose the spuriousness of the theory of bilingualism. If I may be permitted the question, where is this *bilingualism*? This is a simple *monolingualism*, no longer of any given nationality but Russian.

The situation is the same in other spheres of cultural and social life. We hear much said officially about bilingualism, but in reality a single language, Russian, holds sway in official and social life.

We ask: why then this lip-service to a supposed 'bilingualism'?

But let us return once more to the schools. On 17 April 1959, the Supreme Soviet of the Ukrainian SSR issued a decree 'Concerning the Strengthening of the Ties Between School and Life and Concerning the Further Development of Public Education in the Ukrainian SSR'. In Article 9 we read: 'Instruction is conducted in the pupils' mother-tongue.' Exact, exhaustive and quite in the spirit of MarxistLeninist understanding of the nationalities question. But immediately afterwards there suddenly follows: 'Whether the children attend a school with one or another language of instruction, is decided by the parents.' May I ask what kind of a smokescreen this is? Has it not been said clearly enough: 'in the pupils' mother-tongue'? Why then such a crudely anti-pedagogical turnabout: 'is decided by the parents'? After all, this second proposition completely cancels out the first: the parents' decision is predetermined by the political line. The point is that this is precisely what is needed, hence the smokescreen. It was necessary to open the floodgates for the russification of the schools. 'Free decision', of course, 'the will of the parents'. But, if it may say so, neither of these have anything to do with it. A puzzle indeed: will a father send his child to a Ukrainian or to a Russian school, when he knows that later on, in university, his son or daughter will have to switch over to Russian anyway, when Russian will 'make a man' of you, as wrote the *Pravda* correspondent already quoted, whilst Ukrainian will only disgrace you (or as the rustics say: 'You might as well go back to the kolkhoz')? Truly a free decision! Then why should we be surprised at the statistics about the total change-over of schools to Russian-language instruction – 'at the request of the parents' – quoted in the journals *Political Self-Education* and *The Russian Language in the National School*? (Then there is also M. N. Mansvetov boasting in the journal *Problems of History*: 'In Karelia, after numerous requests from parents and pupils, the national [!] schools were changed over in 1958 to Russian-language instruction.') Let us recall the document quoted above: even a hundred years ago the Polish peasants switched to Russian voluntarily, and so did the Latvian peasants and others. And later, when the question of Ukrainian schools was discussed in the State Duma, there appeared a whole delegation of 'Ukrainian peasants' which declared that the Ukrainian peasantry neither understood nor wanted the Ukrainian language but instead understood and wanted the Russian language! – but at that time nobody had tried to call this 'internationalism' and 'Marxism-Leninism'. From the time that Marxists and Leninists first appeared on the historical scene they have always exposed similar phenomena and similar instances of sham 'free choice'. In that very same Duma the Bolshevik H. Petrovs'ky delivered a speech, written by Lenin, which exposed the whole deception and infamy of 'voluntary' russification.

But this is not yet all. Further on, Article 9 holds another great injustice. While in Ukrainian schools the study of Russian is compulsory, in Russian schools in Ukraine the study of Ukrainian is optional: 'depending on a sufficient demand on the part of parents and pupils'. (And further on, once more: if 'the parents and the pupils themselves have chosen this language for study'.)[15] Is this not outright discrimination against the Ukrainian language, an unconstitutional and anti-Leninist classification of languages as 'necessary' and 'unnecessary'? Just imagine someone making the study of chemistry or some other subject dependent upon 'a sufficient demand on the part of parents and pupils'; how many pupils in how many schools would be studying this subject?[16]

Let us cite another historical reference. In its resolution of 19 April 1927, the Central Committee of the CP(B)U ordered that study of the Russian language should be introduced into all schools in Ukraine (which at that time were not conceived otherwise than as becoming eventually 95 per cent Ukrainian) but simultaneously made a reservation on principle: 'However, under no circumstances may this be a cover for attempts to create for Russian culture the dominant position it held in Ukraine under tsardom.'[17]

Isn't there, to put it mildly, some contradiction between what was decided on principle in 1927 and what is done and said today?

Are there not other contradictions too? On the one hand, the resolution of the XII Congress of the RCP(B) that 'the administrative bodies of the national Republics and Regions should be composed mainly of local people who know the language, way of life, manners and customs of the respective peoples', as well as the resolutions of the X and XII Congresses about the training of cadres and professional, technical and other education in the language of the given Republics; and on the other hand what *Pravda* writes today: 'Any display of national separateness in the training and use of workers of various nationalities in the Soviet Republics is inadmissible.' *Pravda*'s formulation is very general and vague, but experience shows that similar formulas against 'separateness' are always brought forward with a definite purpose. These formulas are meant to 'prove' the impossibility of using Ukrainian as the language of instruction in the universities and other educational establishments of Ukraine. They are meant to justify the sending of graduates of Ukrainian universities and technical schools to work in Leningrad and Novosibirsk, whilst graduates in the same subjects are sent from those cities to Ukraine, surely a measure that runs counter to common sense and to the economic and cultural interests of Ukraine. These 'cross-hauls' create situations not unlike the one we have seen at the Kyiv Hydroelectric Station. Is this how truly mutual help with cadres is meant to be?

Here is one more – this time a classical – example of the falsification of theory from N.S. Khrushchev's speech at the XXII Congress:

> Complete unity of nations will be achieved as the full-scale building of communism proceeds ... We come across people, of course, who deplore the gradual obliteration of national distinctions. We reply to them: Communists will not conserve and perpetuate national distinctions. We will support the objective process of the increasingly closer rapprochement of nations and nationalities proceeding under the conditions of communist construction on a voluntary and democratic basis.[18]

What 'unity of nations' is meant here? After all, today there already exists complete unity between most socialist nations in the struggle for peace and the building of communism. Obviously, Khrushchev is speaking of unity but has amalgamation in mind, as his subsequent words prove. But this is a brutal revision of Lenin, who said that nations would exist not only during the period of the building of communism in one country, but for a whole historical era *after* the victory of communism on a *world-wide* scale.

And then: 'Communists will not conserve and perpetuate national distinctions.' This is a completely false formulation which diverts us from the heart of the matter. It is not a question of conservation and differentiation, it is a question of the all-round national development of peoples and their cultures, something for which true communists have always accepted responsibility and which pragmatic businessmen of Khrushchev's type have replaced with assimilation and denationalization.

Finally: 'We will support the objective process ... on a voluntary and democratic basis.' Again, falsification and hypocrisy. First of all, an objective process is a process that takes place by itself, independently of human intentions. But a process directed by the Party and the State (and this is said by Khrushchev and in countless official publications on this subject; e.g., the journals *Voprosy filosofii* [Problems of Philosophy] and *Politicheskoye samoobrazovaniye* [Political Self-Education] stress that the 'rapprochement' of nations is not a spontaneous process but one directed by the Party) is no longer an objectively proceeding but an intentionally induced and 'predetermined' one. Secondly, what sort of 'voluntariness' and democracy is it when the choice has been made beforehand by the leadership; voluntariness indeed if it follows a plan – a 'directed' voluntariness! If the leadership supports (and directs) the 'process', just try to come out against what the leadership supports (and directs)! And if you cannot come out against it (as indeed you cannot), where is 'voluntariness' and 'democracy'?!

In short, as the saying goes, a lie rides a lie, whipping it on with a lie! But the question is: in what cause is Marxism-Leninism being supplanted by time-serving lies or pseudo-theoretical verbiage?

The cynicism in the mendacious garbling of Leninism is reaching such a point that a Doctor (again a Doctor!) of Historical Sciences (again Historical Sciences!), the Party Secretary, not of the Daghestan, but of the L'viv Regional

Committee, and not Abilov, but V. Malanchuk, in his article 'The Power of Great Friendship' advances that purely racist thesis, which we have discussed above, about the Russian language being a 'powerful source of the economic and cultural development of all peoples' and attributes it ... to Lenin. But for some reason he fails to quote Lenin's words in this connection. For, being a 'Doctor' of Sciences, he knows full well that he is doing a piece of falsification, and that it is unthinkable that any such words, expressing a notion of the superiority of the Russian nation and language and the inferiority of others, should ever have passed the lips of Lenin. He knows full well that in reality Lenin said something totally different, namely that it was a harmful thing to force members of other nations to learn Russian, and that in a democratic Russia they would learn it of their own accord.[19] And let us note: in such cases Lenin always spoke about learning the Russian language and becoming familiar with it (which is quite understandable and doubtless necessary), and not about the replacement and displacement of the national languages, against which he spoke out indignantly.

The same V. Malanchuk writes:

> Our great leader, V.I. Lenin, stressed that 'already under capitalism, all economic, political and spiritual life is becoming more and more international. Socialism will make it completely international.'[20]
>
> This is a powerful objective process. To oppose it means to display national narrow-mindedness. In our country sometimes one meets with immature persons who oppose local interests to the interests of the whole State, who attempt to 'snatch' the largest possible slice of the common cake, to take as little part as possible in communal efforts, and to select cadres chiefly

according to nationality. Of course, there are only an insignificant minority of people like this, but to overlook their attempts and not to suppress them at once would be dangerous. The slightest slackening in the struggle against such manifestations could cause serious damage.[21]

As we see, the Doctor of Sciences expresses himself in such a 'code', in such a special jargon, in such 'allegorical' language, that it is not easy for the reader to make much sense of it. Such a 'style' is very fashionable just now, when certain people are afraid to call things by their proper names. But we know very well from experience that 'national narrow-mindedness' and 'local narrow-mindedness' mean the defence of the economic and other needs of the Republics against the excessive appetites of the super-centralists. We know very well that Lenin demanded effective safeguards to prevent the central agencies in Moscow from disregarding the needs of the Republics under various pretexts, and to prevent them from satisfying their own needs at the expense of 'local' needs. Lenin expressed himself sharply and unequivocally about this, suggesting without hesitation that, if it should prove impossible to defend 'local interests' from the centralizers' abuses, the very nature of the Union should be reexamined, preserving it 'only for military and diplomatic affairs'. We have already cited Lenin's relevant declarations.[22] V. Malanchuk, however, is governed by a diametrically opposite principle, and does not stop to think that a society in which 'local interests' and 'the interests of the whole state' are not seen as identical, but as contrary concepts, would be nothing but an unnatural bureaucratic formation, unfit for the main purpose of any state which is to satisfy those 'local interests' of which it is composed. This is precisely why Lenin would not tolerate such a state and demanded guarantees against the Union degenerating into such a one.

The same can be said about cadres. We do not know whom or what Malanchuk had in mind when he condemned the selection of cadres along national lines. If this was, let us say, a cleverly coded protest against the restrictions on the admittance of Jewish youth to universities, we wholeheartedly support this noble-minded protest against discrimination, although we would have liked Malanchuk to protest more openly. But it is not very likely that he was protesting against this. He probably wanted to say something else: that the 'cross-hauls' from Kyiv to Sverdlovsk, from Sverdlovsk to Kyiv, etc., should be stepped up even more. Therefore we must remind him that Lenin demanded the exact opposite: the training of local national cadres in order to develop the economy and culture of the Republics.

As we see, V. Malanchuk mentions Lenin only in order to camouflage anti-Leninist ideas by invoking his name. All of Malanchuk's verbal stratagems are engendered by the wish to conceal and to justify russification, over-centralization and the tacit liquidation of the sovereignty of the Republics. How might Lenin be exploited for this purpose? Malanchuk shows the way. First you have to keep silent about certain documents in which Lenin says clearly and precisely the exact opposite of what the Malanchuks need today. Secondly, you do some shameless falsification, without blushing even a little bit, on other utterances of Lenin's. Lenin speaks of the internationalization of the economic, political and spiritual life of humanity, that is to say, of the interconnection and interdependence of the economic, political and spiritual life of all the nations of the world, of a growing interaction between all groups of humanity – Malanchuk, however, substitutes his principle of all principles: the amalgamation of all the nations of the Union with the Russian nation, and in particular the national dissolution of Ukraine into Russia.

Here it is relevant to draw attention especially to a very common and very treacherous falsification of Lenin. In Lenin's writings there are indeed several statements in favour of the amalgamation of nations. But by amalgamation Lenin meant precisely internationalization in the above sense, that is to say, socio-political unity and rapprochement and a dialectic interaction of nations. This, at least, is how communists throughout the world understand him.

> The aim of socialism, to repeat Lenin, is not only 'to bring nations closer to each other, but also to merge them'.[23] But this merging is viewed not mechanically as the destruction of differences, but dialectically as their mutual stimulation and cross-fertilization.[24]

This has nothing in common with the russifying 'conception' of the highly paid 'Tashkentian gentlemen' and 'Doctors of Sciences' of Malanchuk's and Abilov's ilk.

Secondly, we know that Lenin visualized such a 'dialectic' amalgamation in the distant future: *after* the triumph of the second phase of socialism – communism – on a *world-wide* scale.

Thirdly, Lenin spoke of a spontaneous process of gradual amalgamation which would take place naturally over a long historic period, as a stage of the general evolution of humanity. But what our leaders have in mind is quite different and the exact opposite: a planned and state-managed amalgamation, a clearly outlined process directed from above by appropriate measures, in essence a supplanting of many nationalities, languages and cultures by a single one. What Lenin had in mind was a natural historic evolution of humanity; what is being effected in our country is the artificial russification and emasculation of dozens of nations, in short, the very thing that Lenin fought against.

In recent times *Pravda*, in an attempt to justify the present nationalities policy, has begun to appeal increasingly to supposed laws of economic development which allegedly require a hastened amalgamation of the nations and raise to the level of the greatest good the consistent disregard of their national rights, needs and basic interests. (All these are dismissed with lordly arrogance as 'localism', survivals', etc.) But the Manifesto of the Communist International (adopted at the I Congress of the Comintern, 2–6 March 1919) even then rejected such a feudal-bureaucratic conception of the structure and nature of the future socialist world economy, guaranteed the independence of every people in the economic-cultural world complex, and stressed that such an independence could not harm the cause of unity but was mutually compatible with it. The proletarian revolution 'will enable the weakest and least numerous people to manage the affairs of its national culture freely and independently, without any harm to the unified and centralized European and world economy'.[25]

This 'single economy' which bureaucrats use to intimidate 'nationalists' was not conceived of by Lenin as a nationless economy directed from Moscow or Berlin, but as a universal, multinational whole, 'regulated by the proletariat of all nations'.[26]

There is a lot of talk in our country about the further rapprochement of nations. Rapprochement and mutual enrichment are such undeniably admirable things that we can only welcome them. This means that peoples and cultures become progressively better acquainted with each other, exchange their best spiritual attainments more and more intensively, open up to each other more sincerely, cooperate more closely and purposefully, indirectly modifying and strengthening each other whilst at the same time remaining themselves. In short, rapprochement and mutual enrichment means mutual support, it means many different nations advancing shoulder to shoulder towards a common goal, so that on the day of arrival all will be there – not just one.

However, it is difficult to apply the term 'mutual enrichment' to a process in which one culture and language dislodges another, and in which, in concrete terms, the Russian culture and language are gradually supplanting the Ukrainian more and more, as we have already said. It is even more difficult to apply the term 'mutual enrichment of peoples' to a process in which some of the peoples concerned have already disappeared, some are disappearing, whilst others are tangibly losing their human potential. Perhaps we should not call this 'mutual enrichment' but engulfment or assimilation, chiefly assimilation of others by the Russian nation. We have already cited eloquent data from the current press. Here is the evidence of a solid scholarly work, *The Peoples of the European Part of the USSR*, published in two volumes in Moscow in 1964.

The 1897 census calculated the number of Russians at 55,400,300, the 1959 census – at 114,113,600.

> In the period from 1897 to 1959 the number of Russians on the territory of the USSR has more than doubled. This above-average increase of the total Russian population may be partly explained by the amalgamation of certain groups of other nationalities, in particular of the rather numerous groups of the Ukrainian populations on the Kuban' and in the Northern Caucasus.[27]

As regards the latter we can only add that this 'amalgamation' took place in fact in our own times. Its decisive period was from 1933 to 1937, when Ukrainian cultural-educational centres and schools on the Kuban' and in the Northern Caucasus were dispersed by the Terror, and those people who defended the Ukrainian character of the local population (in fact, Ukrainian) were wiped out. Ever since, many people have even been afraid to admit to being Ukrainians ...

Interesting testimony as to when the relative numbers of Ukrainians decreased so sharply – as it turns out, precisely in the period of the 'unprecedented flowering' of the Ukrainian nation – may be found in the article by V.M. Kabuzan and

G.P. Makhnova, 'The Numbers and Relative Position of the Ukrainian Population on the Territory of the USSR from 1795 to 1959':

> While in the period from 1795 to 1897 the relative number of Ukrainians remained almost unchanged (falling slightly from 22.08 per cent to 21.63 per cent), in the period from 1897 to 1959 it dropped by 3.43 per cent (from 21.63 per cent to 18.20 per cent), although in the 1959 census we have based ourselves on the data for nationality, not for native language.[28]

By language, the decrease is even greater. 'In the period from 1897 to 1959 the relative number of Ukrainians indicating Ukrainian as their mother-tongue has decreased by 6.01 per cent,' and Ukrainians by language constitute by now only 15.62 per cent of the population of the USSR. 'In the period from 1897 to 1959 the relative number of Ukrainians among other East Slav peoples has reduced very noticeably (from 29.90 per cent to 20.63 per cent).'[29]

Are these not eloquent figures?

A number of other nationalities of the USSR do not find themselves in a better situation. Thus the work quoted, *The Peoples of the European Part of the USSR*, attests that 'during the period 1939–59 the absolute number of Mordvins has even dropped by 12 per cent as a result of certain groups of them being assimilated by the Russians'. Today in their own Republic 'the Mordvins amount to slightly over one-third of the population. Even more striking[!] is the example of the Karelians, who constitute only 13 per cent of the population of their Republic.' The absolute number of Karelians has decreased by 25 per cent, the number of Bashkirs by 47 per cent, that of Kalmucks by 79 per cent, of Latvians by 2 per cent, of Estonians by 1 per cent, of Jews by 67 per cent (also as a result of fascist genocide), etc.[30]

THE GAP BETWEEN THEORY AND PRACTICE

It is important to note that in addition to the millions of non-Russians who already consider themselves completely Russian, the 1959 census established a transition group of 10.2 million people who still indicated their own nationality but already considered Russian their native language. 'Groups of people who have changed their language, in course of time usually also change their ethnic (national) identity.'[31] Thus, linguistic russification is the first stage of ethnic russification.

In official *communiqués* on the census results and in current propaganda these 10.2 million are described as a great success of our nationalities policy and of the friendship of the peoples of the USSR. Let us consider this formula calmly. It implies: that the friendship of nations is synonymous with russification;[32] that the aim of our nationalities policy is in the final analysis again russification;[33] and, finally, that tens of millions who have not yet acknowledged Russian as their native language are not yet mature enough to participate in the genuine 'friendship of nations' and to understand the nationalities policy, otherwise they would have gladdened the hearts of the appropriate authorities with a figure of, let us say, 50 million. This, of course, would have been a much bigger 'success' than 10.2 million Russified people. Thus these people are in a certain sense as yet ignorant, second-rate citizens, while those who have exchanged their mother-tongue for Russian are 'preferable'. All this follows inevitably from the official thesis that the 10.2 million non-Russians who have acknowledged Russian as their native language are a 'great success' of our nationalities policy and of the friendship of nations.

Even some of the apologists of 'bilingualism' are forced to admit this is only a transition stage, only a means of reaching the goal of 'language unity'. (Thus, we are the only society in the world which sets itself the goal of wiping out dozens of national languages and replacing them by a single one.) And so N.V. Mansvetov, after giving abundant and clearly irrelevant praise to 'bilingualism', which is supposed to 'contribute' to the development of national languages(!), is forced to admit that 'the road to language unity leads through the widespread acquisition of one of the most prevalent national languages, which under Soviet conditions is the Russian language'.[34]

No matter how many twists you give it, however eloquent you wax, to however unprecedented and unparalleled a flowering you lead the national languages and cultures, the result is the same: the changeover of all the nations of the USSR to the Russian language in the name of 'unity', which for some reason (??) cannot be conceived of without 'language unity'.

Thus, the terms 'amalgamation' and 'assimilation' used by some authors (as in *The Peoples of the European Part of the USSR*) correspond more to reality, to the actual crux of the matter, than the undeniably more pleasant-sounding and desirable 'rapprochement' and 'mutual enrichment', just as the formula 'replacement of national languages by one common language' used by Tsameryan in the article already quoted[35] is more honest than the touching but false 'bilingualism'.

This reluctance to call a spade a spade results in much being obscure to many. Here, for instance, comes a request for an explanation from young Donbas miners. You might think everything has already been explained to them: so many lectures are given about the rapprochement of nations and about bilingualism. And yet it is not clear to them.

To the Editors of Pravda

Dear Editors! We are interested in the question of the development of the Ukrainian language and in this connection in the policy of the Party regarding the Ukrainian language. Should it develop or disappear? We would like to hear an opinion on this from someone in the Institute of Linguistics of the Academy of Sciences of the Ukrainian SSR and someone in the ideological section of the Central Committee of the CPSU. Let them write in the newspaper. It seems to us that this is of interest to many readers, but if it cannot be done in the newspaper, let them explain it in a personal letter to us. Don't take us for some sort of socialist nationalists or chauvinists. The point is that the Ukrainian language and nationality are really in a contradictory position. And they should be pushed one way or the other, depending on what the laws of social development demand.

In the future there will be a single common language on earth and there will be no national divisions. So, perhaps, the Ukrainian people will be the first to lose its language and other national characteristics. This could happen straight away if the remaining schools are switched to Russian-language instruction, and literature will fall away by itself, since nobody will be using the Ukrainian language any more. And since the Party pursues this course, the change-over to the Russian language for communication and instruction should really begin in the elementary school to make it easier for young people to change over after finishing school, since in Ukraine establishments of higher education and technical schools have teaching in Russian and all the rest is completely or mainly based on the Russian language.

Why has nothing been said up to now in the press about this? After all, in the present state of Ukrainian culture, which draws less and less on the resources of national originality, can you call it Ukrainian at all, if it bases itself less and less on the Ukrainian language? A Ukrainian should feel ashamed and unworthy before other nations, since there are almost no contemporary national achievements to be proud of. On the other hand, you can't say that the Ukrainian people have no talent, because the facts testify to the great contribution of Ukrainians in the creation of Russian culture both in Ukraine and in Russia.

But to get us out of this situation, one should discuss this more widely and not leave Ukrainians unsettled. It seems you can be a Ukrainian and not know the Ukrainian language. This is unworthy and shameful. Such a man has no feeling of patriotism. He should not bear the name Ukrainian. But it seems to us that only a man who loves his people can be a true internationalist. To admit to the *assimilation of the Ukrainian nation would today be much more decent than to speak about the Ukrainian people and not hear the Ukrainian language. After all, if the population of Ukraine loses its language it has no right to be called the Ukrainian people.*

All in all, one could still write very, very much about the contradictions in the situation of the Ukrainian language, which everybody knows perfectly well. We would only like this question to be more definite and clearer. If the time for the final russification of the Ukrainian people has come, we should actively work in that direction. If not, we should adopt decisive measures to support the development of the Ukrainian language. It seems to us that both courses will receive the support of the people. However, you could ask the question in the newspaper. But Ukrainian culture can only become original, rich and lofty, and can only satisfy all the needs of the people and hold its own against its replacement by Russian culture, if the Ukrainian language is introduced in all establishments of higher education, in all schools including technical, in offices and organizations, as is proper for a national Republic. Then the native language will become the primary state language. But it seems to us that this is impossible to carry out, since the languages are closely related and there is such a high percentage of Russians in Ukraine. Besides, these Russians are real patriots of their culture and language. There are also many other factors, and still it is not clear to us whether it is right to feel certain of the one way and not the other. For instance, we would like to speak Ukrainian, but we don't know whether this will be correct. Won't this be a survival of the past, won't we slow down the correct march of development, won't we do harm to internationalist feelings? Yet we love all nationalities, including our own Ukrainian one.

N.V. Yankovs'ky, N.I. Pavlyuchenko – miners

Pravda handled this letter as countless letters of the same kind are handled everywhere. It sent it to another department, so that the latter could pass it on to an even lower department, until it got lost somewhere for all eternity ... And indeed, what can you answer to such ingenuousness, which for some reason refuses to be content with elastic commonplaces and 'camouflage tales' and insists on a straight answer: should there be a Ukrainian language 'with all the ensuing consequences', or should there not be a Ukrainian language, also 'with all the ensuing consequences'. And this ingenuousness does not even suspect what a sore spot its unsanctioned curiosity has happened unintentionally to touch upon ...

1   Lenin, *CW*, XXIX, p. 206.
2   X *s'yezd RKP(B)*, p. 206.
3   XII *s'yezd RKP(B)*, p. 515.
4   Ibid., pp. 495–6.
5   Article 123.
6   Lenin, *CW*, XX, p. 224. (Lenin's italics.)
7   L. Tairov, 'Desyat' – i vse molodtsy!' *Pravda*, 14 January 1965, p. 4.
8   A. Abilov, 'Nekotoryye voprosy internatsional'nogo vospitaniya', *Politicheskoye samoobrazovaniye*, No. 7, July 1964, p. 86.
9   A. Abilov, 'Nekotoryye voprosy internatsional'nogo vospitaniya', *Politicheskoey samoobrazovaniye*, No. 7, July 1964, pp. 80, 86.
10 'The conducting of all business in the Russian language.'
11 'O neobkhodimosti vvesti vo vsekh guberniyakh i oblastyakh Imperii russkiye organicheskiye zakony', *Chteniya*, 1865, III (July–September), Section 5, p. 181.
12 V. N. Karazin, 'Ob uchonykh obshchestvakh i periodicheskikh sochineniyakh v Rossii', *Russkaya starina*, III, 1871, p. 330.
13 I. S. Aksakov, 'O prepodavanii russkogo yazyka v shkolakh Tsarstva Pol'skogo', in his *Polnoye sobranye sochineny*, III, Moscow, 1886, pp. 454–6.
14 'Sblizheniye natsiy i russkiy yazyk', *Russkiy yazyk v natsional'n shkole*, No. 6, 1963, pp. 4–5.

15 'Zakon pro zmitsnennya zv'yazku shkoly z zhyttyam i pro dal'shyy rozvytok systemy narodnoyi osvity v Ukrains'kiy RSR', *Radyans'ka Ukraina*, 19 April 1959, p. 2.
16 Unlike the practice in this country, there are as a rule no optional subjects in Soviet secondary school syllabuses. All pupils study chemistry, physics, biology, mathematics, history, etc.; the only major choice exists in modern European languages, where the pupil has, as a rule, to choose one of the following: English, French, or German. Even this choice is restricted, particularly in the smaller schools, owing to the fact that for economic reasons only one foreign language teacher is appointed.
17 *Kul'turne budivnytstvo v Ukrains'kiy RSR* ..., I, Kyiv, 1959, p. 348.
18 N.S. Khrushchev, *On the Communist Programme*, Moscow, 1961, p. 88.
19 Cf. Lenin, *CW*, XX, pp. 20–21.
20 Lenin, *CW*, XIX, p. 246.
21 V. Malanchuk, 'Sila velikoy druzhby', *Pravda*, 16 December 1965, p. 2.
22 Lenin, *CW*, XXXVI, p. 610. Cf. pp. 104, 150–51 above.
23 Cf. Lenin, *CW*, XXII, p. 146.
24 H. Selsam, *Socialism and Ethics*, London, 1947, p. 187.
25 *Kommunisticheskiy Intematsional v dokumentakh*, 1919–32, Moscow, 1933, p. 57.

26 Lenin, *CW*, XXXI, p. 147. (Italics by the author.)
27 *Narody yevropeyskoy chasti SSSR*, I, Moscow, 1964, pp. 22–3.
28 Kabuzan and Makhnova quote their 1959 census figures for the territory within the 1795 boundaries, i.e., without the West Ukrainian lands.
29 V. M. Kabuzan and G. P. Makhnova, 'Chislennost' i udel'nyy ves ukrainskogo naseleniya na territorii SSSR v 1795–1959 gg.', *Istoriya SSSR*, No. 1, January–February 1965, pp. 34–6.
30 *Narody yevropeyskoy chasti SSSR*, I, pp. 23–4.
31 B.Ts. Urlanis (ed.), *Naseleniye mira; spravochnik*, Moscow, 1965, p. 213.
32 If the renunciation of one's native language and the indication of Russian as one's native language is a success of the friendship of peoples.
33 Otherwise, why should the 10.2 million of those non-Russians who acknowledge Russian as their native language be stressed as a special success of this policy?
34 Mansvetov, op. cit., p. 51.
35 I.P. Tsameryan, 'Velikaya Oktyabr'skaya sotsialisticheskaya revolyutsiya i korennoye izmeneniye natsional'nykh otnosheniy V SSSR', *Voprosy filosofii*, No. 5, September–October 1957, p. 65.

13
The national question is simultaneously a social and a universal historic question

It is wrong to oppose social problems to national problems on the pretext that the former are more important and immediate. National problems are always social problems as well, problems of political class strategy. This has always applied to the Ukrainian question. Furthermore, there is the sphere of foreign policy, about which the v Congress of the Comintern declared: 'The Ukrainian question is one of the most important national questions in Central Europe, and its solution is dictated by the interests of the proletarian revolution in Poland, Romania and Czechoslovakia, as well as in all neighbouring countries.'[1] Naturally, the international importance of the Ukrainian question has grown even more, not only in connection with socialist construction in the neighbouring countries of Europe but also in connection with the revolutionary movement and national construction in Asia and Latin America.

But at present we ought also to consider the internal social aspect of the Ukrainian national question.

Lenin and the Party always stressed how important it was for the proletariat and for socialist construction to resolve the conflict that exists in Ukraine between the Ukrainian-speaking peasantry and the predominantly Russian-speaking proletariat, between the Ukrainian village and the russified city. This in particular is the meaning of the policy of ukrainization. The proletariat, the industrialized city, were to become the active bearers of Ukrainian culture and on this basis to strengthen their alliance with, and their leadership of, the peasantry. Thus the Ukrainian nation should have become a fully-fledged socialist nation in its own right and not some sort of underdeveloped embryo, some ethnographic raw material that carries unforeseen complications for the future. The Ukrainian nation should have unfolded its strength in the proud creation of a socialist statehood ...

Unfortunately, today we can only observe a gap, which is, if anything, wider, between the Ukrainian-speaking village and the Russian-speaking city. Only a total lack of political responsibility can allow us to contemplate this calmly and not notice those complex social clashes which, sadly enough for socialism, are produced by this linguistic and national conflict between the village and the city in Ukraine.[2]

I am sure that in the foreseeable future a Marxist economist and sociologist, analyzing the reasons for our present difficulties in agriculture, is bound to find amongst them the morbid abnormalities in the relations between the village and the city, the social-cultural inferiority complex of the village, the manifold contempt for the village and for village people (not formally, in the official press, but actually, in real life) complicated and intensified in Ukraine by the national factor, the painful national difference between the Ukrainian village and the russified city. A thoughtful and subtle analysis would probably establish that a sense of doom hanging over the nation, the lack of national prospects and of national growth beyond the village boundaries, the denationalizing pressure 'from above', from the city, do not rank least among the factors making for that drop in vitality, that demoralization, indifference to life and drunkenness, which you can often observe among the rural population and which in themselves are a serious social problem.

Likewise, the future sociologist will also note the demoralizing influence of the linguistic-national conflict between the city and the village upon the city itself. Thus the city develops, noticed or unnoticed, certain phenomena and attitudes linked with its objectively colonizing, assimilating and 'consumer' position among the indigenous ethnographic 'raw material'. It loses the sense of kinship with its country and with the surrounding people. The consciousness of its responsibility and duties towards them gets extinguished, and there develops instead a feeling of 'freedom' from these responsibilities, of 'liberation' from all traces of descent, in short, of national denudation. As a result, it is ready to grab at any 'stylish' costume: there is a gaudy semi-culture with claims to raciness – 'the abomination of emptiness'. There develop reflexes of irresponsibility and indifference and a hidden or obvious boorishness (including the notorious: 'Hey, you, kolkhoznik!', 'What's the matter, are you a kolkhoznik?',[3] 'Forgive him, he is from the village', 'First learn to speak like a human being', etc., etc., as we know only too well).

Can there be any talk of developing attitudes of collectivism and fraternity, of being conscious that we are each one of us a man among humanity? Let in particular our honourable humanists finally give this some thought, our 'members of humanity' from the 'allRussian intelligentsia' in Ukraine, who like to talk about the universally human principle but actually themselves contribute to the creation of an atmosphere in which a person's dignity and his whole being can be so crudely trampled down, thereby giving rise to innumerable human dramas. 'If a man say, I love God, and hateth his brother, he is a liar ...'[4]

Whenever a nation is split into two linguistically, with the 'lower' stratum speaking its original language, while the 'higher' stratum speaks another, acquired tongue, this always threatens to create a great social problem and danger. Once when Herzen was in Brussels, he pointed out that the 'educated' section of the Belgians spoke French, while the common people, whom the former despised, spoke Flemish. Herzen saw in this an enormous injustice and danger to democracy: 'This cleavage of peoples into two strata – the one bathed in light and floating like oil over the depth of the second stratum, deep and dark and enveloped in mist – has caused all revolutions to fail.' And with great penetration Herzen passes to the Ukrainian question, with a warning against the seemingly successful linguistic expansion, russification. 'Rather than conquering the South Russian[5] people linguistically, let us begin, gentlemen, with the restitution of their land, and then we will see what language they will choose for speaking and learning.'[6]

Take a close look today at who speaks Ukrainian and who speaks Russian in Ukraine. If you are an honest person, if you can see and interpret what you have seen, if truth is more valuable to you than your blindness and your prejudices, than 'mighty rank and miserable greed', you cannot fail to admit that the linguistic division in Ukraine coincides with social and social-cultural divisions. And will your heart not bleed and your soul ache for 'the insulted and the injured'?

And do not the figures quoted earlier – about the actual dropping behind and disadvantageous position of the Ukrainian nation in a number of decisive spheres of social activity – point to grave social problems that require special investigation?

Finally, national problems have a bearing upon the problems of socialist democracy and interact with them. The rights and liberty of the individual are closely linked with national rights and liberty, just as the dignity and self-consciousness of the individual are linked with national dignity and self-consciousness, since rights, liberty, dignity and self-consciousness are indivisible concepts. National problems bear directly upon the problems of self-government and sovereignty of the people. National development and national diversity are the same as the spontaneity and variety of life, its eternal unfolding and enrichment, while, conversely, a purposeful state-controlled levelling, amalgamation and swallowing-up of nations – all the more, if this happens according to despotic design – is a triumph of obtuse bureaucratic uniformity, regimentation and deadliness. For this reason alone, the processes of denationalization and russification are an immense drag upon the cause of socialist democratism and have an objectively reactionary significance.

Besides, such processes impoverish communist society tremendously and make for irretrievable losses. We say that the national question is subordinated to the class struggle, that it is part of the general question of the struggle for communism. Communism leads to the maximum material and spiritual wealth of humanity, to the development of all its powers and potential, to the preservation and proliferation of all its attainments. Thus we must value the amazing riches left to us in the national multiformity of humanity and the diversity of its national activity, which make the great miracle of human universality. We must value this and develop it. The contrary policy – a policy of squandering, debasing, 'writing off' these riches as scrap, a policy of bureaucratic standardization and 'reduction to a common denominator' – is a crime before communism, and future generations will not forgive us such a bankrupted heritage.

---

1   Ye. Girchak [Hirchak], *Na dva fronta v bor'be s natsionalizmom*, 2nd edn, Moscow–Leningrad, 1931, pp. 213–14.
2   Then there is the aspect of everyday life and its culture which also has its importance: is there anyone who does not know how much humiliation and mockery from the petty-bourgeois public has to be endured, let us say, by a village woman who has come to the city on business. A man from the village, a Ukrainian from the village, why, any Ukrainian who is conscious of being a Ukrainian feels in the cities of Ukraine as in a foreign country, 'in our land, yet not our own', to use Shevchenko's words (his *Povne zibrannya tvoriv u shesty tomakh*, II, Kyiv, 1963, p. 9; an English translation in his *Selected Works*, Moscow, 1964, p. 187).
3   Kolkhoznik: collective farmer (here pejoratively).
4   The I John iv 20 quotation has added connotations in the Ukrainian context, for it appears as an epigraph over Shevchenko's 'Epistle' (his *Selected Works*, Moscow, 1964, p. 173).
5   Ukrainian.
6   I-r [Herzen], 'Po povodu pis'ma iz Volyni, *Kolokol*, No. 116, 15 December 1861, p. 966.

14
The government of the Ukrainian SSR as the spokesman of national integrality; its responsibility for the nation

Throughout the world, Communist Parties consider themselves the spokesmen for their peoples' national interests. And if the French communists inscribe on their banner the famous words of their hero, Paul Vaillant-Couturier, 'We continue France',[1] why should Ukrainian communists not follow their example and say: 'We continue Ukraine'?

Somehow not a single socialist nation (beyond the boundaries of the USSR) shows any desire to disappear from the face of the earth, to liquidate itself (through an ever-growing 'rapprochement', to be sure!) in order to please the degree-holding Abilovs and Malanchuks with their police-like 'internationalism'.

On the contrary, each one of them wants to consolidate itself and develop as fully as possible, each one of them wants, in its own way, to be a model for others, each joins in the universal 'competition' between socialist nations for individual historic 'self-expression' and unique economic-cultural historic creativity. And this 'competition' for a good communist national 'name' is led by the Communist Parties of all these countries.

> In the field of culture there are, in ability, no small and great nations. There are no superior and inferior peoples. Every people, no matter how small they may be, can make their contribution to the general treasure-store of culture. Our nation is small, ours is a small country. We are so much the more interested in qualifying ourselves, because we cannot boast, neither today nor even ten years from now, of such industry and wealth as the big countries possess. But we can and we must be able to boast of a sense of inner culture, to create highly artistic examples of art and in general in the field of science, and in this respect our people too can set examples and serve as models to many other nations.[2]

Will the leaders of Soviet Ukraine (a great people of forty million!) ever be capable of saying anything remotely similar, of saying that history holds something better in store for the Ukrainian nation than 'voluntary' self-liquidation to rounds of applause?!

We know from numerous declarations made by both governments and parties in the socialist countries of Europe and Asia that they consider themselves the spokesmen of their peoples, safeguarding their national interests, and see it as their greatest international duty to assure the fullest development of their peoples' economies and material and spiritual cultures, deeming this to be their most practical contribution to the common cause of Communism. Quite naturally, in keeping with the spirit of Marxism and Communism, these governments and parties consider anything damaging to the economy, culture, prestige or dignity of their nations as a negative factor both for other countries and for the whole international cause of communism. If in any one of these countries – Poland, Hungary, Bulgaria, etc. – one were to observe a relative numerical decrease of the nation, or the assimilation of a great part of its population, or linguistic-national conflicts between city and village, or the national language in an unsatisfactory position, or a decline of national culture, or a lack of the most essential literature in the national language, or a relatively low proportion and quality of national cadres, or something similar – the government of such a country would no doubt be profoundly disturbed and would most assuredly take decisive measures to rescue its people from such a national crisis.

However, nobody can tell how the Government of the Ukrainian Soviet Socialist Republic reacts to just such a situation,[3] the one in which its nation finds itself within the Soviet Union, a Union created for the very purpose of safeguarding the interests – including the national interests – of each Republic.

Back in 1913 Lenin wrote in his 'Critical Remarks on the National Question':

> Lastly, it is beyond doubt that in order to eliminate all national oppression it is very important to create autonomous areas, however small, with entirely homogeneous populations, towards which members of the respective nationalities scattered all over the country, or even all over the world, could gravitate, and with which they could enter into relations and free associations of every kind. All this is indisputable, and can be argued against only from the hidebound, bureaucratic point of view.[4]

Today we have not a mere autonomous district, but our own national state with our own national government; however, this government is unconcerned about the preservation of the national ethnic composition of its country's population (the percentage of Ukrainians in Ukraine, especially Ukrainians by language, keeps steadily falling); it does not care about the national-cultural profile of the Republic, or about providing it with national cadres; it shows no concern for the safeguarding of the national interests of many millions of Ukrainians in other Republics of the Union (as the governments of the Baltic Republics do partially, at least, by supporting, for instance, national student associations in Moscow, whilst Ukrainians have not been allowed to do the same); it does nothing to attract 'members of the respective nationalities scattered ... all over the world', as does socialist Poland for instance (a Ukrainian in the USSR does not even know anything about the political and cultural life of millions of working Ukrainians abroad). A remote and unbelievable past seems to enfold us as we learn about those times when the Plenum of the Central Committee of the CP(B)U, defending the rights of the Ukrainian republican bodies against the overcentralizing tendencies of the Moscow authorities, made such decisions:

> ... To charge the Politbureau actively to investigate all the facts known about breaches of the Constitution and its incorrect implementation on the part of the Union People's Commissariats and other central authorities, raising this question in the Central Committee of the CPSU(B), and also to continue work on the subject of uniting within the Ukrainian SSR all neighbouring territories with a Ukrainian majority in their population forming part of the Soviet Union.[5]

Or the times when you would hear in a report to the X Congress of the CP(B)U:

> We set ourselves the task and we raise the question before the CPSU(B) about the unification of the Ukrainian state as regards the Kursk region, the western part of the Voronezh

region, etc. The national needs of this Ukrainian population ... are not being adequately met.⁶

Or those times when at the XII Congress of the RCP(B) M. Skrypnyk raised the question of the seven million Ukrainians in the Russian SFSR:

> Ukrainians in the Soviet Union not only occupy the territory of the Ukrainian Soviet Socialist Republic, but are also distributed over the territories of the remaining Republics, reaching over seven million in the Russian SFSR. Let us see how those seven million are provided for ... we have ... only 500 schools with Ukrainian as the medium of instruction and then only two technical schools at the secondary level, and at present the existence of these schools is uncertain ... I don't think that such a percentage satisfies the cultural-educational needs of that Ukrainian population and can in any way be considered satisfactory. Obviously, here our practice is divorced from our theory. In this question our theses must be properly embodied into living reality.⁷

Today, forty-two years later, there is no question of schools and technical schools – this is an 'ultranationalist' daydream. But could not the Government of the Ukrainian SSR at least see to it that the millions of Ukrainians outside the boundaries of Ukraine, in the Russian SFSR, receive a modest number of Ukrainian newspapers, magazines, books and radio broadcasts? (After all, the Russians on the territory of the Ukrainian SSR are perfectly well provided with the press and literature, which is not only imported from Russia but is also published extensively in Ukraine. They are likewise provided with schools and higher education in the Russian language.) For the time being, in spite of long-standing demands from the

Writers' Union of Ukraine, the total result is that a few small libraries, collected by the writers themselves, have been sent to the Virgin Lands and to some Kuban' schools ...

The government of Ukraine cannot even settle such trifles as the following. In socialist Poland and socialist Czechoslovakia, the small number of Ukrainians living there publish a good number of books and periodicals in Ukrainian. These can be acquired by Ukrainians from all over the world, but not by a Ukrainian in the Ukrainian SSR. It is, however, possible to subscribe in Ukraine to all other, non-Ukrainian, publications from Poland and Czechoslovakia. And no matter how many times inquiries are made of the appropriate government departments in the Ukrainian SSR, nothing comes of them ...

Is it then worth talking about serious matters?

By failing to abide by Leninist principles on the nationalities policy and national construction, by failing to implement its own laws and resolutions adopted in the 1920s and not repealed to this very day, by failing to guarantee the Ukrainian people a full national cultural life and the actual equality of their culture and language, by neglecting the matter of national-cultural construction and a truly internationalist education, the Government of the Ukrainian SSR fails to fulfil its duties towards the Ukrainian people in whose name it acts, whose money it spends and to whom it is accountable. Neither does it fulfil its duties towards the world communist movement and the future communist society, whose interests demand the maximum development of each socialist nation and the complete health of all the national members of the great communist family.

1   Cf. Jacques Duclos, *Izbrannyye proizvedeniya*, I, Moscow, 1959, p. 300.
2   G. Dimitrov, *Selected Works*, Sofia, 1960, p. 404.
3   Cf. all the facts and figures above.
4   Lenin, *CW*, XX, p. 50.
5   V. Koryak (ed.), *Shlyakhy rozvytku ukrains'koyi proletars'koyi literatury*, Kharkiv, 1928, p. 350.
6   X z'yizd KP(B)U, Kharkiv, 1928, p. 444.
7   XII s'yezd RKP(B), p. 570.

Conclusions

What we have said here by no means exhausts even the principal or most obvious problems and facts concerning the present national situation of Ukraine. But even this is enough to show how complex, abnormal, difficult and – in the full meaning of the word – dramatic this situation is.

And it is not strange or surprising at all, but quite natural and normal, that more and more people all over Ukraine begin to feel deeply disturbed about the fate of their nation. Particularly bitter and often contradictory thoughts arise amongst a large section of our youth. This is borne out by a number of facts. Numerous individual and collective letters are being sent to various authorities, editorial boards, etc. An enormous amount of unpublished, mostly anonymous, poetry and publicistic writing is circulating from hand to hand. (This writing of the masses is often naive and unskilled, but it expresses a cry from the heart.) Various literary evenings and discussions are being organized and only too often prohibited. (How many resolutions have already been adopted by Party authorities against these evenings, and how many people have been punished for them!) A smouldering, vague movement and awakening is felt among Ukrainian youth all over Ukraine. A more indirect pointer to the unsatisfactory situation can be seen in the conspicuous expansion of the staff and a feverish increase in the activities of the KGB, which for some reason has been entrusted with nationalities policy in Ukraine.

In 1923 at the XII Congress of the RCP(B) one of the delegates said: 'Are we really going to force the Chekists to see to it that the non-Russians learn Russian? After all, the native language and native school lead to national consciousness, and national consciousness leads to a desire to know where the peasant's rouble goes.'[1]

I do not know whether the Chekists have their eye on the study of Russian today. But with what zeal and predilection do they (however, let us not call wretched spies and informers by the romantic name 'Chekists') watch the Ukrainian language and everything that is connected with it. Anyone who has anything to do with it could tell quite a story. If necessary, a good-sized notebook could be filled on this subject, for the touching concern of the KGB for matters of Ukrainian culture has lasted a good many years and includes various forms of 'work'. True, among all these forms one has become paramount in recent times: the jaw-breaking 'prohibit, suppress, isolate, put away!'

Attempts are made at justifying the KGB orgy by Philistine twaddle about 'Ukrainian bourgeois nationalism' (meaning any deviation from the russified standard). To speak about the threat of nationalism from a nation that is being russified wholesale is tantamount to shouting at a funeral 'many happy returns of the day' (do you remember in what context Lenin used these words?). What also comes to mind is the little tale about the gentleman who was the first to call out: 'Stop thief!' But even if there are some manifestations of nationalism on the part of some Ukrainians, then first of all one should expose them publicly by stating the facts instead of smothering them in soap bubbles for the entertainment of the Philistines; secondly, one should give some thought to the question, what gives rise to these manifestations of nationalism in the forty-ninth year of Soviet rule? Perhaps there really is something amiss in our life and in our policy? After all, the KGB men can only spread rumours about American dollars for the benefit of the most obtuse Philistines; they cannot themselves believe them, since they know better than anyone else that they are not true. One must think at least a little about the causes of certain social phenomena. People should show at least a modicum of knowledge of Lenin and esteem for him, they should know his clear-cut instruction that it is inadmissible to raise the question of nationalism 'in general', his instruction that there are two kinds of nationalism, that the source of local nationalism is Russian Great-Power chauvinism, and that the latter has to be combated if we wish to kill the roots of the former.[2] People should show at least a modicum of respect for the clear-cut resolutions of the Party Congresses which dealt particularly with this question, so that there would be no more unprompted bureaucratic bungling and no further despotic extirpation policies: 'Since the survivals of nationalism are a particular form of defence against Great Russian chauvinism, a resolute struggle against Great Russian chauvinism is the surest means of overcoming nationalist survivals.'[3]

In our country, however, nobody fights against this chauvinism; on the contrary, it is fanned in every way, and by assuming the guise of internationalism and a communist outlook it dislodges them. On the other hand, any protest against it, even the most elementary protest against the merciless flailing of national dignity, is at once watchfully pinpointed, branded as bourgeois nationalism, and then lengthily and tediously 'eradicated'.

This 'eradication' is by no means limited to the recent arrests, house-searches and interrogations, although now it has found in them its most open and disgraceful expression.

The recent 'informer'[4] commotion attests first of all to the pitiful lack of political sense amongst its instigators. It is said that these worthy officials are racking their brains about the fateful question: is there or is there not an underground organization of nationalists in Ukraine ('nationalists' are of course those who think differently from, and therefore are not liked by, them) and how might such an organization be constructed from those arrested?

The problem of the mythical 'organization' is the product of a complete inability to comprehend the real process, the product of the KGB's divorce from life, the product of an armchair style of thinking. It is the product of a professionally malevolent disregard for the live national-cultural needs of the Ukrainian people. It is at one and the same time an exaggeration and an underestimation of what is happening.

An exaggeration: because the phenomena that worry the KGB so much are isolated sporadic outbursts of a spontaneous nature, whilst the people arrested are simply those who have come to the attention of officials or spies through their lawful actions, which do not conceal any activity of a clandestine nature.

An underestimation: because it is not a question of any organization or group of people, but of something immeasurably greater and deeper – the spontaneous, multiform, widespread, self-originating processes of a nation's 'self-defence' in the face of a clear prospect of disappearing from the human family.

Engels spoke many a time about 'the inevitable struggle of each people for its national existence'[5] and also about the fact that when the life of a nation is threatened 'the struggle to restore ... national existence will absorb everything'.[6]

This constant national self-renewal, self-preservation and self-defence is a powerful collective instinct of a people, an indestructible, unconscious, natural force like the instinct of self-preservation and the force of self-renewal of any organism.

It is these forces of national life that break through spontaneously and unexpectedly everywhere, confront purblind strategists of uniformity with inscrutable enigmas and make nonsense of all the historiosophic designs of Shchedrin's town governors.[7]

These forces are unfathomable and inexhaustible; no technique of political surveillance can keep up with them or control them.

And this is not simply an ethnographic force. Everywhere the socialist national consciousness of Ukrainians keeps awakening still more. It is inseparable from human self-knowledge. And it will keep on awakening and growing under the impact of powerful forces. Economic and social development and progress bring on a democratization of social life, which promotes human dignity and self-awareness. Civic concepts and sentiments are crystallizing, everywhere people begin to raise their heads again. The educational and cultural level of the Ukrainian population is rising, inevitably bringing in its wake a more or less conscious desire to achieve distinction in the world. There is an improvement in the material position of the Ukrainian village, which sends forth more and more youth who are no longer downtrodden and crushed by poverty and cares, but fresh, strong and proud, ready to stand up for their national identity. (Take a look, for instance, at our present village school-leavers who enter establishments of higher education, and compare them with those of ten years ago.) Growing numbers of city youth (in establishments of higher education, schools and factories) embark on a moral and spiritual search, feeling that they have been deceived in some way, that something sacred has been concealed from them. (Do you remember how Kostomarov expressed his first impression of Shevchenko's poetry?

> I saw that Shevchenko's muse had rent the curtain concealing the people's life. How frightening, and sweet, and painful, and intoxicating it was to glance behind it ... Shevchenko's muse broke through some underground vault that for several centuries had been locked with many locks and sealed with many seals, covered with earth, deliberately ploughed over and sown to conceal from future generations the very memory of the spot where there exists an underground hollow.[8])

By thousands of different paths this youth comes to an intuition of Ukraine.

This socialist national consciousness, this certainty of their right and duty to give a good account of their socialist nation to humanity, this desire to see the socialist Ukraine as truly existing and genuinely equal among the socialist family of nations, this feeling of a socialist Ukraine as a national reality and not simply as an administrative geographical term and a bureaucratic stumbling-block – all this is also intensified by a number of universal factors in world history and in the world communist movement. Witness the historic reality of the socialist nations of Europe, which are experiencing an upsurge and a revitalization of their national awareness, and make the elementary comparison, which imposes itself, between their position and that of Ukraine. Witness the fiasco of the miserable notion of nationlessness, of the nationless uniformity of communist society, under the pressure of actual historic reality, of the real historic-national multiformity of communism. Witness the Soviet reader's growing interest in, and acquaintance with, living world communist theory, the theoretical works and ideas of MarxistLeninists from all over the world – works and ideas which turn out to be much more profound, humane and attractive than the stuff that our present newspapers keep chewing over. Finally, witness the upswing of national movements and national values all over the world, Europe included. Not so long ago *Pravda* quite justly observed that the significance of the national factor has grown in even the most industrially developed countries, while our newspapers approvingly quoted de Gaulle's sober words against plans for a 'United Europe':

> A so-called integrated Europe which, in the absence of the strengths of the sovereignty of the peoples and the responsibility of the states, would automatically be subordinated to the protector across the ocean. Thus there would no doubt remain French workers, peasants, engineers, teachers, civil servants, deputies and ministers. But there would no longer be France.

> ... The best interests of the human race
> require that each nation be responsible for
> itself, free from encroachment, and assisted in
> its progress without conditions of obedience.⁹

But the most surprising fact has just been quoted by the *Literary Ukraine* (last year *Za rubezhom* [Abroad] also wrote of this).¹⁰ The Welsh language, which was considered to be on the point of extinction and which in 1921 was spoken in Britain by 930,000 people, is now to become an official language of Wales, since it is now used by 3,000,000!¹¹

All over the world nations are not dying out but, on the contrary, are developing and growing stronger, in order to offer as much as possible to humanity, to contribute as much as possible to the creation of universal human values; especially the socialist nations.

And the Ukrainian nation will not become the outcast of the human race.

More than once in history has the Ukrainian question been declared non-existent and the Ukrainian nation an invention. (Inevitably marks, schillings, francs, dollars, etc., were dragged in.) In his time even Stalin ridiculed such an 'historiosophy' arising from the bottomless moral slough of the imperial town of Foolsborough:¹²

> I have received a note alleging that we Communists are artificially cultivating a Byelorussian nationality. That is not true, for there exists a Byelorussian nation, which has its own language, different from Russian. Consequently, the culture of the Byelorussian people can be raised only in its native language. We heard similar talk [some] five years ago about Ukraine, about the Ukrainian nation. And only recently it was said that the Ukrainian Republic and the Ukrainian nation were inventions of the Germans. It is obvious,

however, that there is a Ukrainian nation, and it is the duty of the Communists to develop its culture. You cannot go against history.[13]

Later Stalin forgot his own admonitions and began to destroy the Ukrainian nation. And with what result? He destroyed several million Ukrainians but did not destroy the nation. And no one ever will. 'You cannot go against history', be it with a red-hot iron, or with the silk bridle of 'bilingualism'. It is futile to go against life itself, even with an army of informers and spies, who will lead you anywhere except towards communism.

You cannot play at communism: you either have to put it into practice or betray it in the name of the 'one and indivisible' barracks. Let us consider calmly what prospects and advantages the present nationalities policy offers. Are these advantages, if they really exist, so considerable that they compensate for the catastrophic losses we talked of earlier? Are they worth the apostasy from Marxism-Leninism?

To judge from certain rather nebulous official ventriloquisms, the present policy of denationalization and russification, of 'reducing everything to a common denominator', is first and foremost dictated by the alleged necessity for a high degree of centralization, in order to achieve construction on a vast scale and a rapid rate of economic development. Perhaps overcentralization really seems to some people to be easier and more efficacious.

But, first of all, not everything that seems easier is really more useful. Even at the XII Congress of the RCP(B) the warning note was sounded:

> Our central authorities begin to regard the administration of the whole country from the point of view of their office armchair convenience. Naturally, it is inconvenient to administer twenty Republics; but then, if everything were

> one, if you only had to press one button to administer the whole country, that would be convenient. From the bureaucratic point of view, naturally, this would be easier, more convenient, and more pleasant. If I were to tell you the story of the struggle the Republics are forced to wage with our central administration, this would be the story of their struggle for survival.[14]

Is it not true that the 'bureaucratic point of view' is winning today? 'Easier, more convenient, and more pleasant' – for the central authorities. And hence the illusion: more useful to the cause.

Secondly, the consideration of economic expediency was never regarded by Marxist-Leninists to be the sole or solely decisive one in such a complex and many-sided matter as the building of a new society, nor in national construction. As early as the X Congress of the RCP(B) in the joint report on the nationalities question the fallacy and danger of 'economism' in the nationalities policy was pointed out: 'Very many comrades among us, imagining themselves to be thinking as Marxists, say: "We are faced with a question that has to be approached from the economic point of view, from the point of view of the profitability of higher economic forms."'[15]

This point of view led directly to what Lenin called 'imperialist attitudes' 'towards our own non-Russian nationalities'.[16] This is why the Party rejected it in the name of national construction in the Republics, 'unprofitable' economically, but vitally necessary and indispensable for national justice and communism. It might have been 'more profitable' to develop industry in the 'centres', and yet they developed it also 'in the borderlands'; it might have been 'more profitable' to manage with Russian cadres, and yet they also trained local ones; the Russian language might have been economically 'more profitable for publishing, the press, education, etc., and yet they developed all the national languages'; and so on, and so forth

– for in the construction of a new, communist society the economic factor is only one of many.

This is always worth remembering: in the nationalities policy a purely economic approach, with advantages in the narrow economic sphere (advantages from the point of view of the 'centre'), lead directly to imperialism and Great-Power mania. This is what Lenin warned us against.

Thirdly, do we derive real, and not simply imaginary, advantages from overcentralization, from the actual obliteration of the Republics' economic sovereignty, and the accompanying policy of intensive russification? Would we not achieve better economic results and would we not win decisively in economic competition with capitalism by adopting a different policy – that of broad economic initiative and independent action on the part of the Republics, a policy which would utilize local resources as much as possible, a policy of healthy social-economic competition between distinctive Republics (unlike the present levelling and depersonalization), a policy based on the broad self-government and independent social and economic activity of the masses, a policy based on spiritual enthusiasm which would doubtless be awakened by the activization of nationalcultural life?

> Far from precluding local self-government, with autonomy for regions having special economic and social conditions, a distinct national composition of the population, and so forth, democratic centralism necessarily demands both. In Russia centralism is constantly confused with tyranny and bureaucracy. This confusion has naturally arisen from the history of Russia, but even so it is quite inexcusable for a Marxist to yield to it.[17]

However, it is not for us to think about this, 'as long as the leaders think'. Though it is hard to see in what way their authority as leaders would suffer and their prerogatives as leaders be threatened, if these questions were made, say, the subject of a nationwide public discussion.

There is one more argument in favour of the present nationalities (or rather denationalization) policy, an argument that is not expressed aloud but can be inferred from the words and actions of many bureaucrats. As long as there are various nationalities, it is thought, we must fear all sorts of separatisms and nationalisms, but if we could quickly mingle the nations and make a single-language hotchpotch, we would have complete peace and quiet. If this point of view were openly expressed, we would have to answer: first of all, no matter how intensively denationalization and russification are pursued, there is no visible end to the 'task'. Even the greatest advocate and theoretician of assimilation, Karl Kautsky, was forced to admit that it was impossible, or too difficult, totally to assimilate a people which has already created its own written language and national culture.[18] Thus it is a dubious procedure to count upon results that cannot be perceived in even the longest historical perspective. Secondly, it is just such a policy of denationalization and russification that is causing ever-growing discontent – a real discontent accompanying imaginary 'successes' – whilst a policy of stimulating national development would produce a situation in which there would be no serious reasons for discontent. Thus, then, what is better, two birds in hand, or one in the bush?[19]

Finally, there is still a third argument, related to the previous one, but, in contrast to it, legalized and widely used in our press and propaganda. This argument is, so to speak, of a military-patriotic nature. It is said that in the face of the threat of an aggravation of the international situation and of military provocations on the part of imperialism, we must intensify our military-patriotic education, especially our education in the spirit of the 'common Fatherland' and in the spirit of a certain idealizing of the 'history of the Fatherland', to which rank a modernized version of the history of the Russian Empire and Russian tsarism is being elevated.[20]

To this it must be replied that a genuine education in communist patriotism, in a patriotic sentiment towards the communist commonwealth of nations, can only be founded on education in communist national patriotism, on a feeling that one's nation is equal and holds its rightful place equal among its equals within a comity of nations. In other words, it can only be based on the sentiment of a communist family and not on unity in the sense of identity. This 'feeling of one family' we should derive only from our communist outlook and our communist practice, and not from the false and decayed foundation of the tsarist 'common Fatherland'.

It is difficult to say what other considerations have become the basis for our present nationalities policy. It is difficult, for, as we have already pointed out, this policy does not wish to appear publicly as it really is but hides behind generalities and coded formulas. Its basic principle is at all costs to avoid calling things by their proper names. In such a situation, how can there be any thought of the open and honest discussion of questions which touch upon what is most sacred and dear to millions their native land, their national heritage. We have already seen what became of attempts to talk about these questions ... As Khrushchev explained with touching laconism to a certain 'messenger' from Ukraine: 'Don't touch this question, you will break your back.'

Again, we see how today all sorts of 'Tashkentian gentlemen' snigger in true Smerdyakov[21] style at Svitlychny and the other arrested men: 'Just look at them! They wanted to be some sort of Bulgaria! We'll knock this nonsense out of them!'

To 'knock out' – one does not have to learn from anybody ... However, in that case, what are we to do with the elementary concepts of communist civic virtues? What are we to do with Lenin's testaments?

> In his last works V.I. Lenin bequeathed to us
> the idea of educating as many people as possible
> 'for whom one can vouch that they will not take

one word on trust, that they will not accept one word that goes against their consciences', who 'will not be afraid to admit any difficulty and will not be afraid of any struggle to achieve their earnestly set goal', the great goal of building a truly human society – communism.[22]

There are those for whom it would be 'more convenient' to have toadies instead of such people. So as to bring about such an idyllic state it is so tempting to 'knock' honesty, conscience and principles out of people with the fist of the state and the prison cell.

So then: in the fiftieth, the seventy-fifth and the hundredth year of Soviet rule you will still be sacking people because of literary evenings; you will still be smuggling secret tape-recorders into places where friends meet; you will still be dispersing public discussions with squads of KGB and *sambists*;[23] you will still be arresting people for reading books; you will still be constructing 'nationalist organizations' in the dungeons of the KGB; you will still be confiscating private typewriters; you will still be checking and 'thinning out' the personal libraries of the builders of communism, and dragging the latter from pillar to post, 'breaking their backs', slandering them, terrorizing them, doing all that you are doing now, which Lenin described in these words: '... base persecution for "separatism", the persecution of people who are unable to defend themselves, is the very limit of shamelessness ...'[24]

Well, perhaps there will be a police with brute force enough for the job. But will it not lead the communist cause up a blind alley? Will it not be too obvious a betrayal of communism, too nasty a besmirching of its radiant ideals in the sight of all humanity?

Today is not the last in the world's history. Sooner or later everything will fall back into place. And if not tomorrow, then the day after tomorrow we ourselves will have to pay dearly for each injustice and mistake committed today, for each concealment and each deception, for each attempt to 'trick' nature, history, the people ...

And in this matter, the nationalities question, sooner or later we will have to return to truth, we will have to return to Lenin, to Lenin's nobility of mind and sense of justice – to Lenin's nationalities policy. But the sooner the better.

There is no need of clever mental acrobatics here: this policy was adequately worked out both in its main principles and in the whole breadth of its practical approach. It was precisely formulated in Lenin's last notes and in the resolutions of Party Congresses. Its main points are: the correction of the actual inequality or lagging behind of the smaller nations in various spheres of material and spiritual life; concessions from the larger nation to smaller ones; the inadmissibility of any one nation, language or culture being more highly privileged than others within the boundaries of the USSR; the observance of the sovereignty of the Republics and its protection from the encroachments of centralizers on no matter what specious grounds; the maximum national-cultural development of all Republics on the basis of national languages, cultures and traditions; a resolute struggle against Russian Great-Power chauvinism as the main threat to communism and internationalism; the development of a communist national self-awareness in all nations, and, on these foundations, true internationalist education in the spirit of brotherhood and mutual assistance.

Appropriate practical measures for Ukraine were thoroughly elaborated in the resolutions of the CP(B)U and in the decrees of the Government of the Ukrainian SSR. We only have to rescue them from oblivion and the Stalinist-Khrushchevist attitude of 'not giving a damn' for them, show them to the people, and in a common effort start working for their implementation.

At the same time, it is a simple matter (and extremely necessary) to avoid that element of administrative coercion and that 'campaign' atmosphere which quite understandably frighten many people in the very word 'ukrainization'.

A forced, official 'ukrainization' from above would only compromise ukrainian culture and language, especially when many people do not understand the need for it. In practice it might be implemented in just this way – in absurd and antagonizing fashion.

When I quoted examples of 'inconspicuous' coercion into russification, I did not do so in order to propose its supplanting by coercion into ukrainization. Not at all, I quoted them in order to show those who do not see that *there is* coercion into russification in our country and that the 'voluntariness' of russification is only apparent, only *seeming*. I propose to counter this coercion with one thing only: *freedom* – freedom for the honest, public discussion of national matters, freedom of national choice, freedom for national self-knowledge, self-awareness and self-development. But first and last comes freedom for discussion and disagreements. Why should the present nationalities policy have so much to fear from this? Whence such a fear of the human word and such an inquisitorial fury against it? Why do official representatives flee so shamefully from those evenings and discussions at which the nationalities question suddenly comes up? Why do they prohibit, break up and gag, instead of coming and explaining matters, instead of carrying their point in honest discussion, and convincing in frank and open conversation? Why do they not have discussions with groups of students rather than summoning them individually to one office after another, grilling them behind closed office doors, expelling them and terrorizing them?

Let us discuss all aspects of the nationalities question honestly and frankly. We can but benefit from this. Let all points of view be expressed. There is no doubt that, through the strength of logic and argumentation, through the strength of truth and conscience, through the strength of human decency and care for the common weal, that the point of view to win will be the one showing a truly communist understanding of internationalism, the point of view which will proclaim: the inadmissibility of any injustice towards any nation in the world no matter what calculations, advantages or considerations of 'necessity' may be advanced to excuse it; the general responsibility of the human family for the plenitude of each member, each nation in the world; the most propitious development – unlimited in time and effort – of each nation in the name of humanity and of communism; cooperation and fraternity in the name of the growth and consolidation of each, and not in the name of seniority, engulfment and uniformity.

Then it will become comprehensible and obvious that we have to begin with the most important thing, that is the propagation of those ideas of Lenin, those ideas of Marxism-Leninism and world communism which are now concealed, evaded or falsified; we have to begin with the development of a communist national self-knowledge and self-awareness and a communist understanding of internationalism. At the same time we must overcome the psychological inertia deriving from chauvinism, Great-Power ideology, national liquidationism, national boorishness and bureaucratic standardization. Such a work of national enlightenment and education would create the requisite spiritual and psychological conditions for all the other measures needed to stimulate the national political and cultural life of the Soviet Ukraine. Once her political and cultural life have taken on a real, rich and vital meaning, once they have acquired ideological attractiveness and become an inspiration to millions of Ukrainians, they would in their turn become 'mighty levers of communist construction, they would help to awaken and mobilize forces and reserves hitherto unregarded and make for a manifold increase in the contribution of Ukraine to the common effort of the peoples of the USSR and the whole socialist camp.

Then will the Soviet Ukraine truly become a unique jewel in the multiform socialist world, then will she give to humanity fully of her powers.

Then it will not be necessary to keep a watch on every Ukrainian word, on every Ukrainian thought, it will not be necessary to expend great efforts and enormous sums on surveillance, 'suppression' and 'eradication' ...

And it will not be necessary to fill the KGB's 'isolation wards' with those people whose only crime is that they love Ukraine with true filial affection and are troubled by her fate, those people who have the right to say in the words of Shevchenko:

> Our path was straight, and there is not
> A grain of falsehood in our souls.[25]

1   *XII s'yezd RKP(B)*, p. 578.
2   Cf. Lenin, CW, XXXVI, pp. 607, 609.
3   *KPSS v rezovyutsiyakh*, I, p. 715.
4   'Fiskal'nyy': Lenin's expression.
5   Marx and Engels, SC, p. 400.
6   Ibid., p. 294.
7   Shchedrin's town governors: an allusion to his satire Istoriya odnogo goroda (1870). *Pravda*, 14 January 1965, p. 4.
8   N. Kostomarov, 'Vospominaniye o dvukh malyarakh', in *T.G. Shevchenko v vospominaniyakh sovremennikov*, Moscow, 1962, pp. 1512.
9   General de Gaulle's national broadcast on the evening of 27 April 1965, *Le Monde*, 29 April 1965, p. 2. [Translation by the editors]
10 The Literary Ukraine article is based on a report 'Let Welsh speak Welsh, Government is urged' in the *Daily Mail*, 26 October 1965, p. 9.
11 'Nareshti-vyznannya', *Literaturna Ukraina*, 30 November 1965, p. 4. Apropos, Britain's communist press started a campaign in defence of the future of the Welsh language.
12 Foolsborough: gorod Glupov of Shchedrin's satires mentioned previously.
13 *X s'yezd RKP(B)*, p. 213; English translation in J.V. Stalin, *Works*, V, Moscow, 1953, pp. 48–9.
14 *XII s'yezd RKP(B)*, p. 580.
15 *X s'yezd RKP(B)*, p. 194.
16 Lenin, CW, XXXVI, p. 611.
17 Lenin, CW, XX, p. 46.
18 K. Kautsky, *Die Bifreiung der Nationen*, 2nd edn, Stuttgart, 1917, p. 23.
19 'Two birds in hand ...': in the original, the proverb is inverted to reinforce the point by giving it an unusual twist: 'what is better, a sparrow in the sky or a crane in the hand?'
20 Cf. Sakharov's article note 142.
21 Smerdyakov: a character from Dostoyevsky's *The Brothers Karamazov*.
22 A. Rumyantsev, 'O partiynosti tvorcheskogo truda sovetskoy intelligentsii', *Pravda*, 9 September 1965, p. 3.
23 Sambists: here, 'auxiliaries' or 'muscle-men' used by the KGB. (The original meaning: people practising sambo, short for samozashchita bez oruzhiya, self-defence without weapons, a Russian version of Karate.)
24 Lenin, CW, XIX, p. 267.
25 T. Shevchenko, 'Dolya', in his *Povne zibrannya tvoriv u shesty tomakh*, II, Kyiv, 1963, p. 299; an English translation in his *Selected Works*, Moscow, 1964, p. 245.

Postscript to the second edition

Bohdan Krawchenko

Ivan Dzyuba, sharing the alarm of a large section of the Ukrainian public at the series of political arrests in Ukraine in August and September 1965, submitted *Internationalism or Russification?* to the Soviet Government and the Party in December the same year. In this work he exposed the present Soviet leadership's nationalities policy as being both un-Leninist and liable to lead to disaster, and appealed for a return to Leninist principles. But first and foremost, he appealed for an honest and frank public discussion of all aspects of the nationalities question.

Dzyuba's work, though firmly based on Marxism-Leninism and incontrovertibly argued, has to date not been published in the Soviet Union; yet its publication there could have been the beginning of precisely just such a discussion as would have greatly improved the relations between the nations of the USSR. Peter Archer[1] in his Preface to the first English edition commented on the magnitude of the 'loss if a contribution to the debate such as this document is denied publication among those whom it most concerns'.

Nevertheless, Dzyuba's work became known in manuscript to many members of the Ukrainian public; as for the Soviet Government and the Party, the press and other media controlled by them, these had for years shown no open reaction to his work. (It may, however, have influenced official policies in some respects, but so far there is no conclusive evidence on this point, and speculation would be idle.)

The publication in the West, in the summer of 1968, of *Internationalism or Russification?*, first in English and then in the original Ukrainian, did not produce a single ripple in the Soviet official press for twelve months. However, as it now transpires, a lengthy 'refutation' of Dzyuba's book was being prepared during these months by one Bohdan Stenchuk and published in Kyiv in July–August 1969 by the Ukrainian SSR Association for Cultural Relations with Ukrainians Abroad.[2] Moreover, in April–May 1970, the same Association published a 196–page translation of this book entitled *What I. Dzyuba Stands For, and How He Does It* (Once more about the book *Internationalism or Russification?*).[3] Although the Association which has published the book is termed 'public', i.e. non-governmental, its intimate connection with certain powerful state agencies is well known.[4] The special prominence given to Stenchuk's book by the Soviet Government is obvious from the fact that a pile of copies for distribution to callers has been seen in at least one major Soviet embassy in the West (as is well known, run-of-the-mill Soviet books are normally distributed in the West by appointed local commercial booksellers who receive them from Mezhdunarodnaya Kniga). Both the Ukrainian and the English versions were printed in ten thousand copies each, this considerable edition being designated only for circulation abroad.[5]

In view of all this, it is natural to regard Stenchuk's book as an officially sponsored reply to Dzyuba aimed at his readers abroad. In content and purpose patently a denunciatory review of Dzyuba's work, it runs into practically half the length[6] of his book. This fact alone demonstrates how seriously Dzyuba's book is taken, since it was deemed to need a counter-blast of these dimensions.

When the first edition of *Internationalism or Russification?* was published it was introduced as 'a carefully documented study' 'remarkable for its courageous statement of the facts combined with the depth and scope of its scholarly analysis'. Now, Stenchuk asserts that 'Dzyuba's book has nothing in common with conscientious scientific investigation, and especially not with a study conducted from the positions of Marxism-Leninism'; also he claims that 'Dzyuba's book reflects and interprets reality incorrectly, mutilates the ideas of proletarian internationalism, and has the aim of inculcating a petty-bourgeois nationalist world outlook in its readers'; furthermore he asserts that Dzyuba adduces 'arbitrarily selected or even simply invented facts and little things, which by the way very often have nothing at all to do with the questions that are being examined', and that Dzyuba 'systematically distorts the ideas and statements of Marx and Lenin, quotations from their works, Party documents ...' (S.,[7] 153–4).

A formidable indictment indeed, obviously requiring close examination in any circumstances.

Stenchuk pursues two main lines: he attacks Dzyuba's exposition of Marxist-Leninist principles and policies on the nationalities question, and denies the correctness of his factual data and assertions.

It would take another book to dispose in detail of Stenchuk's every argument, while his doctrinaire attitudes on points of dogma as now established in the Soviet nationalities policy are of little interest, since they are repeated, with infinitesimal variations, in all those Soviet scholastic writings on the subject published under official auspices in the USSR.[8]

To exemplify Stenchuk's method it may therefore suffice to mention a few instances in which he 'refutes' or 'unmasks' Dzyuba by questioning the truth of facts cited by him; matters of doctrine will be left mostly without comment.

Here is the first example: Dzyuba calculates the numbers of specialists with higher education per 10,000 Russians and Ukrainians in the USSR, and the numbers of students per 1,000 of each of these nationalities in the Ukrainian SSR (D., 184–5). Stenchuk quotes Dzyuba's figures, but fails to name the official Soviet source of Dzyuba's data (mentioned in footnotes) which are at the basis of the calculations, and describes them, without bothering to verify (to do this he only had to get the generally known 1959 census data), as 'figures of a doubtful nature from his [Dzyuba's] personal "statistics"' (S., 102). A check on Dzyuba's arithmetic, given below, shows his figures to be quite correct, and Stenchuk's allegation patently libellous.

	Population in tens of thousands (1959 census)	Numbers of specialists with a higher education in the USSR (1 December 1960)		
		Absolute figures	Per each 10,000	Per cent ratio to USSR average
USSR total	20,883	3,545,234	170	100
Russians	11,411	2,070,333	182	107
Ukrainians	3,725	517,729	139	82

(The ratio of Ukrainian specialists, 82 per cent, is 18 per cent lower than the USSR average, or, as Dzyuba notes, than the ratio of Ukrainians in the USSR, which comes to the same thing.)

In the Ukrainian SSR:

	Population in thousands (1959 census)	Student numbers, 1960–61	
		Absolute figures	Per 1000 population
Ukrainians	32,158	260,945	8
Russians	7,091	125,464	18

When it comes to censuses, Stenchuk does not hesitate to do some falsifying himself, whilst accusing Dzyuba of this. Not surprisingly, he finds it convenient to do this with the 1926 census, believing himself safe since only a few libraries in the West have copies of its results. Objecting to Dzyuba's pointing out the mass resettlement of Ukrainians outside

Ukraine and their replacement by the mass immigration of Russians (D., 42), Stenchuk asserts that 'facts, not [Dzyuba's] empty declarations, tell a different story', that according to the 1959 census the Ukrainians comprised '76.8 per cent of the population of the Ukrainian SSR (as compared to 74.2 per cent in 1926)', and that, 'as you see, there's not even a hint of that "crisis" which haunts Dzyuba' (S., 64–5). The first figure is true enough, and can be confirmed from many reference works; not so the second one. However, when ultimately the relevant data are found, it transpires that the second figure is 80 per cent,[9] and that Dzyuba's fear is, after all, fully justified. If this were not proof enough, Stenchuk's falsification was shown up in a popular Kyiv journal,[10] now easily accessible, a few months after the first publication of his book.

Referring to, and misrepresenting, a source, particularly when it is not easily accessible, is Stenchuk's favourite device. Another typical example: he gives a 1959 statistical table of mixed marriages and adds: 'won't I. Dzyuba exploit it, too, as proof of the ruination of the Ukrainian nation? ... May he not fight to have the marriage[s] of Ukrainians to persons of another nationality forbidden? Did not the national-deviationists, who are so dear to Dzyuba's heart clamour for precisely that in their time?' Stenchuk's reference purporting to give the source of this last assertion says: 'See XII Congress of RCP(B), Stenographic report, p. 161' (S., 95–6, 165). It is bad enough to condemn someone for an opinion he only may hold, just because some other individual (albeit his friend) has expressed it. But who were those national-deviationists, and what exactly did they advocate? The 1923 Russian edition of the report of the XII Congress of the RCP(B) to which Stenchuk refers[11] is available in the original perhaps only in one or two libraries in the West, and Stenchuk's reader will have to take his word on trust. But if he does succeed in tracking down one of these two copies he will find, on page 161, a quotation from a decree 'On Citizenship of the Socialist Soviet Republic of Georgia' saying that 'The citizenship of Georgia is lost: by a Georgian citizen if she marries a foreigner' – a provision not unlike that found in many other countries in the world, which no sane – or honest – person will interpret as a *prohibition* of marriages with foreigners. Stenchuk must have been sure that his falsification would pass undetected; unfortunately for him, the rare book he referred to is now available in a reprint, and the above quotation can easily be seen by anyone interested.¹² Added if any lies in the fact that a ban on marriages with foreigners was *in fact* imposed, though not by Georgian, Ukrainian or Estonian 'national-deviationists', nor by any 'capitalists', but by a body which, by definition, can never be suspected of any 'deviations', national or otherwise: the Presidium of the Supreme Soviet of the USSR in Moscow. The exact title of its decree was 'On the Prohibition of Marriages between Citizens of the USSR and Foreigners', dated 15 February 1947; it was repealed on 26 November 1953,¹³ though even now such marriages are greatly discouraged.¹⁴

Sometimes Stenchuk challenges Dzyuba for stating some item of common knowledge and not quoting chapter and verse for it. This he does when, e.g., Dzyuba mentions that 'it is held that the nationalities question was solved once and for all in 1917',¹⁵ and therefore all criticism is stifled (D., 57); 'Marxist-Leninists never did and don't now consider any such thing', Stenchuk asserts (S., 42). In fact, this view has been held all the time since the Revolution; the majority of the army held it in 1923 according to a contemporary witness (D., 76), and it can be constantly found in Soviet print ever since; it will suffice to quote the latest, highly authoritative, example: 'The nationalities question was solved in the Soviet Union long ago and for ever. It was solved by the Great October Socialist Revolution.'¹⁶ Stenchuk gets into deeper waters when in his zeal to refute Dzyuba he misrepresents Lenin as well: 'Neither Lenin nor our Party ever considered them [the Borot'bist party] as Communists, as Dzyuba claims' (S., 46, D., 99). Stenchuk says this without heeding the fact that 'Borot'bist Communists' (kommunisty-borot'bisty) is Lenin's own expression, and is clearly quoted as such by Dzyuba on the same page.

Dzyuba deplores the concealment of the past attainments of Ukrainian culture from the present-day reader; he enumerates some forty names of historians, writers, poets, literary and sociological scholars and economists, including those active in the 1920s (and mostly liquidated during the Terror of the 1930s: cf. Notes, pp. 226–7 above), and regrets that their *works* (NB) are not published nowadays (D., 212–6), making it clear that he means after the 1920s. All this was undeniably true at the time of Dzyuba's writing (late 1965); Stenchuk, however, singles out this passage for a particularly vicious attack. Some writers he declares to be politically unacceptable; for others he provides bibliographies of critical writings about them, but nothing by them; in a few cases he finds that their selected works have in fact been published, but only after the date of the completion of Dzyuba's manuscript, or else quotes titles of their works published back in the 1920s; for some he even announces that their selected works are *in preparation*; all this he does with an air of triumphant superiority, calling Dzyuba 'a dishonest or simply a poorly informed individual' and peppering pages with vulgarisms. The only relevant facts which Stenchuk produces are that a volume of M. Pavlyk's *selected* works was published in 1959 (nothing since), and there was a two-volume edition of N. Ziber's economic works printed in Russian in Moscow in the same year, but his works on Ukrainian law are still not republished. (S., 106–18)

For reasons of space it is possible to mention in passing only a few more examples of Stenchuk's misuse of statistics. He refers to Dzyuba's assertion that the percentage of Ukrainian schools has been decreasing lately in favour of the Russian ones (D., 191–2) and remarks that 'facts, however, don't bear this out', quoting the 1968–9 figures, 23,036 Ukrainian and 5,505 Russian schools; instead of proving Dzyuba wrong by supplying data for preceding years, he quickly adds: 'The essence of the matter, however, isn't this' (S., 97–8). This is a pity, because if he had given data for any preceding year of the past decade or two, he would have shown Dzyuba to be right; e.g., in 1955–6 there were six Ukrainian schools to each Russian one, while in 1968–9 there were only four (NB: on average, a Russian school is twice the size of a Ukrainian one). Quite regularly, when Stenchuk casts doubts upon Dzyuba's statements, Dzyuba turns out to be correct. His estimate of the percentage of Ukrainian books in libraries (D., 178) is dubbed by Stenchuk 'invented figures', but he fails to supply any of his own (S., 98). Meanwhile, one can read reports in the official Soviet press confirming this state of affairs even in the best school libraries (D., 238–9). Stenchuk objects to Dzyuba's adducing 1957 data showing that, proportionally, there were only half as many Ukrainian scientists and scholars as Russian ones (ethnically) (D., 123–4). This he 'corrects' by quoting 1966 figures for scientists and scholars in the USSR and in the Ukrainian SSR (territorially) (S., 104–5). The two sets of figures are obviously incompatible, and (from D., 185) it is clear why.

Thus, one could – given space – deal with virtually all the statistical and other data quoted by Stenchuk, with similar results.

In the 'ideological' field, Stenchuk's main objection is that Dzyuba's quotations from Marx, Engels, Lenin, Party congresses, etc., are too selective and not extensive enough. There is no need to examine this charge here, since, as Stenchuk rightly remarks, 'the reader can do it himself with the books by the classics of MarxismLeninism and the documents at hand' (S., 60), and the reader may also be interested to see which parts of Dzyuba's own words and quotations are omitted from Stenchuk's versions, and what are the actual wider contexts (often very telling) of Stenchuk's quotations from the authorities. There is at least one occasion when Stenchuk sternly rebukes Dzyuba for quoting a shorter passage (from the American Communist philosopher, H. Selsam, D., 52) than he himself would have liked (S., 58–9) without noticing that the essential part of the 'missing' portion is in fact reproduced by Dzyuba elsewhere (D., 269–70).

Having shown a complete disregard for facts, Stenchuk is equally free in his conclusions. Quite unjustifiably he asserts that Dzyuba calls for 'national oppression' (S., 86), 'compulsory Ukrainianization' (S., 132, 135), and 'the establishment of some sort of closed borders between Russia, Ukraine and the other republics' (S., 135, referring to D.,193, in particular point II), ignoring Dzyuba's clear statement against forced ukrainization (D., 304). Equally arbitrarily Stenchuk asserts that Dzyuba 'makes game of Communist ideas' (S., 144) or has a 'bourgeois-nationalist' world outlook (S., 27).

Attempting to remove to some extent this impression of arbitrariness, Stenchuk quotes from Dr S. Oliynyk's Preface to the Ukrainian edition: '"outside the borders of the USSR Ivan Dzyuba with his book, as though with a reflector, threw a broad beam of light through the fog of indifference, ignorance, half-truths and even deliberate confusion, that covered up this real problem" (national question – Author).' Stenchuk considers this quotation to be implicit[17] proof, recognized by a bourgeois-nationalist "Doctor of Science", that there's not even a whiff of Marxism in Dzyuba's book, that his opus is only a "reflector" for nationalist "studies" (S., 146) – a typical *non-sequitur*. But if Dr Oliynyk is, for Stenchuk, such an irrefutable authority on Dzyuba's Marxism, here is a clearer statement from him: Dzyuba 'belongs to those Marxist researchers who keep within the framework of the Soviet Constitution'.[18]

Stenchuk similarly twists Peter Archer's Preface:

> British Member of Parliament Peter Archer in his preface to the English edition of *Internationalism or Russification?* estimates Dzyuba's book in a somewhat more restrained manner, but also from the positions of anti-communism; he sees

Dzyuba as a revisionist and considers that his book places serious economic and social interests on the agenda and defines the way for Ukraine to go out of the USSR, and therefore, a practical way of undermining the USSR from within (S., 149).

The degree of distortion is easily ascertained. There is no mention in Peter Archer's Preface of Dzyuba's 'revisionism'; on the contrary, he is quite emphatic that 'Certainly the author of this essay writes as a committed MarxistLeninist.'

It would be very revealing to examine which parts of Dzyuba's study are passed over by Stenchuk without comment because there he cannot contradict him, not even by the means of falsification or misrepresentation. A full list of such instances would be too long; some examples will have to suffice.

Thus Stenchuk does not comment on the fact that Ukrainian schools in the RSFSR were all abolished (in the early 1930s) and never reintroduced after Stalin's death (cf. D., 289); nor on the Army as an instrument of russification (D., 202–4, 231); nor on the destruction of Ukrainian culture and intellectuals in 1933–7 (D., 196); nor on the extermination of Ukrainian Communists, both Borot'bist and Bolshevik (D., 99). In this last case, Stenchuk's evasion is no 'oversight': he in fact quotes the first three lines of the paragraph in question, leaving out the rest, from 'and later exterminated' onwards (S., p. 44). He cannot, however, always avoid these issues completely; and his moral worth is vividly illuminated by his formula 'certain actions that occurred in the 1930s and were brought about by the cult of the individual' (S., 81) – his euphemistic way of referring to the Terror whose victims numbered tens of millions.

But Stenchuk's most blatant evasion concerns the very cause which drove Dzyuba to write his work. He manages to avoid mentioning the political arrests of 1965, together with all the KGB's other repressive measures and activities directed against nationally conscious Ukrainians, although

Dzyuba refers to these matters at length (D., 32–9, 98, 187, 291–3, 301–2, 307); by avoiding what Dzyuba presents as the cardinal issues in the present-day situation, Stenchuk leaves Dzyuba's stand on them unchallenged.

Not surprisingly, as Stenchuk's book was not made available to the general Soviet reader, no reviews of it appeared in the internal Soviet press. But its appearance marked the beginning of an intensive campaign against Dzyuba in the Ukrainian SSR. The first move was an article entitled 'The Place in Battle. Concerning a litterateur who has found himself on the other side of the barricades' by L. Dmyterko. There is no evidence that Dmyterko had actually seen Dzyuba's work. On the other hand, it is clear that he had Stenchuk's book as his text; there is no overt reference to it in his article, but the quotations from Dzyuba's Ukrainian *émigré* reviewers as well as from David Floyd's review in the *Daily Telegraph* (27 June 1968) point clearly to Stenchuk as their source. Taking Stenchuk's fabrication as incontrovertible and without quoting a single word from Dzyuba's book (apart from the title), Dymterko declares: 'Before us is not only a falsification of Marxism-Leninism but also a cynical mockery. This, incidentally, is also noticed by Sir Peter Archer who in the Preface to the English edition of the book *Internationalism or Russification?* unambiguously calls Dzyuba a revisionist.' The only specific charge against the contents of Dzyuba's work which Dmyterko puts before the Soviet reader is that he 'quotes fragments from K. Marx's and F. Engels's letters in his own, low-quality translations, cuts them short at the point which suits him, and misrepresents and distorts their essence. He performs similar operations on V.I. Lenin's immortal works. All this he needs in order to prove Marx, Engels and Lenin as allegedly putting first not the social and class questions but the nationality questions.'[19]

The rest of Dmyterko's invective has nothing to do with the contents of the book, but with the alleged attempted transmission of its manuscript to Czechoslovakia. He makes much of the allegation that in December 1965 at the Soviet–Czechoslovak border station, Chop, during a customs check, nineteen different documents were discovered on the person of a Czechoslovak citizen, M. Musinka,[20] including a typescript copy of Dzyuba's *Internationalism or Russification?* with his letter to the CC CPU, his article 'Shevchenko and Khomyakov' prepared for publication abroad,[21] and a selection of poems compiled by him.[22] These named items at least (if not all the nineteen documents) were confiscated. Moreover, Dmyterko quotes from Musinka's alleged explanation: 'The letter to the CC CPU I received from Ivan Dzyuba in Kyiv on 4 December 1965. There had been a prior agreement between me and Dzyuba about the handing over to me of the aforementioned documents...'[23] Dmyterko alleges that this was later confirmed by Dzyuba.[24]

At pains to prove that Dzyuba's first aim was to send his manuscript abroad (albeit into the then friendly Czechoslovakia), Dmyterko still has to concede that he did in fact send his manuscript, together with the covering letter, to the CC CPU, but in order to demonstrate Dzyuba's order of priorities, alleges that this was done later, in January 1966.

Dmyterko also makes heavy weather of the fact that *Internationalism or Russification?* is not the only work by Dzyuba to have got abroad, and that his articles, speeches and other material are regularly published and enthusiastically praised in various Ukrainian *émigré* periodicals.

A month later, another article appeared in the Soviet Ukrainian press under the title 'In Spiritual Exile', in the form of a letter to the Editor signed by two writers and seven journalists and referring to 'the article in *Literaturna Ukraina* of 5 August "The Place in Battle"'. This new article contains no mention of *Internationalism or Russification?*, but it is asserted there that 'The acquaintance with I. Dzyuba's output in a number of hostile publications convincingly shows that ... he has entered upon the path of preaching little theories, long since bankrupt, about the artist's independence of society, about art being above and beyond class, and about national exclusiveness and national isolation which he elevates to the absolute.' Echoing Dmyterko's accusations, the authors of the article then taunt him with being 'in the service of the vultures of anti-communism', and 'having gone over to the camp of nationalist mercenaries'. Taking Stenchuk's and Dmyterko's fabrications as proof, they conclude that 'I. Dzyuba's moral fall, his desertion and the deceptiveness of the platform adopted by him are cogently revealed'; showing no surprise and without asking why, they assert that 'thus a man who received higher education in a Soviet institute, who lives in our midst and even holds a membership card of the Soviet Writers' Union of Ukraine, has become a second voice to the fierce enemies of the Fatherland'. Their declared purpose in writing is to deny the assertions of the *émigré* writers that Dzyuba voices the aspirations of the younger generation and to declare that they, the writers of the letter, 'are indignant about the behaviour of I. Dzyuba who still bears the designation of member of the Writers' Union of Ukraine', and indignant that 'formally being in the ranks of this very authoritative organization, he engages in activity directly opposed to the high calling of a Soviet man of letters'. And, finally, the ominous question: 'As a matter of interest, what is the opinion of the Writers' Union of Ukraine regarding this?'[25] This 'popular request' was soon acceded to, and within a few weeks 'the Dzyuba affair' became a subject for discussion at the Kyiv writers' organization in the same way as, at about the same time, 'the Solzhenitsyn affair' was being discussed by the writers' organization of his home city, Ryazan'. According to an unofficial report, from among the many Kyiv writers who spoke at the meeting only two demanded Dzyuba's expulsion, accusing him of the divulgence of a state secret. In reply to Dzyuba's query, as to what secrets were meant, since in his work he had no access to classified information, one of the speakers retorted: 'Is the disclosing of our Party's nationalities policy not the divulgence of a state secret?' All the others refused to vote for Dzyuba's expulsion and spoke against the two. The meeting lasted for five hours, and the chairman of the meeting, V. Kozachenko,[26] adjourned the vote for two weeks. However, the full meeting was not reconvened; instead – and this is confirmed in an official report[27] – Dzyuba was expelled at the smaller meeting[28] of the Executive Committee only of the Kyiv writers' organization under the chairmanship of Kozachenko. After this, the matter was put by the same Kozachenko before the meeting of the Presidium of the Writers' Union of Ukraine at the end of December 1969.[29]

This official report reiterated the familiar charges that Dzyuba's 'speeches and articles with a nationalistic flavour and with the catchwords of political anarchism and, finally, his brochure *Internationalism or Russification?*, published abroad and written from politically erroneous un-Marxist positions, have become food for the enemies of the Soviet system', pointed out that he had been criticized in the press, viz. in the article 'The Place in Battle'[30] 'and in some other publications',[31] and announced that the reason for Dzyuba's expulsion was his failure to 'draw any conclusions from this criticism'.

After Kozachenko, the Presidium was addressed by Dzyuba himself who read out the following statement, in which, far from recanting, he reaffirmed his stand:

To the Presidium of the Writers' Union of Ukraine

Latterly, my name has often been mentioned in the West, in particular in the milieu of Ukrainian émigrés, and not infrequently in contexts which are unpleasant to me. Sometimes 'sympathy' and 'solidarity' with me is expressed by people over there with whose anti-Communist views I have never had and do not propose having anything in common. Some circles do not hesitate even to interpret my work in the spirit of anti-Soviet propaganda. Sometimes the empty politicizing talk goes so far that I am declared to be nothing more nor less than a leader of a nationalist underground allegedly existing in Ukraine. Such provocative ravings would be merely ridiculous if they did not find their grateful audience, thereby endangering my civic reputation.

Therefore, I deem it necessary to give this reminder that, as a Soviet litterateur, I have taken, and am taking, a civic stand which has nothing in common either with the ideology of Ukrainian bourgeois nationalism or with any conceptions of enmity among peoples and of hatred of humanity. I have always endeavoured to consider nationality problems – just as, in fact, all other problems – from the viewpoint of the principles of scientific communism and of the teaching of Marx, Engels and Lenin, perceiving the prospects for their successful solution to lie along the road towards the fulfilment of Lenin's legacy and the Communist construction.

I have been and shall be with my people, my life and work are inseparable from the life and work of Soviet society. And everything which I write exists for me and has sense in my eyes only in such a connection. I do not accept the designation 'nationalist', whatever meaning anyone may attach to it, because I proceed from a deep respect for every people and do not conceive of any patriotism outside the ideals of the friendship and mutual understanding of peoples, outside the universal human problems and values.

26 December 1969
Ivan Dzyuba

In addition, it is reported that Dzyuba 'expressed regret that some of his manuscripts had got abroad and into the disreputable hands of various falsifiers, and promised to adhere to the requirements of the statutes of the writers' organization and to be concerned together with all writers for the further flowering of Soviet Ukrainian literature'.

Nineteen writers spoke in the discussion, among them B. Chaly, the first signatory of the letter to *Molod Ukrainy* against Dzyuba. According to the report, 'the writers spoke unanimously and frankly about serious errors in I. Dzyuba's literary and public activity'. Such unanimity seems, however, hardly likely; Ivan Drach, for instance, who himself had expressed concern about the 1965 arrests, was among the speakers and surely could not have condemned his fellow-protester and co-signatory of the 'Protest of the 139' mentioned above.[32] The same could probably be said of a number of others.

Yu. Zbanats'ky (presiding) noted in his summing up: 'Dzyuba has been greatly remiss with respect to the writers' organization and our people. Yet the critic's [Dzyuba's] speech and written statement give one grounds to believe that he sincerely wishes to stay within our ranks.'[33]

It would seem clear that a pro-Dzyuba majority carried the day, apparently not without intervention from somebody in higher authority in Kyiv, but its precarious victory over the powerful hardline minority had to be expressed in a compromise resolution, which is officially reported to have been adopted unanimously, and which 'acknowledged as correct the decision of the Kyiv writers' organization concerning I. Dzyuba whose activity had been contrary to the Statutes of the Writers' Union of the USSR'; but, taking his declaration into account, and strictly admonishing him to be guided by the principles of the Union and 'to take an active part in the literary process on the basis of the Marxist-Leninist teaching and an irreconcilable struggle with the bourgeois ideology', 'the Presidium considers it possible to let I. Dzyuba remain in the Writers' Union'.

---

1   Peter Archer was a Labour Member of Parliament from 1966 to 1992. He was a founder member of Amnesty International.
2   B. Stenchuk, *Shcho i yak obstoyuye I. Dzyuba*. (Shche raz pro knyhu *Internatsionalizm chy rusyfikatsiya?*), URSR, Tovarystvo kul'turnykh zv'yazkiv z ukrayintsyamy za kordonom, Kyiv, 1969, 196 pages (in Ukrainian).
3   The author's name is erroneously transliterated in the English edition, both on the cover and on the title-page, as Stanchuk. All references below are to this English edition unless otherwise stated, but the author's name will be given in its correct form, Stenchuk.
4   The same applies to analogous societies for relations with other 'nationals' abroad as well as to the Soviet Committee for Cultural Relations with Compatriots Abroad.

5   Soviet books meant for circulation within the USSR (as well as abroad) carry on the last page a considerable amount of publication data, including the number of copies printed. Those printed for abroad only display hardly any such data; this is the case with Stenchuk's book. Nor does the entry in the USSR central bibliography referring to the Ukrainian edition (*Knizhnaya letopis*', No. 47, 1969, entry 38568) show the number of copies (though this information is always given there for 'ordinary' books). The figure of 10,000 copies each is, however, quoted here on completely reliable information.

6   Not counting the 26-page bibliography

7   'S.' will refer to pages in Stenchuk's book (English translation), and 'D.' to the pages of the present book..

8   Stenchuk (S., 171–96) lists nearly two hundred such books and articles on the nationalities question published from 1964 to 1968, and abstracts of theses in the same field examined in 1964–7. No doubt some future researcher into the official Soviet policy on it will be grateful for this systematic list. In places it makes quite curious reading; for instance, under the subheading 'The National Policy of the CPSU' among the total of 34 titles we find, in the Ukrainian edition (pp. 174–6), no less than three books with absolutely identical titles, rendered into English (S., 176–7) as *The Flowering and Drawing Together of Nations in the Process of the Construction of Communism*, or with slight variations, by various authors: G. Apresyan (Moscow University, 1965), V.A. Pustovit (Kyiv, 1966), both in Russian (*Rastsvet i sblizheniye natsiy v protsesse stroitel'stva kommunizma*), and O.M. Horpinko and M. Velikolug (Kyiv, 1967), in Ukrainian, in addition to some eight books and articles with only one or two words in the title transposed or changed (e.g. 'period' instead of 'process'). It is also significant that all those thesis abstracts listed by Stenchuk (the Ukrainian edn. pp. 186–95) which are published by universities situated in nonRussian republics are in Russian, and never in the language of the republic. Thus, he inadvertently confirms Dzyuba's assertion about the russification of higher education (D., 157), although this fact is concealed in Stenchuk's English translation, all titles being given in English only (S., 188–96).

9   The data found, e.g., in *Vsesoyuznaya perepis' naseleniya 17 dekabrya 1926 g. Kratkiye svodki. Vyp. iv. Narodnost' i rodnoy yazyk naseleniya SSSR*, Moscow, 1928, pp. 3, 23, are: Ukrainian SSR population, 29,018,187; therefrom, Ukrainians male, 11,257,032; female, 11,961,828; Russians male, 1,330,519; female 1,346,647. Hence the totals and percentages can be calculated: Ukrainians, 23,218,850 or 80 per cent; Russians 2,677,166 or 9.2 per cent.

10   H. Yurchenko writes in *Ukraina* (No. 2, 11 January 1970, p. 3) that in the 1926 census '80 per cent of the population called themselves Ukrainians' in the Ukrainian SSR.

11   *XII s'yezd RKP(B)*, Moscow, 1923 (Stenchuk quotes the original Russian title in the Ukrainian edition of his book, p. 26, fn. 1).

12   *XII s'yezd RKP(B)*, Moscow, 1968, p. 177.

13   *Istoriya Sovetskoy Konstitutsii (v dokumentakh)* 1917–1956, Moscow, 1957, p. 891.

14   'Cf. Erik de Mauny, *Russian Prospect*, 1969, p. 181, and also the top-level Anglo-Soviet barter deal in 1969 of Soviet spies for Mr Gerald Brooke and some Soviet brides of Englishmen.

15   It should be noted that the Ukrainian edition of Stenchuk's book carries references to Dzyuba's Ukrainian edition; these page references have been taken over into Stenchuk's English translation, instead of being replaced by references to Dzyuba's first English edition. This creates quite unnecessary difficulties for the English-speaking reader, when he wishes to check the context of Stenchuk's references. Also, Stenchuk's translator himself rendered into English all the quotations from Dzyuba occurring in

Stenchuk's Ukrainian edition, instead of using the available first English edition. (It was indeed available to Stenchuk: cf. p. 242 below.) In the present postscript, however, Stenchuk's page references to Dzyuba's Ukrainian edition are replaced, when quoted, by references to the present edition, and similarly, when Stenchuk's and this edition's English: renderings differ, the latter is preferred. Thus, Stenchuk's translator renders the above phrase as 'It is considered that the national question ...', etc.

16   General-Lieutenant D. Dragunsky, a Deputy of the Supreme Soviet of the Georgian SSR, twice Hero of the Soviet Union, writing in *Pravda*, 27 February 1970, p. 5.

17   In the Ukrainian version (p. 156) bezzaperechny, which means 'irrefutable' rather than 'implicit'.

18   S. Oliynyk's Preface to Dzyuba, *Internatsionalizm chy rusyfikatsiya?*, Munich, 1968, p. 19.

19   How untrue this charge (again borrowed from Stenchuk) is may be seen, e.g., from Dzyuba's reference to *Capital* (D., 29) and by verifying the context of all quotations in that, or any other, chapter. Also it is not true to say that to attach a very great importance to the nationalities question is un-Marxist; to quote the contemporary American Communist philosopher H. Selsam whose views Stenchuk evidently wholeheartedly approves (cf. S., 59), 'The Marxist, rather than ignoring the nation and the resultant national question, takes it with unexampled seriousness' (H. Sekam, *Socialism and Ethics*, London, 1947, p. 179).

20   M. Musinka: a research worker at the Presov Faculty of Philosophy, P.J. Safarik University of Kosice, eastern Slovakia.

21   Then, it will be remembered, Novotny was still in power in Czechoslovakia. About that time, some articles and literary works by Ukrainian authors, both living and dead, which either were not published in the USSR or were to be published only subsequently, appeared in print in Czechoslovakia perfectly legally under the Communist government's authority, both in the original and in translation.

22   Apparently not Dzyuba's own poems. Earlier in the same year the Prague publishing house Svet sovetu ('The World of the Soviets', specializing in Soviet literature) produced an anthology of thirteen young Ukrainian poets, some poems appearing there before their publication in the USSR (cf. D., 142).

23   The complete quotation as given by Dmyterko. The abridgement is his.

24   There is so far no other evidence to confirm any of Dmyterko's allegations, which, if partially or fully true, would appear to be based on the border guards' or the KGB's records. Dmyterko's indignation about Musinka is particularly unconvincing, since despite this alleged incident Musinka subsequently continued being mentioned in very favourable contexts in the journal *Vitchyzna*, whose editor-in-chief happens to be Dmyterko himself; Musinka is described e.g., as 'a young scholar folklorist from Presov' or 'a well-known Ukrainian folklorist in Czechoslovakia' (*Vitchyzna*, 1967, Nos. 2, 4; 1968, No. 8; also the Kyiv academic journal, *Radyans'ke literaturoznavstvo*, 1969, No. 6).

25   It is significant that only two Writers' Union members were found to sign this letter; some journalists had to be drawn in to swell the numbers.

26   V. Kozachenko: the Party Committee secretary of the Kyiv branch of the Party organization of the Writers' Union of Ukraine until early 1969, then the chairman of the Executive Committee of the Kyiv writers' organization. Known for his attacks on Ivan Svitlychny before the latter's arrest (cf. p. 217 above) in *Literaturna Ukraina* (27 April 1965) and on the signatories of the 'Protest of the 139' (Lit. Ukr., 21, 24 May and 27 December 1968; cf. M. Browne (ed.), *Ferment in Ukraine*, London, 1970, pp. 191–8).

27 *Literaturna Ukraina*, 6 January 1970, p. 3.
28 Said to have taken place late in November.
29 This meeting is understood to have taken place on 26 December.
30 Again, no mention of Dmytreko's name.
31 Apart from the one letter to the Editor, no other such articles appear to have been printed in the Soviet internal press between 5 August and 26 December 1969.
32 Cf. note 394, note on Drach in the section 'People'.

33 Dzyuba's failure to recant was commented upon by a hard-liner Party *apparatchik* in the Institute of Literature of the Academy of Sciences of the Ukrainian SSR, I. Bass, who had written an article, half of which consisted of attacks against three of Dzyuba's articles on Ukrainian literature which had been published abroad. When Dzyuba's above statement to the Union's Presidium appeared in print, Bass pointed out in a postscript to his article that Dzyuba had 'not acknowledged a single one of his errors'. (I. Bass, 'U pokhodi proty istyny', *Radyans'ke literaturoznavstvo*, No. 1, 1970, pp. 65–70.)

Editors' notes

Notes by Resistance Books

- The chapters titled 'The author and his book' and 'Postscript to the second edition' were published in previous editions under the name of M.I. Holubenko. The author's actual name, Bohdan Krawchenko, is used in this edition.
- The names of cities in this edition have been changed from Russian to Ukrainian.
- The dates of death of people listed in the previous editions have been added when that is known.
- The text in this edition has been edited to include the notes and corrections in the Appendix of the earlier editions.
- Notes by Weidenfeld and Nicolson to the 1968 and 1970 editions, and reproduced in the Pathfinder Press 1974 edition.
- Some references in the original work to sources not available in Britain have been replaced in the text of the editions by references to other, available, editions of the same sources. Wherever a source exists not only in the original language but also in a standard, or authorized, English translation, the English edition is always quoted, usually without any change. Some exceptions to this rule, occurring on pp. 22, 57, 61, 65 [in the earlier editions] are noted below. If no published English translation of a source has been found, the original source is referred to, and translation is made directly from it, e.g., Dzyuba translates Togliatti from *Pravda*'s Russian into Ukrainian, but

in this book Togliatti's quotation has been translated straight from Italian into English; the original publication is cited and not *Pravda*, which is in fact given as the source of this quotation by Dzyuba.
- References to the very rare 1923 edition of XII *s'yezd RKP(B)* have been replaced in the second edition by references to the 1968 reprint, which has become generally available since the appearance of the first edition of this book.

Tables

Table 1: Book production in Russian and in other languages

Titles

Year	USSR total	In Russian	%	In other languages	%
1964	78,204	58,351	75	19,853	25
1965	76,101	57,521	76	18,580	24
1966	72,977	54,968	75	18,009	25
1967	74,081	56,225	76	17,856	24
1968	75,699	57,498	76	18,201	24

Copies (in thousands)

Year	USSR total	In Russian	%	In other languages	%
1964	1,252,934	1,017,882	81.2	235,052	18.8
1965	1,279,268	1,038,411	81.2	240,857	18.8
1966	1,260,478	1,012,515	80.3	247,963	19.7
1967	1,243,551	978,883	78.7	264,668	21.3
1968	1,334,005	1,052,534	78.9	281,471	21.1

Table 2: Book production in the Ukrainian SSR and that in the Ukrainian language

Titles

Year	Ukr SSR total	% of USSR total	Ukrainian SSR in Ukrainian language	% of Ukrainian SSR total	USSR in Ukrainian language	% of USSR total
1964	7,492	9.6	3,266	44	3,270	4.2
1965	7,251	9.5	2,998	41	3,003	3.9
1966	7,486	10.2	3,021	40	3,026	4.1
1967	6,861	9.3	2,842	41	2,855	3.8
1968	7,615	10.1	2,944	39	2,950	3.9

Copies (in thousands)

1964	112,281	9.0	78,031	70	78,761	6.3
1965	110,742	10.7	77,489	70	78,442	6.1
1966	109,732	10.8	79,366	72	80,059	6.3
1967	115,712	9.3	87,325	75	88,608	7.1
1968	126,475	9.5	96,202	76	98,673	7.4

Table 3: Periodicals

Narodnoye khozyaystvo SSSR v 1964 godu, Moscow, 1965,
pp. 722–3; *Narodnoye ... v 1965 godu*, Moscow, 1966, pp. 732–7;
Pechat' SSSR v 1966 godu. Statisticheskiye materialy, Moscow, 1967,
pp. 10, 56, 59, 95, 156; ... *v 1967 g.*, pp. 10, 56, 59, 95, 158; ...
v 1968 g., similar pages.

			Titles			
Year	USSR total	Therefrom in the languages of Union Republics except Russian %	Ukrainian SSR total	% of the USSR total	Therefrom in the Ukrainian language	% of the USSR total
1964	3,833	693	18	240	6.3	113	2.9
1965	3,846	658	17	256	6.7	108	2.8
1966	4,342	700	16	288	6.6	120	2.8
1967	4,704	722	15	323	6.9	126	2.7
1968	5,109	768	15	391	7.6	146	2.9
			Copies (in millions)			
1964	1,217.7	168.6	13.9	66.7	5.5	57.9	4.8
1965	1,547.6	190.3	12.3	77.7	5.0	67.6	4.4
1966	1,955.8	229.2	11.7	96.4	4.9	85.8	4.4
1967	2,295.7	301.7	13.1	123.7	5.4	111.7	4.9
1968	2,362.3	346.4	14.7	141.4	6.0	128.4	5.4

Table 4: Newspaper publishing statistics

The figure of '765' Ukrainian-language newspapers in 1963 has been corrected in the subsequent volume (*Narodnoye khozyaystvo sssr v 1964 godu*, Moscow, 1965, p. 728) to 1,906. Moreover, the 1950 and 1963 figures are not in fact comparable, as the 1963 figures include collective farm newspapers, whilst the 1950 figures do not. There were 1,353 collective farm papers in Ukraine in 1963 (and only 271 in the rest of the USSR), appearing on average once a month with runs of about 750 copies per issue (*Pechat' sssr v 1963 godu*, Moscow, 1964, pp. 60, 95), Truly comparable newspaper publishing statistics for 1963–6 on which the following table is based are available in the annual volumes: *Pechat' sssr v 1963 g.*, pp. 60, 95–6, ... *1964 g.*, pp. 75, 126, ... *1965 g.*, pp. 67, 187, ... *1966 g.*, pp. 67, 187, ... *1967 g.*, pp. 66, 188, ... *1968 g.*, pp. 66, 188, in which collective farm papers are consistently excluded from the language analyses.

Titles

Year	USSR total	Ukrainian SSR total	language	In Ukrainian	% of the USSR total	% of the Ukrainian SSR total
1950	7,831	1,192	15	972	11	82
1963	5,167	1,013	20	639	12	63
1964	5,067	932	18	607	12	65
1965	6,253	1,104	18	742	12	67
1966	6,528	1,114	17	758	12	68
1967	7,087	1,285	18	890	13	69
1968	7,307	1,289	18	897	12	70

Copies (in millions)

Year	USSR total	Ukrainian SSR total	language	In Ukrainian	% of the USSR total	% of the Ukrainian SSR total
1950	6,998	872	12.4	575	8.2	66
1963	18,292	1,817	9.9	1,229	6.7	68
1964	19,917	2,004	10.1	1,440	7.2	72
1965	23,057	2,064	9.0	1,466	6.4	71
1966	24,462	2,324	9.5	1,606	6.6	69
1967	26,654	2,743	10.3	1,879	7.0	68
1968	27,810	2,966	10.7	2,009	7.2	68

Table 5: Student numbers in 1963-9 (in thousands)

Narodnoye khozyaystvo SSSR v 1963 godu, Moscow, 1965, p. 579; ... *v 1964 godu*, p. 691; ... *v 1965 godu*, p. 701; *Strana Sovetov za 50 let*, Moscow, 1967, p. 280; *Narodnoye khozyaystvo sssr v 1967 godu*, p. 803; ... *v 1968 godu*, p. 694.)

Academic year	USSR total	Russians	%	Ukrainian	%
1963-4	3,260.7	1,987.9	61	476.4	14.6
1964-5	*figures not available*				
1965-6	3,860.5	2,362.0	61	558.6	14.5
1966-7	4,123.2	2,494.7	61	590.2	14.3
1967-8	4,310.9	2,599.5	60	600.1	13.9
1968-9	4,469.7	2,675.9	60	616.9	13.8

People

The trials of Zalyvakha, P., Horyn', B., Horyn', M., Hryn', M., Rusyn, I., Martynenko, O. and Hevrych, Ya. were in camera, in contravention of Soviet law on this point. They were all charged with 'anti-Soviet propaganda and agitation', and sometimes (as in the cases of Hevrych and Martynenko) this charge was qualified also as 'nationalist'. With the exception of Hryn', whose sentence was suspended, they were all deported after the trials and appeals to the Pot'ma Camps in the Mordvin Autonomous SSR (south-east of Moscow).

Aksakov, I. S. (1823–86): Russian Slavophile writer and journalist, editor and publisher of the newspapers *Den'* and *Moskva*. Son of S. T. Aksakov.

Amangeldy lmanov (1871–1919): one of the leaders of the Kazakh uprising of 1916, from 1917 to 1919 leader of Red partisans in Kazakhstan against the Kazakh nationalist Alash-Orda government. Killed by his own followers, who switched to the anti-Soviet side.

Antonov, O.K. (1906–84): Corresponding Member of the Ukrainian SSR Academy of Sciences; Hero of Socialist Labour, an alternate member of the CPSU Central Committee, deputy of the USSR Supreme Soviet, Lenin Prize laureate.

Bazhan, M. (1904–83): leading Soviet Ukrainian poet; scholar, member of the Academy of Sciences, Ukrainian SSR, and of the Central Committee, CPU. Shevchenko Prize laureate.

Berezovs'ky, M. (1745–77): Ukrainian composer, in Italy from 1765 to 1775, where an opera of his was performed in Livorno in 1773. Also wrote choral church music.

Boychukists: followers of the Soviet Ukrainian painters, the brothers **M. and T. Boychuk** (1882–1937 and 1896–1922) who established the Ukrainian monumentalist school of art, which combined Byzantine and early Renaissance motifs with those of Ukrainian folk ornamentation.

Bratun', R. (1927–95): Soviet Ukrainian poet, CPSU member. Editor of *Zhovten'* (an organ of the Writers' Union of Ukraine) from October 1963 to April 1966, when he was demoted, becoming a member of the editorial board.

Chuprynka, H. (1879–1921): Ukrainian poet. Shot for participation in an anti-Soviet uprising.

Dovzhenko, O. (1894–1956): the most outstanding Soviet Ukrainian film director; also writer and graphic artist. One of the founders of Ukrainian cinematography.

Drach, Ivan (1936–2018): Soviet Ukrainian poet, the most prominent member of the 'sixties group'.

Dray-Khmara, M. (1889–1939): Soviet Ukrainian poet, philologist, translator and scholar, an authority on Ukrainian and Serbian literature. Arrested in 1935, he died in the Kolyma labour camps. A selection of his poetry (Vybrane, Kyiv, 1969) has since appeared. Rehabilitated.

Fylypovych, P. (1891–1937): Soviet Ukrainian neo-classicist poet, literary scholar. Arrested and executed in 1937. A selection of his works has been said (1969) to be in preparation for publication. Rehabilitated.

Hevrych, Ya. (1937– 2009): a student of the Kyiv Medical Institute. Arrested at the end of August 1965 and sentenced in Kyiv on 11 March 1966 to five years in strict regime camps, reduced on appeal to three years.

Hordiyenko, K. (?–1733): leader (otaman) of the Zaporozhe Cossack Host at the time of Mazeppa; he sided with Mazeppa in the latter's attempt to achieve secession of Ukraine from Russia.

Horyn', Bohdan (1936–?): Soviet Ukrainian literary and art critic and scholar, research worker in the L'viv Museum of Ukrainian Art. Arrested on 26 August 1965 and sentenced in L'viv on 18 April 1966 apparently to three years in strict regime camps. Released in August 1968, forbidden to return to L'viv, and works in occasional jobs in the L'viv Region.

Horyn', Mykhaylo (1930–2013): Soviet Ukrainian psychologist (cf. V. Vukovich, 'V tsekh prishol psikholog', *Izvestia*, 16 February 1965). Arrested and sentenced together with his brother Bohdan to six years in strict regime camps. In December 1966 put for six months into prison inside the camp for having in his possession a copy of Dzyuba's *Internationalism or Russification?* in Ukrainian in manuscript, although members of the KGB in the camp subsequently admitted to his brother that it was not an anti-Soviet document (cf. M. Browne (ed.), *Ferment in Ukraine*, London, 1970, p. 148). For writing a protest about the inhumanity of the camp administration in illtreating in June 1967 a prisoner's mother who came to visit him, M. Horyn' was transferred in July 1967 for three years to the Vladimir Prison, notorious for its appalling conditions (ibid., pp. 108–10, and A. Marchenko, *My Testimony*, London, 1969, pp. 103–204).

Hrinchenko, B. (1863–1910): Ukrainian writer, ethnographer and philologist, best known for his monumental *Dictionary of Ukrainian* (4 vols, 1907–9).

Hrushevs'ky, M. (1866–1934): the most outstanding of Ukrainian historians; scholar, statesman, head of the Ukrainian national government, the Central Rada (1917–18), member of the Academies of Sciences of the Ukrainian SSR and the USSR. Partially rehabilitated in 1966.

Hryn', M. (1928–?): a senior researcher at the Institute of Geophysics, Kyiv. Arrested in late August 1965, sentenced in Kirvin March 1966 to three years, but the sentence was suspended in view of his full admission of 'guilt' and recantation. After release he was reinstated as a junior researcher.

Hryn'ko, H.F. (1890–1938): a leading Borot'bist, joined the CP(B)U in 1920, occupied high governmental posts in the Ukrainian SSR and the USSR, the last one being that of Commissar for Finance of the USSR. Arrested in 1937 and shot. Now rehabilitated.

Ivchenko, M. (1890–1939): Soviet Ukrainian writer. Died in virtual exile in the Caucasus. His works banned since 1930.

Kalynovych, M. (1888–1949): Soviet Ukrainian philologist, authority on Ukrainian, Sanskrit and Romance languages and on Russian and modern French literatures. Member of the Ukrainian SSR Academy of Sciences.

Karavans'ky, S. (1920–2016): Soviet Ukrainian philologist, poet, translator. Arrested in 1944, sentenced on 7 February 1945 to 25 years' detention. After 16 years and 5 months in prison and in labour camps, amnestied on 19 December 1960. Re-arrested on 13 November 1965 and deported to the Pot'ma Camps, without a trial, to serve the rest of his original sentence. For writing protests to higher authorities and for reading documents about the situation in Ukraine transferred in summer 1967 to the Vladimir Prison together with M. Horyn'. Early in 1970, his sentence was increased to 30 years for smuggling documents out of the prison.

Kenesary, Qasim-uli Sultan (Kasymov) (1802–47): leader of the Kazakh anti-Russian revolt, 1837–47.

Khmel'nyts'ky, Bohdan (1595–1657): Hetman of Ukraine, outstanding Cossack leader of a successful revolt against Poland (1648–54), founder of the Ukrainian Cossack State.

Khvyl'ovy, M. (1893–1933): Soviet Ukrainian writer, critic and publicist, CP(B)U member, famous for his slogan 'away from Moscow' and advocating cultural orientation towards Europe. Committed suicide in the face of persecution in Ukraine.

Koryak, V. (1889–1939): Soviet Ukrainian literary critic and scholar. Exiled by the tsarist government in 1915–17 for revolutionary activity. CPSU (B) member from 1920. Arrested in 1937, he died in a Siberian labour camp. Rehabilitated.

Koshyts' choir (1919–1924): a national Ukrainian ensemble under the direction of O. Koshyts' (1875–1944), conductor, composer and ethnographer. After the establishment of Soviet rule in Ukraine in 1920, the ensemble left for Western Europe and North America.

Kosiv, M. (1934–?): L'viv University lecturer in Ukrainian literature. Arrested in late August 1965, suffered a severe coronary thrombosis when in prison, released five months later. Eventually found employment as a schoolteacher in the L'viv Region.

Kostenko, Lina (1930–?): Soviet Ukrainian poetess, a prominent member of the so-called 'sixties group' of young Ukrainian writers.

Kupala, Yanka (1882–1942): the greatest Byelorussian poet. The poem alluded to is 'A khto tam idzye?' (1905–7).

Kurbas, L. (1887–1942): leading Soviet Ukrainian theatre director, known for his expressionist experiments; introduced the latest West European achievements to the Ukrainian stage. Exiled to Siberia in 1933, where he died in a labour camp. Now rehabilitated.

Lysenko, M.V. (1842–1912): the leading Ukrainian composer; ethnographer, conductor and civic leader, founder of the national trend in Ukrainian music.

Makharadze, F.I. (1868–1941): Georgian communist, occupied leading positions in the Party and the government of the Georgian SSR.

Malyshko, A. (1912–1970): Soviet Ukrainian poet, member of the CPSU and of the Committee of the Writers' Union of Ukraine; several State Prizes and decorations, including two Orders of Lenin.

Martynenko, O. (1935–?): a senior engineer of the Kyiv Geological Prospecting Research Institute. Arrested on 28 August 1965 and sentenced to three years in strict regime camps, now free. Both he and Rusyn were sentenced in Kyiv on 25 March 1966 (together with a Kyiv University laboratory assistant, Mrs Yevheniya Kuznetsova (1913–68), arrested on 25 August 1965 and sentenced to four years in strict regime camps; mortally ill, she 'recanted', was released, apparently in summer 1967, and died a year later.)

Mayboroda, H. (1913–1992): Soviet Ukrainian composer, chairman of the Composers' Union of Ukraine, deputy of the Ukrainian SSR Supreme Soviet.

Mazeppa, Ivan (1644–1709): Hetman of Ukraine, led a war of secession from Russia in alliance with Charles XII of Sweden against Peter I.

Mdivani, Budu (1877–1937): a Georgian communist leader, one-time Premier of Soviet Georgia. Arrested and executed in 1937.

Mentsyn'sky, M. (1876–1935): Ukrainian tenor, appeared in leading roles in Wagner's and Verdi's operas in European cities, including London.

Murav'yov, Count M.N. (1796–1866): 'the Hangman': notorious for his extreme cruelty in the suppression of the uprisings of 1830–31 and 1863 in Poland, Lithuania and Byelorussia where he was the Governor-General.

Myshuha, O. (1853–1922): Ukrainian tenor of world reputation (known by the name of Filippi), he performed at all the major European opera centres and taught in the music schools of Kyiv, Warsaw and Stockholm.

Nikovs'ky, A. (1885–1942): Soviet Ukrainian literary critic, scholar and authority on West European literature. Convicted together with Yefremov; died in a labour camp.

Parashchuk, M. (1878–1963): Ukrainian sculptor, studied in Paris under Rodin. After 1924 in Sofia.

Pavlyk, M. (1853–1915): West Ukrainian writer, prominent in the Ukrainian Radical Party in Galicia. A selection of his works (*Tvory*) was last published in Kyiv in 1959.

Petlyura, Simon (1877–1926): a leader of the Ukrainian Social-Democratic Workers' Party, a leading member of the Ukrainian Central Rada (1917–18), chairman of the Directory (1919–20), C.-in-C. of the Ukrainian national armies from 1917 to 1920 against the Bolsheviks and the White Guards. Assassinated in Paris in 1926.

Petrovs'ky, H.I. (1878–1958): a Ukrainian old Bolshevik, occupied prominent Party and government posts until 1938. Head of the Bolshevik faction in the Fourth Duma.

Pidmohyl'ny, V. (1901–1941): Soviet Ukrainian writer and translator, arrested in 1934, died in a Siberian labour camp. Rehabilitated.

Pryzhov, I. (1827–1885): Russian historian, the author inter alia of *Malorossiya (Yuzhnaya Rus') v istorii yeyo literatury s XI po XVIII vek*, Voronezh, 1869.

Purishkevich, V.M. (1870–1920): a founder of the Union of the Russian People (cf. Shul'gin).

Rusyn, I. (1937–?): an engineering geodesist. Arrested on 28 August 1965 and sentenced to one year in strict regime camps.

Ryl's'ky, M. (1895–1966): one of the most outstanding Soviet Ukrainian poets, literary critic, scholar, member of the Ukrainian SSR Academy of Sciences, translator into Ukrainian of foreign classics and literary idol of the younger generation of poets in Ukraine.

Sadovs'ky, M.K. (1856–1933) (stage name of M.K. Tobilevych): Ukrainian actor and stage director, founder of the Ukrainian modern theatre.

Safarov, G.I. (1891–1942): leading Bolshevik, editor of *Leningradskaya pravda*, member of the 'new opposition' within the Party. Expelled from it in 1934, died in a labour camp.

Semenko, M. (1892–1938): Soviet Ukrainian futurist poet and literary critic. Arrested in 1937 and executed. Rehabilitated.

Shkurupiy, G. (1903–1937): Soviet Ukrainian futurist poet and prose writer. Arrested in 1934 and shot in 1937. A selection of his works (*Vybrane*, Kyiv, 1968) has since appeared. Rehabilitated.

Serpilin, L. (1912–?): Soviet Ukrainian writer, CPSU member.

Shamil (1798–1871): leader of the 'Holy War' (1820s–60s) of the Caucasian peoples against Russian colonial oppression.

Shestopal, M.: an assistant professor in the faculty of journalism, CPSU member, known for his speech at the Ukrainian language conference held in Kyiv on 11–15 February 1963. Dismissed from the University and expelled from the Party.

Shevchenko, Taras (1814–1861): the greatest Ukrainian poet whose poetry has not only laid the foundations of modern Ukrainian literature and literary language, but whose ideas have inspired the development of the modern Ukrainian national movement. Born a serf, he was critical of the social, political and national injustices of the tsarist regime, and arrested and exiled for ten years. Ever since Shevchenko has been the personification of the Ukrainian people, of their national aspirations and goals, and their spiritual leader.

Shul'gin, V. (1878–1976): Russian politician and political writer, a leading member of the Union of the Russian People (founded in 1905, known as 'the Black Hundred';

a forerunner of the fascist movements of the 1930s), a staunch anti-Bolshevik *émigré* leader after the Revolution. Returned to the USSR in 1944 (according to some accounts – cf. *The Times*, 7 December 1965 – he was at that time arrested by the Russians in Prague) and sentenced possibly to 25 years' detention. He was amnestied in 1956. In 1960 he wrote an 'Open Letter to Russian Emigres', published in *Russkiy golos* (New York) (cf. *Izvestia*, 17 December 1960). His letter to Khrushchev praising the CPSU programme appeared in *Pravda*, 1 October 1961.

Skrypnyk, M. (1872–1933): Ukrainian communist leader, Party member since 1897. Occupied high posts in the Party, Soviet Ukrainian governments and the Comintern. Committed suicide when accused of nationalism. Now rehabilitated.

Slisarenko, O. (1891–1937): Soviet Ukrainian writer. Arrested and executed in 1937. A volume of his selected works (*Bunt*, Kyiv, 1965) has appeared since the completion of Dzyuba's study. Rehabilitated.

Smolych, Yu. (1900–1976): Soviet Ukrainian writer and publicist; CPSU member, twice decorated. Member of the Presidium, Writers' Union of Ukraine. Two books of his memoirs have since been published in Kyiv: *Rozpovid' pro nespokiy* (late 1968) and *Rozpovid' pro nespokiy tryuaye* (1969).

Sosyura, V. (1898–1965): an eminent Soviet Ukrainian lyrical poet, popular among the young Ukrainian poets.

Stel'makh, M. (1912–1983): Soviet Ukrainian writer and ethnographer, deputy chairman of the Council of the Union, Supreme Soviet of the USSR; several decorations, including Order of Lenin (1967).

Svitlychny, I. (1929–1992): prominent Soviet Ukrainian literary critic. Arrested in late August 1965 and released at the end of April 1966.

Tychyna, P. (1891–1967): one of the most outstanding Soviet Ukrainian poets and a literary critic; under pressure during the late 1920s, he became the official ode writer, and followed a strictly conformist line.

Vaillant-Couturier, P. (1892–1937): one of the founders of the French CP, writer, editor of *L'Humanité* (1926–37).

Voynarovs'ky, A. (1680–1740): I. Mazeppa's nephew and confidant. After Mazeppa's downfall, lived in exile in Hamburg. Kidnapped and taken to Russia, he was deported to Siberia where he died. K. Ryleyev wrote a poem, 'Voynarovsky', which also influenced Pushkin's 'Poltava'.

Vynnychenko, V. (1880–1951): Ukrainian writer and publicist, member of the two Ukrainian national governments, the Central Rada and the Directory (1917–20), later an *émigré* in France.

Yakovlev, Ya.A. (Epshteyn) (1896–1939): one of the most prominent old Bolshevik leaders in Ukraine, a member of the Central Committee of the RCP(B) and CPSU(B); later in charge of Soviet agriculture. In 1937 he was sent from Moscow to carry out the purge in Byelorussia; was himself shot two years later. Now rehabilitated.

Yefremov, S. (1876–1937): Soviet Ukrainian literary scholar and critic; member of the Ukrainian national governments (1917–20); member of the Ukrainian Academy of Sciences. For allegedly organizing the Union for the Liberation of Ukraine he was sentenced in 1930 to ten years in prison, where he died.

Yevshan, M. (1889–1919): Ukrainian literary critic, officer in the Ukrainian national army (1917–19).

Yohansen, M. (1895–1937): Soviet Ukrainian poet and prose writer, linguist and literary scholar. Arrested and executed in 1937. A small selection of his children's stories only (*Kit Chudylo*, Kyiv, 1968) has since appeared. Rehabilitated.

Zalyvakha, P. (1925–2007): Soviet Ukrainian artist and art teacher. Arrested at the end of August 1965 and sentenced in Ivano-Frankivsk in March 1966 to five years in strict regime camps.

Zatons'ky, V. (1888–1938): Ukrainian communist, occupied high posts in the Party and the government of the Ukrainian SSR. Arrested in 1937 and executed. Now fully rehabilitated.

Zerov, Mykola (1890–1941): Soviet Ukrainian neo-classicist poet, literary historian, critic, translator of classical and French literature, an authority on the literature of antiquity. Arrested in 1935, died in a Siberian camp. A selection of his works (*Vybrane*, Kyiv, 1966) has since appeared. Rehabilitated.

Ziber, N. (1844–1888): author of works on Ukrainian common law. His selected economic works (*Izbrannyye ekonomicheskiye proizvedeniya* in 2 vols) were published in Moscow in 1959.

Index

With names, the dates of birth and death are given when known. A brief description is provided, except for: persons whose data appear in the section of People, persons described sufficiently fully in the author's own text, persons generally well known. Also, of course, no description is provided when nothing has been found in sources consulted.

Some congress speakers not identified by name in the text are none the less indexed under their names as well as under the appropriate Congress entry, e.g., the 'delegates to the XII Congress' alluded to on p. 171 are identifiable as Makharadze and Mdivani by reference to the 'RCP(B) ... Congresses... XII' Index entry.

References are to text pages. Italicized figures refer to the pages of the Notes.

Transliteration of geographical names in the Index (and throughout the book) is in conformity with The Times Atlas.

Abilov, A., 256, 257, 262, 267, 270.
Aesop (7th–6th c. B.C..), 218.
Africa, 120, 144, 194, 228.
Aguls, 258
Aksakov, I. S. (1823–86), 260.
Aksakov, S. T. (1791–1859), 246.
Alexander II (the Liberator) (1818–81), 188, 259.
Alexis (1629–76), 122.
Algeria, 53.
Amalgamation of nations, see also assimilation, 79, 80–86, 269, 270, 275, 283.
Amangeldy Imanov (1873–1919), 335.
Annexations, 116, 121, 125, 136, 245.
Antisemitism, 111, 156, 363, 364.
Antonov, Oleh. (1906–1984), 29.

Antonovych, V. (1834–1908), 213.
Archipenko, A. (1887–1964), 218.
Argentinian, 145.
Armenians, 85, 183, 219.
Army, 134, 202, 204, 231, 298, 313, 317.
Arrests, political (1965), 29–31, 98, 204.
Art, 219, 232–233.
Artists' Union, 210.
Asia, 122, 123, 136, 144, 194, 280, 286.
Assimilation of nations, 81, 82, 85–87, 131, 224, 266, 272, 275, 277, 287, 301.
  See also amalgamation,
Astrakhan, 112, 114.
Aswan, 144.
Australia, 53.
Austria, 214.
Austro-Hungarian Empire, 134.
'Autonomization', 62, 65.
Averchenko, A. (1881–1925), 216.
Azerbaijan SSR, 168.
Azerbaidjani, 107, 206.
Azov Sea, 112.

Badinguet (Napoleon III), 52.
Bahaliy, D. (1857–1932), 123, 196.
Bakunin, M. (1824–76), 44, 246.
Baltic, Soviet Republics, 87, 113, 114, 168, 187, 288.
Banderists, 154.
Bashkirs, 141, 273.
Baturin, 166.
Bazhan, M. (1904–1983), 216.
Belgians, 282.
Berezovs'ky, M. (1745–77), 218.
Berlin, 271.
Bibikov, D. (1792–1870), Minister of the Interior, extreme reactionary, 248.
Bilets'ky, O. (1884–1961), Ukrainian Literary scholar, 91.
'Bilingualism theory', 260–262, 274, 275.

'Black Hundreds', 136.
Black Sea, 113, 122.
Bloch, J., 64.
Bobrinsky, Count V. A. (1868–?),
  extreme right in the Duma, 137.
Bodyans'ky, O. (1808–1877), 214.
Bohomazov, O. (1880–1930),
  Soviet Ukrainian painter, 219.
Bondarenko, V. V. (1907–?), 166.
Book publishing, data, 178–183, 240–241.
Books, Russian, import, 177–178.
Books, Ukrainian, availability, 177–178.
Borot'bists (Ukrainian Communist Party), 99.
Bortnyans'ky, D. (1751–1825), 218.
Bosporus, 112.
'Boychukists', 219.
Bratun', R. (1927–?), 212.
Braun, O. (1872–1955), 208.
Britain, 208, 297.
Brotherhood of Cyril and Methodius, 150.
Brussels, 282.
Bukharin, M. (1888–1938), 62.
Bulgaria, 286 302; Bulgarians, 167.
Bunin, I. (1870–1953), 114, 215.
Buryat, 261.
Butovych, M. (1895–1961), Ukrainian painter and engraver, 218.
Byelorussia, 129, 130, 148, 164.; Byelorussians, 129, 136, 147, 148, 167, 297.

Cadres, national, 169, 253, 269, 287, 288;
'exchange of', 115, 168, 184.
Canada, 53.
Cape Province, 53.
Karelian, 273.
Caspian Sea, 112.
Catherine II (the Great), 120, 128–130, 133, 135, 147, 153.
Caucasus, 117, 141, 246, 272.
Central Asian peoples, 119, 122.
Central Europe, 280.
Central Executive Committee, 194, 229, 230.
Central Rada, 72.
Centralization, 78, 159, 161, 169, 170, 269, 298, 300.
Chaadayev, P. (1794–1856), 129.
Cherkassians (Ukrainians), 153.
Chernihov province, 124.

Chernyshevsky, N. (1828–89), 44, 114, 245.
China, 137.
Chubyns'ky, P. (1839–84), 213.
Chukovsky, K. (1882–1969), 249.
Chuprynka, H. (1879–1921), 216.
Chuvash, 167.
Cinema, 22, 23, 145, 159, 187, 192, 207, 212.
Cities and towns, 204–205, 209, 280–282.
Club of Young Writers and Artists in Kyiv, 36, 154.
Colchis (Mingrelia and Imeretia), 117.
Colonial heritage of Russian Empire as 'ancestor' of USSR, 117–137; Russian colonialism, 125, 131, 141, 148; Russian petty bourgeoisie's colonialist attitudes, 106–107.
Colonies, 53, 120.
Colonizers of Africa, 120.
Comintern, see International, Third.
Committee for State Security (KGB),
Commonwealth of nations, communist, 60, 302.
Communist International, see International, Third.
Communist Party of Slovakia, Central Committee 1952 resolution, 96, 97.
Communists, Ukrainian, extermination of, 317.
Conquest, causes decline, 123–139.
Consciousness, national, 17, 46, 92, 93, 95–97, 193, 291, 292, 294, 295.
Constitutional and actual position of Ukrainian SSR, 34.
Cossacks, 20, 114, 248.
Council of People's Commissars of the Ukrainian SSR, 67, 75, 209, 229, 230.
Councils of National Economy, 157, 161, 162.
CP(B)U, Central Committee, 1927 declaration to Comintern, 194–195; resolutions, 239, 264; Plenum, 1927 theses, 94, 169, 215; 1923 Conference, 70–72; Congresses: X, 203, 289; XI, 196–197, 133; XII, 196.
CPSU(B), 83, 93, 288.
CPU, 25, 26, 30, 31, 319.
Crimea, 117, 121, 123, 165; Tartars, 121.
Crisis of Ukrainian nation, 42–43.
Cultural Association of Ukrainian Workers (KSUT), Slovakia, 96.

Cultural-educational centres, 192, 193, 236, 272.
Culture, Ukrainian, 35, 286–290; discussion on the state of (April 1965), 35.
Cyril and Methodius, 150, 248.
Czechoslovakia, 21, 93, 96, 165, 204, 280, 290, 318; Czechs, 84, 210.

Dadenkov, Yu. (1911–?), 187.
Daghestan, 258, 266.
Dante Alighieri (1265–1321), 217.
Decolonization of Russia, 141–142.
Denationalization, 43, 166, 224, 225, 248, 249, 266, 298, 301.
'Denationalization' of Russian, 249–250.
Denikin, A. (1872–1947), 109.
Derpt (Tartu), 116.
Deviation, Russian nationalist, in the Party, 100, 194–195.
Diesterweg, F. A. (1790–1866), 224,225.
Dimitrov, G. (1882–1949), 286.
Discussion of nationalities policy, stifled, 56, 100; essential, 60, 304–305.
Disdain for nationalities question, 58, 68.
Dissatisfaction with nationalities policy, 36.
Dmitriy, Bishop (Sechenov) (1708–67), 133.
Dnieper, 54, 113, 114, 148, 213.
Dobrolyubov, N. (1836–61), 44.
Don, 113, 194.
Donbas, 21, 182, 275.
Donetsk, 21, 231.
Dovhan', R., 236.
Dovzhenko, O. (1894–1956), 232.
Dovzhenko Film Studio (Kyiv), 144, 211.
Drach, I. (1936–?), 29, 212, 323.
Drahomanov, M. (1841–1895),16, 128, 213.
Dray-Khmara, M. (1889–1939), 216.
Duclos, J. (1896–1975), 290.
Duma, State, 124, 127, 134, 148, 263.
Dutch possessions, 53.
Dutt, R. Palme (1896–1974), 131.
Dymshits, V. (1910–1993), Deputy Chairman of USSR Council of Ministers, 156.

Economic approach in nationalities question, 71–76, 296–299.
Economic indices of the Ukrainian SSR, 161.
Economists, 214.

Education, Ministry of, Ukrainian SSR, 234.
Education, national, lack of, 42, 96.
Elizabeth (1709–1761), Empress of Russia, 64, 69, 76.
Emigration, 166–167.
Engels, F. (1820–1885), 80; against overstressing economic side, 64; on: colonies, 53; German national movement, 51–52, 92; Irish question, 54, 126; national independence and oppressor nations, 125; Polish claims to Ukrainian territories, 55; Russian Empire, 55, 112, 116, 127, 136; struggle for national existence, 293; Terror, 37.
England, 50, 52, 126; the English, 52, 80, 113, 120, 126, 142.
Estonian SSR, 115; Estonians, 85, 116, 273, 313,
Europe, Central, 280.
Europe, socialist nations of, 296.
'Exchange of cadres', 115, 168, 184.

Famine (1933), 196.
Far East, 165.
Fichte, J. G. (1762–1814), 224.
Filipenko, A. (1912–?), Soviet Ukrainian composer, 232.
Financial position of the Ukrainian SSR, 163.
Finland, 117.
Firsov, V., 112.
Flemish language, 282.
Folk art and customs, 206, 220; song, 237; folklore, 314.
Folklore, Institute of (Kyiv), 238.
Foolsborough, 297.
Fourier, C. (1772–1837), 80.
France, 130, 285, 296.
Franko, Ivan (1856–1916), eminent Ukrainian writer and scholar, 154, 215.
Franko Academic Dramatic Theatre, Kyiv, 211.
Fraternal aid, Russian, 120, 141.
French, the, 53, 130, 296; communists, 285, 228; 'Marxists', 27; language, 228.
Friendship of nations,86, 90, 107, 115, 124, 168, 200, 274.
Frunze, M. (1885–1925), 71.
Fylypovych, P. (1891–1937), 216.

Gagauzi, 167.
Galicia, see Western Ukraine.
Georgia, 21, 122, 146, 312; Georgian, 156, 158, 228, 254; Georgians, 128, 107, 167
German Empire, 134; Germany, 20, 52, 53; Germans, 53, 84, 298.
Glazyrin, 154.
Goethe, J. W. (1749–1832), 217.
Gogol, N. (1809–52), 245.
Gor'ky, M. (1868–1936), 79, 87, 153.
Gradovsky, A. (1841–89), 47, 48, 51.
Gramsci, A. (1891–1937), 88.
Greeks, 50.
Grigorovich, D. (1822–1899), 114.
Gumilyov, N. (1886–1921), 114.
Gypsies, 167.

Hanseatic League, 113.
Haydamaks, 248.
Health, Ministry of, Ukrainian SSR, 234, 235.
Helvetius, C. (1715–1771), 130.
Herzen, A. (1812–70), 17, 44, 45, 114, 121, 127, 129, 245, 247, 283; on: Belgium, 282; Ukraine, 121, 247, 195; her independence, 127.
Hetmanate, 123, 124.
Hevrych, Ya. (1937–?), 29.
Historic and social thought, 214.
History, falsification of, 111–132
Holovats'ky, Ya. (1814–1888), 213.
Homer (9th c. B.C.), 217.
Hordiyenko, K. (?–1733), 128.
Horyn', B. (1936–?), 29.
Horyn', M. (1930–?), 29.
Hrabovs'ky, L. (1935–?), 211.
Hrabyanka, H. (?–1738), 213.
Hrinchenko, B. (1863–1910), 215, 363.
Hrushevs'ky, M. (1866–1934), 128, 213.
Hryn', M. (1928–?), 29.
Hryn'ko, H. (1890–1938), 70, 71, 253.
Huba, V., 211.
Human rights, 282–284.
Hungary, 91, 137, 204, 286.
Hydroelectric power station, 167, 168.

Icon art, 219.
Il'chenko, Yu., 212.
Il'men', Lake, 113.

Imeretia (also Colchis), 117.
Import of Russian books, periodicals, 177.
Importance of nationality, 43–55.
India, 53, 120, 280.
Industrial development of the Ukrainian SSR, 163–164.
International, 256; First, 51, 79; Second, 82, 175; Third, 111, 140, 161, 194–195; guaranteed national development of Ukraine, 192–193; national policy, 176; on ukrainization, 93–94; Manifesto, 271.
International Film Festival (Mar del Plata), 144.
International prestige involved in nationalities question, 66.
Ireland, 52, 126, 142.
Isakov, I. (1894–?), 112.
Ishchuk, A. (1908–?), 35.
Istoriya rusov, 213.
Ivan IV (the Terrible) (1530–84), 121.
Ivano-Frankivsk, 28.
Ivanov, S. P. (1906–?), 145.
Ivchenko, M. (1890–1939), 216.

Jews, 65, 167, 175; fascist genocide of, 271; Khrushchev on, 156; persecution of, in tsarist Russia, 136; restrictions on university admissions of, 269; Russified, 201; in Ukraine, 195.
Journals, 212.

Kabuzan, V. M., 272.
Kalmucks, 273.
Kalynets', I. (1939–?), 210.
Kalynovych, M. (1888–1949), 216,
Kamenev, L. (1883–1936), 62.
Kapustin, M. Ya. (ca. 1845–?), 134.
Karacharov, 113.
Karavans'ky, S. (1920–?), 186, 187.
Karazin, V. N. (1773–1842), 123.
Karelia, see Karelian ASSR.
Karmans'ky, P. (1878–1956), 217.
Katkov, M. N. (1818–1887), 119, 148, 149, 151, 245.
Kautsky, K. (1854–1938), 53, 82, 83, 84, 301.
Kazakh SSR, Ukrainians in, 164, 178.
Kazakh school, 261.
Kazan', 121.

Kenesary (1802–1847), 128.
KGB, see Committee for State Security.
Kharkiv, 143, 230, 231.
Khmel'nyts'ky, B. (1595–1657), 123, 155.
Kholodny, M. (1940–?), 33, 210.
Kholodny, P. (1876–1930), Ukrainian painter, 218.
Khrapovitsky, A. V. (1749–1801), 147.
Khrushchev, N. (1894–1971), 85, 253, 302, 304; nmchauvinist measures taken by, 60; violated Leninist nationalities policy, 36, 43; on: Jews, 156; rapprochement of nations, 68, 266; Russian conquests, 129.
Khvyl'ovy, M. (1893–1933), 100, 216.
Kyiv, 145, 154, 211, 269; arrests (1965), 28; film studio, 144, 207, 212; Institute of Folklore, 238; Philharmonic, 217; schools, 239; theatre, 211.
Kindergartens, day nurseries, 168, 233.
Kirghiz SSR, 139; the Kirghiz, 139.
Klyuchevsky, V. (1841–1911), 214.
Kokovtsov, V. N. (1853–1943), Prime Minister of Russia (1911–14), 175.
Kolokol, periodical ed. by Herzen and Ogaryov, 45.
Korop, 166.
Koryak, V. (1889–1939), 216.
Kos-Anatol's'ky, A. (1909–1983), Soviet Ukrainian composer, 232.
Koshyts' choir, 218.
Kosiv (village), 219.
Kosiv, M. (1934–?), 29.
Kostenko, L. (1930–?), 29, 210.
Kostomarov, M. (1817–85), 214, 295.
Kosygin, A. (1904–1980), 164.
Kotsyubyns'ky, M. (1864–1913), 33; see also *Shadows of Forgotten Ancestors.*
Kryvy Rih, 238.
Krushel'nyts'ka, S. (1873–1952), Ukrainian opera singer, 218, 232.
Kuban', 165, 272, 290.
Kulish, P. (1819–1897), 214.
Kupala, Yanka (1882–1942), 129.
Kurbas, L. (1887–1942), 232.
Kursk region, 165, 194, 288.
Kuznetsova, Ye. (1913–?), 218.
Kyreyko, V. (1926–?), 29.
Kyrychenko, H. (1939–?), 210.

Lafargue, P. (1842–1911), 80.
Language, native, value of, 221–227; Ukrainian: condition of, 31, 42.
Language 'barrier', 200–202; conflict, 280–284, 286.
Latin America, 280.
Latvia, 146.
Latvians, 107, 128, 146, 156, 167, 183, 205, 263, 273.
Lazarevs'ky, O. (1834–1902), 214.
Lenin, V. I. (1870–1924), 70, 74–75, 93, 104–105, 114, 121, 128, 157, 192, 194, 200, 235, 253–254; against: antisemitism, 157; assimilation, russification and Russian chauvinism, 82–83, 145; on: grave errors in the implementation of nationalities policy, and need for discussion, 56–57; equality of nations, 191; building of national states and cultures in Soviet Republics, 62; city and village conflict, 280; educating builders of communism, 304; international culture, 87–88; Katkov, 148–149; training specialists in Soviet Republics, 167–168; ukrainization, 167–169.
Lenin's Works (CW), specific references to: (1912 – May 1914) vol. XVIII, on: Herzen, 45, 246; XIX, internationalization of world society, 268–269; against persecution for 'separatism', 303–304; on: Ukraine's population, 42; XX, learning Russian, 266; national autonomous areas, 287, 299–300; nationalities in Russia, 80; against inequality of nationalities, 187, and languages, 255; on: tsarist Empire, 120; oppressed nation's nationalism, 214; Marx's views on national movements, 63, and on Ireland, 126; (December 1914–July 1916) XXI, on: tsarist Russia and need to liberate nations she oppresses, 126, 138; XXII, merging of nations, 269–270; Engels's view on Russian Empire, 128; (June 1917) XXV, on Ukrainian people under tsarism, 105–106; (1918–June 1920) XXVII, on: control of authorities, 31; statistics, 174; XXIX, Russian chauvinist communists, 253; bourgeoisie's cosmopolitanism, 46; theory and practice gap, 251; XXX, Ukrainian language, 222;

importance of national question in Ukraine, 64, and possibility of her secession, 101; the Borotbist communists, 99; their and the Bolsheviks' attitude to Ukraine's independence, 98–99, 151; roots of Russian chauvinism, 105; XXXI, future of nations, 83–84, 182; single world economy, 270–271; equality of nations, 175; (October–December 1922) XXXIII, against Russian chauvinism, 55, 104, 111, 156; XXXVI, Lenin's 'Testament' ('The question of nationalities ...'), 57, 64–65, 103; on: 'Autonomization', 65–66; 'freedom to secede', 189; Russian chauvinism, 32, 155, and safeguards against it, 189; Russified:- non-Russians, 223, 249; spite in politics, 31; meaning of internationalism, 38; two kinds of nationalism, 103–104, 234, 292; need for oppressor nation to make up for actual inequality, 66, 104, 175–176, 293; use of national languages, 221–222, 268; nationals to draw up detailed code, 55, 57, 223, 268; limiting scope of the Union, 159, 268; this decentralization less harmful than loss of international prestige, 66, 159–160, 267, 300.

Lenin's *Sochineniya*, 3rd edn., XVI, Petrovsky's Duma speech 'On the nationalities question' (June 1913), 124, 127, 136, 264.

Lenin's unpublished speech on the nationalities question (December 1919), 66, 108.

Lenin's 'Testament' ('letters'), publication demanded (1923), 66, 77; published (1956), 57, 77; execution, 104–105.

Leningrad, 211, 265.

Leninist nationalities policy, concern about non-implementation of (1923), 67, 70–77; main points of, 303–305; grave violations of, 28, 43, 60.

Leonov, L. M. (1899–?), 249.

Leontovych, M. (1877–1921), Ukrainian composer, 232.

Lermontov, M. (1814–1841), 245, 246.

Levyts'ky, V. F. (1854–1939), 214, 215.

Libraries, 238–239.

Linguistic conflict, 280–284, 286; see also Language.

Literary discussions, 291; readings, rulings against, 33, 291; scholarship, 216.

Literature, 207, 209–210, 215–216, 232, 276.

Lithuanian SSR, 183.

Livonian Knights, 113.

'Localism', 'local interests', 157, 267, 268, 271.

Lukash, M. (1919–?), 217, 218.

Lunacharsky, A. (1875–1933), 88, 89, 207, 208, 215, 246.

Lutsk, 28, 233.

Luxemburg, Rosa (1871–1919), 55, 74.

L'viv, 28, 165, 212, 219, 238, 266; Council of National Economy, 157, 161, 162, 165.

Lyatoshyns'ky, B. (1895–1968), Soviet Ukrainian composer, 232.

Lysenko, M. V. (1842–1912), 232.

Lyudkevych, S. (1879–1979), Soviet Ukrainian composer, 232.

Machiavelli, N. (1469–1527),130, 133, 134.

Magazines, 212.

Makharadze, F. (1868–1941), 67.

Makhnova, G. P., 273.

Maksymovych, M. (1804–1873), 214.

Malanchuk, V. (1928–?), 267–270, 285.

Malyshko, A. (1912–1970), 29.

Mamaysur, B. (1938–?), 210.

Manastyrs'ky, A. I. (1878–?) and his son, V. A. (1915–1992), Soviet Ukrainian painters, 232.

Mandel'shtam, O. (1891–1938), 216.

Mansvetov, M. N., 263, 274.

Mar del Plata, 144.

Markov, Ye. (1835–1903), 123.

Martynenko, O. (1935–?), 29.

Marx, K. (1817–1883), 136, 235; against idea of nations as 'antiquated prejudices', 79–80; and Ziber, 214; Capital, 63; on: French 'Marxists', 63; Irish question, 52, 54, 126; nationality, 46.

Marx and Engels, on: 'barracks communism', 55, 82, 198; struggle for national existence, 92.

Marxism-Leninism, does not ignore nations, 51–55; teaching on nationalities question violated, 32.

Mayakovsky, V. (1893–1930), 106.
Mayboroda, H. (1913–?), 29, 232.
Mayboroda, P. (1918–?), 29, 232.
Mazeppa, I. (1644–1709), 122, 133, 246.
Mdivani, B. (?–1937), 158.
Mehring, F. (1846–1919), 53.
Mentsyns'ky, M. (1876–1935), 218.
Meyer, S. (1840–1872), 52.
Mikoyan, A. (1895–1978), 251.
Mingrelia (also Colchis), 117.
Mongolian invasion, 145.
Mordvins, 133–134, 273.
Moscow, 17th c., 123; pre-revolutionary, 139; capital of: RSFSR, 160, 162, 268; USSR, 162, 178, 211, 241, 271, 272, 288, 313, 314.
Murav'yov, M. (1796–1866), 117.
Muscovite Russia, 124.
Muscovites, 122.
Mushak, Yu., Soviet Ukrainian classical scholar, 218.
Music, 218, 238.
Musin-Pushkin, Count A. A. (1760–1805), 122, 245, 246.
Mykhal'chuk, K. (1841–1914), Ukrainian philologist, 224.
Mykolaychuk, O., 35.
Myshuha, O. (1853–1922), 218, 232.

Napoleon III (1808–1873), 52.
'Narrow-mindedness', national and local, 101, 268.
Nation, definition, 41.
'National', negative connotation given now to the concept, 88.
'Nationalism', allegations of, 29–31, 292–293, 303.
Nechuy-Levyts'ky, I. (1838–1918), Ukrainian writer, 215.
Nejedly, Z. (1878–1962), 92.
Nekrasov, N. (1821–78), 114.
Neva, 113.
Newspapers, 241–242; statistics, 177, 179, 197–199, 133.
Nicholas I ('Palkin', 'the Big Stick') (1796–1855), 117, 129, 249.
Nicholas II (1868–1918), 128, (Romanov) 137.
Nihilism, national, in: Russian Empire, 44, 145; Party, 59, 62, 67, 94, 170.

Nikovs'ky, A. (1885–1942), 216.
Nishchyns'ky, P. (1832–96), Ukrainian composer, 232.
Nizhniy-Novgorod, 134.
North, the, peoples of, 123; Ukrainian resettlement to, 42.
North-Western Region (Byelorussia), 129.
Norway, 127.
Novakivs'ky, O. (1872–1935), Ukrainian impressionist painter, 218.
Novhorod-Siverskiy, 166.

Obal', P. (1900–1987), Ukrainian painter and engraver, 218.
Ochakov, 113.
Odessa, 186, 187, 207, 231.
Ogaryov, N. (1813–1877), see Kolokol.
Orgnabor, 42, 164, 165.
Orlov, Count A. F. (1786–1861), 150.
Osyka, L., 212.

Painting, 219.
Palme Dutt, R. (1896–1974), 131.
Paradzhanov, S. (1924–1990), 31, 211, 212.
Parashchuk, M. (1878–1963), 218.
Paskevich, I. (1782–1856), 117.
Paul, Archdeacon of Aleppo (17th c.), 124.
Paustovsky, K. (1892–1968), 249.
Pavlyk, M. (1853–1915), 214, 314.
Pavlyuchenko, N. I., 277.
Penza, 148.
Periodicals, publishing data, 179; Russian, import, 177–178; Ukrainian, from Poland and Czechoslovakia, 289–290.
Perov, V. (1833–1882), Russian painter, 233.
Persia, 137.
Peter I (the Great) (1672–1725), 117, 122, 129, 133, 245.
Petersburg, 122, 139.
Petlyura, S. (1877–1926), 72.
Petrovs'ky, H. (1878–1958), 124, 127, 263.
Petrykivka, 219.
Petryts'ky, A. (1895–1964), Soviet Ukrainian painter and stage designer, 219, 232.
Phidias (431? B.C.), 50.
Philharmonic, Kyiv, 237.
Picasso, P. (1881–1973), 218.
Pidmohyl'ny, V. (1901–1941), 216.

Pizarro, F. (1478–1541), 120.
Plato (429–327 B.C.), 50.
Pobedonostsev, K. (1827–1907), 120.
Podolyns'ky, S. (1850–1891), 214.
Poetry readings, official, directive on, 34, 291.
Poland, 15th–17th c., 123, 194; 19th c., 14, 54, 135, 150, 259; early 20th c., 127; in World War I, 137; inter-war, 214, 280; today, 93, 165, 204, 286, 288, 290.
Poles, 18, 54, 134, 136, 167.
Policy, nationalities, changes, errors and crimes in, 60.
Polish, 228.
Polish revolutions, 134, 259.
Political arrests (1965), 29–31, 98, 293.
Poltava, 112; province, 124.
Polytechnic Institute, Odessa, 186.
Polyukh, I., 211.
Population, Russian, increasing ratio, 80; Ukrainian, no increase, 42–43; relative numbers, 273, 288; outside Ukrainian SSR, 280–290.
Portuguese possessions, 53.
Potebnya, O. (1835–1891), eminent Ukrainian philologist, 86, 225, 249.
Pot'ma camps, 335.
Prague, 211.
Print, Ukrainian, abolition of restrictions, 221.
Privileged position of Russian, and Russians, 254–265.
Prymachenko, Mariya (1908–1997), Soviet Ukrainian ceramic artist, 219.
Pryzhov, I. (1827–1885), 44, 246.
Publishing, 176–184, 197–198, 240–243.
Purishkevich, V. (1870–1920), 137.
Pushkin, A. (1799–1837), 122, 245, 246.
Pushkin, Count, see Musin-Pushkin,
Pyatakov, G. (1890–1938), 62.
Pymonenko, M. (1862–1912), Ukrainian painter, 232.

Radio, 166, 178, 242, 254, 289.
Radio-Telegraphic Agency of Ukraine (RATAU), 242.
Radishchev, A. (1749–1802), 128, 129.
Rakovsky, Kh. (1873–1941), 17, 67, 75, 201.

Rapprochement of nations, 80, 81, 85, 265, 266, 270, 271, 275, 285.
RCP(B), Central Committee, Politbureau, 1919 resolution, 221; December 1919 Conference, 66; Congresses: VIII, 202; Lenin, 251; X, Burnashev, 106; Mikoyan, 251; Safarov, 19, 57, 139; Stalin, 137, 297; Zatons'ky, 58, 108. 110, 253; resolution on the nationalities question, 192, 230, 264; XII, 194; Hryn'ko, 70, 71; Makharadze, 67; Mdivani, 158–159; Rakovsky, 67, 75, 291–292; Skrypnyk, 73, 202–203, 289; Stalin, 109, 298; Yakovlev, 19, 66, 79, 201; resolution on the nationalities question, 68, 104, 105, 158, 169, 206, 223, 235, 264, 294.
Repin, I. (1844–1930), 233.
Repressions (1963–5), 33, 98, 100, 294.
Resettlement, Russian and Ukrainian, 42.
Reshetnikov, F. (1841–71), Russian writer, 114.
Restrictions on Ukrainian print, abolition of, 219–221.
Riga, 205.
Roman Empire, 130, 134; Romans, 28, 134.
RSDWP resolution on equality of nations, 82.
Romania, 93, 204, 280.
Rumyantsev, Count P. (1725–1796), 135.
'Russia, one and indivisible', 108–111, 115, 129, 132, 152, 158.
Russia prison of nations, 116, 174, 245.
Russian priority, 110.
Russian SFSR, 163, 164; book import from, 177; Ukrainian population in, 166, 178, 194.
Rusyn, I. (1937–?), 335.
Rutul, 258.
Ryleyev, K. (1795–1826), Russian poet, Decembrist, 246.
Ryl's'ky, M. (1895–1966), 217.

Sadovs'ky, M. (1856–1933), 232.
Safarov, G. (1891–1942), 17, 57, 139.
St Petersburg, 122, 139.
Sakharov, A. M., 128–129.
Saltykov-Shchedrin, M. (1826–1889), 112, 204, 294.

Sambists, 303.
Samovydets', pseud., probably of Rakushka-Romanovs'ky, R. (1623–1703), 213.
Schlisselburg, 113, 114.
Schmidt, C. (1863–1932), 63.
Scholars, scientists and postgraduates statistics, 185–186.
Schools in Daghestan, 258.
Schools in Ukraine, 155–158, 168, 193, 200, 276–272; russification of, 124; by Catherine II, 135; 1927 CP(B)U resolution, 264; ukrainization of, 196; 1959 decree, 60, 261–262; statistics, 199, 231; Ukrainian: teaching, 232–233; libraries, 238–239.
Schools, non-Russian, in USSR, 226–227; Ukrainian, in: Czechoslovakia, 96–97, 166; Poland, 166, 259; RSFSR, 289.
Scientific, scholarly and technical publishing data, 180–182.
Scientific Research Institute of Communications, poetry reading (8 December 1965) in, 34.
Sculpture, 218.
Secession right of the Soviet Republics, 98, 188–189; possibility of, Ukraine's, 100.
Sechenov, Bishop Dmitriy (1708–1767), 133.
'Second native language', 188, 255; see also 'bilingualism'.
Self-government, 300.
Selsam, H. (1903–1970), 316.
Semashko, 248.
Semenko, M. (1892–1938), 216.
Semi-culture, 282.
Semirech'ye region, 139–141.
Serpilin, L. (1912?), 29.
Settlements, Ukrainian, in the Russian SFSR, 165.
Shadows of Forgotten Ancestors, Ukrainian film, after M. Kotsyubyns'ky (1864–1913), 144, 211, 212.
Shamil (1798–1871), 128.
Shchedrin, M. (1826–1889), 112, 204, 294.
Shcherbyts'ky, V. (1918–1990). 28.
Shelest, P. (1908–1996), 25, 27.
Shestopal, M., 20, 37, 100.
Shevchenko, T: (1814–61), 21, 23, 29, 34, 147, 153, 154, 196, 214, 215, 228, 230, 246, 295, 307, 319.

Shevchenko jubilees, 230; memorial evening, Machine Tool Factory (March 1965), 35, 153; monument, meetings at (1964–5), 35, 153; destruction of stained-glass window (1 March 1964), 34.
Shevchenko Scientific Society, L'viv, 214.
Shishkin, I. (1832–1998), Russian painter, 216.
Shkurupiy, G. (1903–1943?), 216.
Shostakovich, D. (1906–1975), 211.
Shul'gin, V. (1878–1976), 100, 110, 111, 115.
Siberia, 17th–19th c., 117–118; peoples of, 117–118; Radishchev in penal servitude, 130; post-1917: construction projects, 168; place of deportation, 153; of Crimean Tartars, 212; Ukrainian settlements in, 165, and resettlement to, 43, 164.
Skrypnyk, M. (1872–1933), 100, 176, 253; speeches at: CP(B)U 1923 Party Conference, 71; X Congress, 40; RCP(B) XII Congress, 73–75, 202, 289; works not published now, 215.
Sleptsov, V. (1836–1878), Russian writer, 114.
Slisarenko, O. (1891–1937), 216.
Slovakia, 96, 97.
Smena Vekh, 109, 111.
Smerdyakov, 302.
Smolych, Yu. (1900–1976), 210.
Social sciences, 213–215.
Socialism as the philosophy of the Ukrainians, 41.
Socialist commonwealth, 41, 194.
Socialist legality, 28.
Soloukhin, V. (1924–?), 249.
Solov'yov, S. (1820–1879), historian, 122, 214, 245.
Son ('Dream'), film, 154.
Sosyura, V. (1898–1965), 216.
Sovereignty, Ukrainian, progressive loss of, 42.
'Soviet nation' or 'people', theory of a single, 87–88.
Spanish possessions, 53.
Stalin, (1879–1953), 42, 68, 76, 304; against: Kautsky, 83–84; 'local nationalism', 103; on: Byelorussian and Ukrainian nations, 298; derussification, 204; *Smena Vekh* idea, 204–206.

Stalin's antisemitism, 103; 'autonomization' idea, 65; extermination of Ukrainian communists, 100, and Ukrainian intelligentsia, 95, 197; proposed Chamber of Nationalities, 77; toast to the Russians, 110; ukrainophobia, 60, 153; violation of Leninist nationalities policy, 36, 43.
Stalinist era crimes, 31, 60.
Stalino (now Donetsk) region, 21, 240.
Stel'makh, M. (1912–1983), 28.
Stepovy, Ya. (1883–1921), Ukrainian composer, 232.
Struve, P. B. (1870–1944), 153, 256.
Student associations, national, 288.
Students and graduates statistics, 183–185.
Stus, V. (1938–1985), Soviet Ukrainian poet and critic, 22, 210.
Sverdlovsk, 269.
Svitlychny, I. (1929–1989), 31, 302.
Sweden, 113, 127.
Syl'vestrov, 211.

Tadzhik SSR, 183.
Tallinn, 115.
Tanyuk, L., 211.
Tartar, 179; Tartars, Crimean, 121, 123.
Tartu (Derpt), 115–116.
'Tashkentians', 204, 270, 302.
Tchaikovsky, P. (1840–1893), 233.
Tel'nova, 154.
Ten, Borys, pseud. of Khomychevs'ky, M. (1897–?), 217.
Teplov, G. (1711–1779), 130.
Terlets'ky, O. (1850–1902), 214.
Ternopil', 28.
Terror (1932–1937), 195–196, 273.
Textbook publishing data, 182–183.
Theatre, 95, 187, 191–192, 209, 211.
'Third Rome', 132.
Timoshenko, V. V., 129.
Togliatti, P. (1893–1964), 93.
Trade Unions, World Congress in Warsaw, 154.
Transcaucasia, 165, 187; see also Caucasus.
Translation, literary, 217–218.
Trials, political (1966), 179–180.
Trush, I. (1869–1941), Ukrainian painter, 232.

Tsakhurs, 258.
Tsameryan, I. P., 275.
Tsvilyk, P. (1891–1964), Soviet Ukrainian ceramic artist, 219.
Tugan-Baranovs'ky, M. (1865–1919), 214.
Tula, 203.
Turgenev, I. (1818–83), 17, 114, 246, 248.
Turkestan, 108, 139.
Turkmen SSR, 183.
Turks, 132.
Tychyna, P. (1891–1967), 216.

Ukrainian Communist Party (Borotbists), 99, 192.
Ukrainian communists exterminated, 99–100.
Ukrainization and its end, 60, 94–95, 168–169, 191–199, 200, 209, 230, 281, 305, 316.
Ukrainization (1920s), 194, 196.
Ukrainka, Lesya (1871–1913), famous Ukrainian poet, memorial evening (31 July 1963), 34.
Ukrainophobia, 60, 152–153, 223.
Unemployment, 164.
United Nations, 144.
Universal union of humanity distinct from assimilation, 85.
Universities, Baltic and Transcaucasian Republics, 187.
Universities, Ukrainian SSR, 169; Afro-Asian students, 144; Russian as language of instruction, 144, 176, 186, 231, 263, 265, 275, 289; student numbers, 184.
Universities, USSR and RSFSR, student numbers, 185.
University of Kyiv, discussion on Ukrainian culture (27 April 1965), 35, 154; repressions in, 35, 100 Shevchenko stained-glass panel, 35.
University of Tartu, 115–116.
Unpublished writings, 291.
Upishnya, 219.
Urals, 117, 165.
Urlanis, B. Ts., 166.
Ushinsky, K. (1824–1871), Ukrainian educator, 226, 260.

USSR, as a free union, idea now abandoned, 98, 101–102; identified with Russian Empire, 111–130, 138, 143–144.
Uzbeks, 206–207.

Vaillant-Couturier, P. (1892–1937), 285.
Vasyl'kivs'ky, S. (1854–1917), Ukrainian painter, 232.
Velychko, S. (ca. 1670–after 1728), 213.
Village, 280–282, 294–295.
Virgin Lands, 166, 290.
Vogt, A. (ca. 1830–ca. 1883), 52.
Voguls, 117–118.
Volga, 149.
Volhynia, 148.
Voloshin, M. (1878–1932), 216.
Voronezh region, 165, 288.
Vovk (Volkov), F. (1847–1918), 214.
Voynarovs'ky, A. (1680–1740), 246.
Vynnychenko, V. (1880–1951), 215.

Wales, 297.
Warsaw, 17, 117, 154, 211.
Well for the Thirsty, Ukrainian film, 212.
Welsh language, 297.
Western Ukraine, 18, 42, 164–165, 185, 214.
Writers' Union of Ukraine, 21, 22, 23, 212, 290.

Yakovlev, Ya. A. (1896–1939), 17, 66, 77, 201.
Yalta, film studio, 207.
Yankovs'ky, N. V., 277.
Yaroslavl', 134.
Yefremov, S. (1876–1937), 216.
Yenikal, 112.
Yermolov, Gen. A. (1772–1861), Governor of Georgia (1818–27), 117.
Yevshan, M. (1889–1919), 216.
Yiddish, 177.
Yizhakevych, I. (1864–1962), Soviet Ukrainian painter: 232–233.
Yohansen, M. (1895–1937), 216.
Yurkevych, L. (Rybalka) (1885–1918), Ukrainian left-wing Social Democrat, 18, 214.
Young Writers' and Artists' Club, 36,154.

Zalygin, S. (1913–2000), 31.
Zalyvakha, P. (1925–?), 29.
Zan'kovets'ka, M. (1860–1934), eminent Ukrainian actress, 232.
Zatons'ky, V. (1888–1938), 58, 108, 110, 253.
Zerov, M. (1890–941), 216.
Ziber, N. (1844–1888), 214, 314.
Zinov'yev, G. (1883–1936), 62.
Zlatovratsky, N. (1845–1911), 246.

Abbreviations

Chteniya: Chteniya v Imperatorskom obshchestve istorii i drevnostey rossiyskikh pri Moskovskom universitete.

CP(B)U: Communist Party (Bolsheviks) of Ukraine (1918–1952).

CPSU: Communist Party of the Soviet Union (1912–1991).

CPSU(B): Communist Party of the Soviet Union (Bolsheviks) (1925–52).

CPU: Communist Party of Ukraine (1925–1952).

KPSS v rezolyutsiyakh: *KPSS v rezolyutsiyaki resheniyakh s'yezdov, konferentsiy i plenumov TsK*, 7th edn, Moscow, 1953.

Lenin, CW: V. I. Lenin, *Collected Works*, Moscow, 1960–

Marx and Engels, SC: K. Marx and F. Engels, *Selected Correspondence*, Moscow [1956].

RCP(B): Russian Communist Party (Bolsheviks) (1919–25).

Solov'yov, *Istoriya*: S. M. Solov'yov, *Istoriya Rossii*, 15 vols, Moscow, 1959–61.

X *syezd RKP(B)*: *Desyatyy s'yezd RKP(B). Mart 1921 goda. Stenograficheskiy otchot*, Moscow, 1963.

XII *s'yezd RKP(B)*: *Dvenadtsatyy s'yezd RKP(B). 17–25 aprelya 1923 goda. Stenograficheskiy otchot*, Moscow, 1968.

Appendix
Speech by Ivan Dzuba at Babyn Yar

29 September 1966

Babyn Yar, near Kyiv, is the site of the largest single mass shooting of Jews in German-occupied Europe. The memorial event in 1966 was the first in Kyiv to honour the victims. Organised by Jewish and Ukrainian activists, the event turned the tide on the historical recognition of the Babyn Yar massacre after decades of official silence and antisemitism.

The initial phase of the killings occurred between September and November 1941. The first of the massacres was of Kyiv's Jews on 29–30 September 1941. The killing only stopped when the Nazis were driven from Kyiv on 4 November 1943. An estimated 150,000 people were murdered at Babyn Yar under the German occupation, it has become a symbol of the 'Holocaust by Bullets'.

POSTSCRIPT BY IVAN DZYUBA TO THE PUBLICATION OF HIS SPEECH

It was in the last ten days of September 1966 that Viktor Nekrasov passed me a message through friends asking me to come to his house before 1pm on 29 September. I guessed what this was about. After all, 29 September was a special day in the life of many Kyivans. On that day some Kyivans took bouquets of flowers with verses of mourning to that edge of the city, the name of which is sadly remembered throughout the world: Babyn Yar. Other Kyivans on that same day racked their brains about how to prevent a large gathering of the first group in that place. And a third group of Kyivans acting on the orders of the second group zealously stalked the first group and 'took measures' if they needed to against the most agitated among them.

However, 29 September 1966 was not just the next anniversary of the beginning of the Babyn Yar tragedy, but its 25th anniversary. A quarter century of grief remembered, whose remembrance was explicitly prohibited, unwanted and malicious as far as the authorities were concerned, a stance reinforced by the government unleashing a programme of public works to change the actual topography of Babyn Yar.

I was in Viktor Platonovych's home at the specified time. There I saw his friends from the Kyiv Studio of Scientific and Popular Cinematography. Led by Heli Snehirov, they were getting ready to film something: they were expecting more people than usual to be there. If the gathering was not banned it would be given at least some form of ritual. When we got to Babyn Yar we were struck by what we saw there. All the surrounding hillocks and parks were covered by many people in distinct groups – thousands and thousands of people. Yet this uncoordinated element was here as a single living being. Suffering had set onto their faces while people's eyes seemed out of place and time. They were looking into the depths of time and they saw the frightening picture of what had not and would never become the past for them. The shadow of horror long ago and some kind of human loss of way hung over Babyn Yar. Thousands of people, silent and immobilised in the tumult, embodied the muted cries of a whole people.

People were silent but this was an insistently questioning silence. People wanted to listen, listen and hear something important said. So, when word got around that 'writers have arrived', people converged on us, pulled us apart in different directions. Everyone (Borys Dmytrovych Antonenko-Davydovych had joined us on his own initiative) was surrounded by a tight crowd who demanded 'Say something, at least something!' One had to improvise, though we spoke about what we well knew and was hurting inside.

Someone taped our speeches, and in a few days they appeared in samizdat, then in its infancy. Naturally 'the powers that be' demonstrated they thoroughness and 'militancy', applying 'educational' and administrative measures to those who had transgressed. The first victims were the cinematography studio workers. The film they took was confiscated and they were punished by various fines. My speech at Babyn Yar was added to the 'criminal evidence' against me that the KGB had already gathered.

Translation by Marko Bojcun

Ivan Dzyuba's speech

There are events, tragedies the enormity of which make all words futile and of which silence tells incomparably more – the awesome silence of thousands of people. Perhaps we, too, should keep silent and only meditate. But silence says a lot only when everything that could have been said has already been said. If there is still much to say, or if nothing has yet been said, then silence becomes a partner to falsehood and enslavement. We must therefore speak and continue to speak wherever we can, taking advantage of all opportunities, [for they] come so infrequently.

I want to say a few words – one-thousandth of what I am now thinking and what I would like to say here. I want to address you as men – as my brothers in humanity. I want to address you Jews as a Ukrainian – as a member of the Ukrainian nation to which I proudly belong.

Babyn Yar is a tragedy of all mankind, but it happened on Ukrainian soil. And therefore, a Ukrainian has no right to forget it any more than a Jew. Babyn Yar is our common tragedy, a tragedy for both the Jewish and Ukrainian nations.

This tragedy was brought on our nations by fascism.

Yet one must not forget that fascism [could] neither begin nor end in Babyn Yar. Fascism begins in disrespect to man, and ends in the destruction of man, in the destruction of nations – though not necessarily in the manner of Babyn Yar.

Let us imagine for a moment that Hitler had won, that German fascism had been victorious. One can be sure that the victors would have created a brilliant and 'flourishing' society which would have attained a high level of economic and technical development and made all the same scientific and other discoveries that we have made. Probably the mute slaves of fascism would eventually have 'tamed' the cosmos and flown to other planets to represent humanity and earthly civilization. Moreover, this regime would have done everything in order to consolidate its own 'truth' so that men would forget the price they paid for such 'progress,' so that history would excuse or forget their enormous crimes, so that their inhuman society would seem normal to people and even the best in the world. And then, not on the ruins of the Bastille, but on the desecrated forgotten sites of national tragedy, thickly choked with sand, there would have been an official sign: 'Dancing Here Tonight.'

We should therefore judge each society not by its external technical achievements but by the position and meaning it gives to man, by the value it puts on human dignity and human conscience.

Today in Babyn Yar we commemorate not only those who died here. We commemorate millions of Soviet warriors – our fathers – who gave their lives in the struggle against fascism. We commemorate the sacrifices and efforts of millions of Soviet citizens of all nationalities who unselfishly contributed to the victory over fascism. We should remember this so that we may be worthy of their memory, and of the duty which has been imposed upon us by the countless human sacrifices, hopes and aspirations that were made.

Are we worthy of this memory? Apparently not, since even now various forms of human hatred 'are found among us – [including one] we call by the worn-out, banal, and yet so terrible [name], antisemitism. Antisemitism is an 'international' phenomenon. It has existed and still exists in all societies. Sadly enough, our own society is also not free of it. Perhaps there is nothing strange about this – after all, antisemitism is the fruit and companion of age-old barbarism and slavery, the foremost and inevitable result of political despotism. To conquer it – in entire societies – is not an easy task, nor can it be done quickly. But what is strange is the fact that no struggle has been waged here against it during the post-war decades; what is more, it has often been artificially nourished. It seems that Lenin's instructions concerning the 'struggle against antisemitism' are forgotten in the same way as his precepts regarding national development of the Ukraine.

In Stalin's day, there were open and flagrant attempts to use prejudices as a means of playing off Ukrainians and Jews against each other – to limit the Jewish national culture on the pretext of Jewish bourgeois nationalism, Zionism and so on, and to suppress the Ukrainian national culture on the pretext of Ukrainian bourgeois nationalism. These cunningly prepared campaigns wrought damage on both nationalities and did nothing to further friendship between them. They only added one more sad memory to the harsh history of both nations and to the complex history of their relationship.

We must return to these memories, not in order to open old wounds, but in order to heal them once and for all.

As a Ukrainian, I am ashamed that, as in other nations, there is antisemitism here; that those shameful phenomena which we call antisemitism – [and which are] unworthy of mankind – exist here.

We Ukrainians must fight in our midst against all manifestations of antisemitism or disrespect towards the Jew.

You Jews must fight against those in your midst who do not respect the Ukrainian people, the Ukrainian culture, the Ukrainian language – against those who unjustly see a potential antisemite in every Ukrainian.

We must outgrow all forms of human hatred, overcome all misunderstandings, and by our own efforts win true brotherhood.

It would seem that we ought to be the two nations most likely to understand each other, most likely to give mankind an example of brotherly cooperation. The history of our nations is so similar in its tragedies that, in the Biblical motifs of his 'Moses,' Ivan Franko recreated the story of the Ukrainian nation in terms of the Jewish legend. Lesia Ukrainka began one of her best poems about Ukraine's tragedy with the line: 'And you fought once, like Israel …'

Great sons of both our nations bequeathed to us mutual understanding and friendship. The lives of the three greatest Jewish writers – Sholom Aleykhem, Itskhok Peretz and Mendele Moykher-Sforim – are bound up with Ukraine … The brilliant Jewish publicist, Vladimir Zhabotinsky, fought on the Ukrainian side in Ukraine's struggle against Russian Tsarism and called upon the Jewish intelligentsia to support the Ukrainian national liberation movement and Ukrainian culture.

One of Taras Shevchenko's last civic acts was his well-known protest against the antisemitic policies of the Tsarist government. Lesia Ukrainka, Ivan Franko, Boris Hrinchenko, Stepan Vasylenko and other leading Ukrainian writers well knew and highly valued the greatness of Jewish history and of the Jewish spirit, and they wrote of the suffering of the Jewish poor with sincere sympathy.

Our common past consists not only of blind enmity and bitter misunderstanding – although there was much of this, too. Our past also shows examples of courageous solidarity and cooperation in the fight for our common ideals of freedom and justice, for the well-being of our nations.

We, the present generation, should continue this tradition, and not the tradition of distrust and reserve.

But sadly enough, there are a number of factors which are not conducive to letting this noble tradition of solidarity take firm root.

One of these factors is the lack of openness and publicity given to the nationalities question. As a result, a kind of 'conspiracy of silence' surrounds the problem. The attitude in socialist Poland could serve as a good example for us. We know how complicated the relations between Jews and Poles were in the past. Now there are no traces of past ill-feeling. What is the 'secret' of this success? In the first place, the Poles and the Jews were brought closer together by the common evil of the Second World War. But we, too, had this evil in common.

Secondly – and this we do not have – in socialist Poland relations between nationalities are the subject of scientific sociological study, public discussion, inquiries in the press and literature, and so on. All of this creates a proper atmosphere for successful national and international enlightenment.

We, too, should care about and exert ourselves – in deed rather than just in word – on behalf of this kind of enlightenment. We must not ignore antisemitism, chauvinism, disrespect towards any nationality, a boorish attitude towards any national culture or national language. There is plenty of boorishness in our midst, and in many of us it begins with the rejection of ourselves – of our nationality, culture, history and language – even though such a rejection is not always voluntary nor the person involved to be blamed.

The road to true and honest brotherhood lies not in self-oblivion, but in self-awareness; not in rejection of ourselves and adaptation to others, but in being ourselves and respecting others. The Jews have a right to be Jews and the Ukrainians have a right to be Ukrainians in the full and profound, not merely the formal, sense of the word. Let the Jews know Jewish history, the Jewish culture and the Yiddish language, and be proud of them. Let the Ukrainians know Ukrainian history, the Ukrainian culture and language, and be proud of them. Let them also know each other's history and culture and the history and culture of other nations, and let them know how to value themselves and others – as brothers.

It is difficult to achieve this – but better to strive for it than to shrug one's shoulders and swim with the current of assimilation and adaptation, which will bring about nothing except boorishness, blasphemy and veiled human hatred.

With our very lives we should oppose civilized [forms of] hatred for mankind and social boorishness. There is nothing more important for us at the present time, because without such opposition all our social ideals will lose their meaning.

This is our duty to millions of victims of despotism; this is our duty to the better men and women of the Ukrainian and Jewish nations who have urged us to mutual understanding and friendship; this our duty to our Ukrainian land in which we live together; this is our duty to humanity.

About the publishers

RESISTANCE BOOKS is a radical publisher of internationalist, ecosocialist and feminist books. Resistance Books publishes books in collaboration with the International Institute for Research and Education (iire.org), and the Fourth International (fourth.international). For further information, including a full list of titles available and how to order them, go to the Resistance Books website.

info@resistancebooks.org
www.resistancebooks.org

THE INTERNATIONAL INSTITUTE FOR RESEARCH AND EDUCATION is a centre established in 1982 for the development of critical thought and the exchange of experiences and ideas between people engaged in struggles. The IIRE provides activists and academics opportunities for research and education in three locations: Amsterdam, Islamabad and Manila. The IIRE publishes *Notebooks for Study and Research* in several languages which focus on contemporary political debates, as well as themes of historical and theoretical importance.

iire@iire.org
www.iire.org

www.ingramcontent.com/pod-product-compliance
Lightning Source LLC
Chambersburg PA
CBHW032025290426
44110CB00012B/671